ABROAD IN ENGLAND

ABROAD IN
ENGLAND

Frank Entwisle

Illustrated by John Bigg

W·W·NORTON & COMPANY
· NEW YORK · LONDON

PRINTED IN GREAT BRITAIN BY
ST EDMUNDSBURY PRESS, BURY ST EDMUNDS, SUFFOLK.

For Tina Rice, Pat Adams, Margie Segar, Sheila Hill, Eileen Crosby, Ann Segar of Liverpool 8 and my own Dan . . . who will inherit.

Stranger, if you passing meet me and desire to speak to me
  why should you not speak to me?
And why should I not speak to you?

Walt Whitman

I went out into the churchyard where the green stones nodded together, and I took up a handful of earth and felt it crumble through my fingers, thinking that as long as one English field lies against another there is something left in the world for a man to love.

'Well,' smiled the vicar as he walked towards me between yew trees, 'that, I am afraid, is all we have.'

'You have England,' I said.

H. V. Morton *In Search of England*

CONTENTS

List of Illustrations

Acknowledgments

The author and publisher would like to thank the following for permission to quote from their works: the estate of the late Jocelyn Brooke (see pages 40–1); Chatto & Windus for the Ivor Gurney extract (see page 224); Mr Fred Reed (see page 162) and Mr Laurie Lee (see pages 229–30). The lines from Paul McCartney's 'Let 'em In' on page 29 are used by permission of M.P.L. Communications Ltd. Copyright © by M.P.L. Communications Ltd.

The publisher would also like to thank the various persons and institutions who provided reference material for some of the illustrations. We would particularly like to mention the Photographic Librarian of the Central Electricity Generating Board, the Public Relations Officer at British Rail Regional Headquarters in York, the City of Liverpool Public Relations Office, and the Reverend Peter Durnford of St Just in Roseland.

PREFACE

In the Spring of 1926 a young Fleet Street journalist called Henry Vollam Morton set off from London in a blue, bull-nose Morris to trundle round England. A year later – the year when I was born – he published an impression of the journey. *In Search of England* sold a million copies and people buy it still today.

It was not a work of scholarship. It did not set out to explore the English psyche. It contained no political, economic or social analysis. (He did not mention the General Strike, which occurred while he was travelling. It might even be said that the England he described had already disappeared on Flanders Field.) Yet, there it is still, on the bookshelves of a thousand vicarages and gentle English homes – still re-read with affection, along with all the books that followed when he climbed back into his car and set off again to interview seagull-egg collectors, tramps and vergers and to rhapsodise about Lindisfarne and Hull and York and a kind of England the book-buying Southern Railway commuter yearned for.

Oh, it was grand to be an Englishman in the 1930s with your slippers hoisted on the fender, a sherry at your elbow, the five-bob-a-week maid out at the pictures and the latest of that nice Mr Morton's books in your hand. And even lovelier to plan a holiday in the Morris Cowley with Mr Morton in the glove box. How far away the guns of Flanders sounded. Who would not take up arms for Ponders End?

That other England altogether, whose capital was Jarrow, was beyond the imagination of such readers, perhaps beyond their capacity to bear more pain. But even there, among the silent shipyards, in the grim schools where Empire Day was sincerely celebrated with dozens of little halfpenny flags in skinny fists – even there, Mr Morton's England was more real, more believable, than the activities of the Bright Young Things chronicled in the papers. Truer even than the descriptions of working-class squalor by Saint George Orwell who wrote remarkably like an old-Etonian toff among the Hottentots.

H. V. Morton wrote of an England in which the English wanted to believe. The English, whose deeds (good and bad) have influenced more people than any other nation did not, in general, hunger for past greatness. They yearned for a vague memory of semi-rural bliss – the good old days that never really happened – a decent enough dream. Perhaps Morton sought unconsciously to satisfy it as the land of Ramsay Macdonald, Stanley Baldwin and the Vicar of Stiffkey took to the country lanes in long shorts and Austin Sevens. And as he tootled through the counties the spec builders were nailing laths on ten thousand semi fronts in imitation of Tudor mansions, the manufacturers of little wrought-iron gates and lead-latticed windows were doing well and there had not been such a call for cheap stained-glass door panes since Edward VII's reign. For the fleeting peace English men and women wanted to be reassured that 1914–18 had all been a dreadful interruption, that God (and Roy Fox) had returned to his heaven and that all was once more right with the English world. Morton reassured them.

I do not denigrate Mr Morton. I praise him. Even if I were not an admirer of his craft and a reveller in some of his period descriptions – I read them first when I was a schoolboy in a depressed shipyard town and my own vision of England was permanently stained by some of his bright pigments – it would be insensitive to disregard a book that has given delight to so many for so long.

Nor do I deprecate his readers. Nor their dreams. For being an Englishman, I still share them in my way. Nor their apparent complacency. Given their recent history, how else could they have been expected to think and feel.

And it was H. V. Morton who inspired my own journey. The idea sprang from a conversation with Harold Evans, then Editor of *The Sunday Times*, during which we realised that Morton had set out on his search fifty years before. We decided on this book as a kind of celebration.

I had no intention of following exactly the same route or deliberately comparing the England of the 1920s with that of the 1970s. Still less did I intend to pronounce on the English psyche or the social condition of the country (both of which, however, and despite all recent troubles, I believe to be in tolerable health).

Like Morton, I set out to entertain myself in the country I love best of all. Should anyone discern a reflection of the contemporary English mood, I hereby declare it was accidental. Like *In Search of England* this too is just a ramble. If, on these terms, it pleases – well and good.

Personal and family affairs have intervened between the actual journey and the compilation of the book. I hope that will not have harmed it. To my patient bank manager, Bob Carmichael of my local Lloyds, to true friends like Jackie Charlton, the football manager, and my beloved sister-in-law Alice Roffe who gave advice and help, to my stoic editor

Esther Whitby who I have tried sorely, to dozens of helpers along the wayside who offered hospitality and aid, but most of all to my dear wife Sally who has been a ruthless critic and has borne a writer's moods and emergencies with humour, I offer my everlasting gratitude.

1

I set out from Calais, am delayed by an admiral in cycle clips and waylaid by a guest of the Dalai Lama. All of which makes me ponder on the nature of Englishness in the most taciturn and heavily fortified town in England.

1

I SAT in a cool little bar in Calais. And having no taste for the light, yellow liquid which the French call *bière*, I sipped rosé from a dainty glass on a slender green stem like everyone else.

For some reason, I had been befriended by an old man wearing bicycle clips who was referred to as 'l'Amiral'. It must have been some whimsical neighbourhood joke, for the only nautical characteristic he displayed was a gentle swaying whenever he committed himself to his long, spindly legs – as if the bar floor was the deck of a packet boat in a mid-Channel swell. Each time a newcomer stepped in from the heat of the obscure side-street, he or she elaborately shook hands, first with the proprietor, then with my new *copain* ('Bonjour, Monsieur l'Amiral'), next with me

('Bonjour, Monsieur'), and then with every other customer in turn.

Eventually, and perhaps because of my presence, the conversation at the small tables turned to England. I had read a recent news story about a party of French schoolgirls visiting Palace Yard, Westminster, who had taunted the House of Commons policemen with mocking cries of 'Breetish Leyland! . . . Breetish Leyland!' collapsing into laughter after each sally. Today I expected something a little more adult. A fusillade or two, perhaps, of that pithy, worldly-wise, Gallic cynicism that lovers of France appreciate so much.

A large man, not dissimilar in construction from the Michelin man of the tyre advertisements, said: 'You ask me, M'sieu, whether I would rather be French or English' – I had of course put no such question – 'and I reply, *English!*'

I must have shown disbelief, for he gave me an injured look and proceeded to clinch the argument after his fashion. 'Believe me, M'sieu, before I retired I was in the textile trade. The machines we used came from Nottingham to Calais ĩn *boats!*'

Obviously some nuance of his reasoning had escaped me, so he went on to explain that his great-grandfather had been English, that his nephew had married an English girl and now lived in Manchester (no, alas, he had never crossed to England himself), and if I remained unconvinced that he would readily abandon his nationality because of his admiration for le *Système Anglais,* I had only to ask anyone else in the bar and they would tell me that they too would prefer to be English. Seventy-five per cent of the people of Calais wanted to be English, I was assured gravely by several nodding heads.

To a young pastry-cook who later said much the same I suggested that perhaps le *Système Anglais* was looking a bit shaky these days. 'Ah, but we have the faith in England,' he said. 'It is necessary for the French and the English to hold hands and swim together.'

Now I honour the tradition that the French are the most logical race in Europe. Maybe, with a little practice, even a French pastry-cook and an English journalist could accomplish this aquatic feat. But I wondered whether the anglophile attitudes of my French companions resulted from an excess of politeness and hospitality, of summer heat and rosé, or whether, quite simply, it was all a mildly roguish amusement to lighten a drowsy afternoon. It doesn't matter really. I enjoy the memory. Partly because I love the French and all their logical illogicalities as all sensible Englishmen should, partly because it all took place on the eve of my own adventure into England, but mostly because it happened – the handshaking, the workmen's minute glasses of wine – only twenty-two miles from the bar of the Prince Regent in Dover's Market Square.

How it is that two nations could have lived within sight of one another for a thousand years or so and yet remained so different, is at once a mystery and a delight.

Vive l'Amiral!

2

For weeks Europe had baked in the fierce heat of early summer. The wine growers of Germany and France had already hinted at a vintage year. Serious German families were turning mahogany on the *playas* of Majorca and the Costa Brava and defending their Siegfried Lines of sand against teenagers from Birmingham and Luton. Communism with a sunny face was making parliamentary noises from a rickety but eternally ebullient Italy. Spain had a king again and perhaps, after a few more assassinations, might stagger at last into the sunshine.

The news from England was as usual. Britain too, it seemed, was sweltering. But the newspapers and radio programmes spoke alarmingly not of vintages but of a five-year drought. Britons, the headlines informed the world, were suffering not only from the lassitude of summer but from a surfeit of history, possibly a terminal illness. The demoralised Englishman gazed into his palm and saw a pound note withering before his eyes, then tottered off to the betting shop before it disappeared entirely. The ancient elms had Dutch disease and the only battle being fought on England's beaches was a paranoid skirmish against little dogs imported by bewildered ladies from a Europe that the bureaucracy seemed to think was ridden with rabies. The mad Ulsterman assaulted from the rear, and John Bull wearily turned the other cheek. Chauvinist Scots cried for their oil and their liberty, as if the last had not been their greatest gift from England. There was even fear about the survival of parliamentary democracy. Then there was Race. For England, hinted some US commentators, it was only a matter of time . . .

At least that was the picture composed each day by the journalists and politicians. And waking every morning to the BBC and the newspapers, that was what some Englishmen were coming to believe.

. . . Out in the Pas-de-Calais the merchant ships of the world moved in a procession northwards up the coast of Europe. Beneath the surviving radar masts of World War II standing on the blinding white cliffs above Dover, two Russian destroyers skipped jauntily down-Channel towards the Med.

Up on the boat deck of the Sealink ferry I was approached by a pretty schoolteacher from Dunkirk.

'Excuse me, Sir. Are you English?'
'Yes.'
'Would you be so kind as to sign your autograph in my pupils' books?'
'Of course. But why?'
'Oh, they are fascinated by everything English,' she said.

So I found myself scrawling my signature across the ruled pages in a dozen exercise books belonging to French teenagers on a day trip to Dover and Canterbury where each would be able to fill more *cahiers* with the autographs of the similarly obscure. I tried to imagine a party of English adolescents on an outing to Calais doing the same – and I couldn't. Will I ever fully understand the French?

I went down to the bar though it was still early morning, partly to escape the children and partly because of a childish but excusably English impulse to buy a beer before opening time within sight of Dover.

The English coast was gently heaving and tilting in the square of the window. Why is it, I wondered, that the big bluff of Cap Blanc Nez and the neighbouring coast, with Calais on its little plain, look so Continental? Yet the Kentish coast – Shakespeare Cliff, Castle Hill and the break where Dover lies – look so English, though both were of a piece when Britain was joined to the mainland and the Thames was a tributary of the Rhine. Calais looks like an *entrance* to Europe. An invitation. The cliffs of Dover are a barrier, a screen behind which the most un-Continental of Europeans (and from this I exclude the Scotch and Welsh) conduct their mysterious suburban lives.

The white cliffs that curtain from passing seamen the orchards, hop fields and villages of Kent, seem to conceal a thousand enigmas of such a kind that even England's offspring, from North America to the Antipodes, marvel at her perversities – and once in a while at some illogical gallantry. I wondered over my Worthington E whether this was an entirely English notion. Or did Bonaparte and Hitler have such thoughts as they looked over from France?

Then I remembered that strange and haunting passage written by a Greek traveller who approached these shores a few centuries before Julius Caesar. 'There in the north, where ice, water and air mingle, is, without doubt, the end of the earth . . .' he noted. 'There I have seen the lung of the sea, for across those vast sandy foreshores and wide desolate creeks, the sea moves in and out with a slow breathing rhythm.'

The place where the sea breathes. The end of the earth. That may be a feeling that preceded even Pytheas the Greek and was held by the Carthaginians who traded for British tin centuries before him. Sometimes I sense it lingers in the French mind to this day as they observe the English and their mysterious land. If so, Dover can do little to dissolve the mists.

4

Calais, looks, sounds, feels like a city. Dover – a sallyport and haven of imperial fleets and armies, and still the most extravagant fortified place in Britain – lies in a little cleft between the Kentish cliffs like a small country town.

I landed. I collected the vehicle that was to be my home for months, drove to the municipal car park and drew in alongside a caravan. An oldish woman, handsome face darkened by exposure to the weather, was sweeping up outside the doorway. At first I thought she was talking to herself but when I wound my window down I realised she was addressing me.

'It's a year today . . . exactly a year . . . since we left England,' she was telling me, 'and we don't know quite what to expect.' Her husband was away shopping and she asked me about food prices in her educated southern accent. Dover stewed in the mid-morning heat, and there in the car park cleared by German gunfire thirty-five years before, she told me how they had spent the last twelve months travelling through Europe, Persia, Baluchistan, India and Kashmir . . . how they had escaped when their caravan was snatched by a flood of melted Himalayan snow . . . how, one fragrant, moonlit night in a Jain temple she had debated with a consumptive monk – gentle, young and dying – whether it would be a mortal sin to eat an egg . . . then how she had negotiated her husband Tom's seventieth birthday present – an audience with the Dalai Lama. 'A happy birthday,' said the 14th incarnation of the Buddha.

This was not the first Odyssey of Jean and Tom Rising. They had taken to the wandering life when Tom, a headmaster from Penzance, had reached retirement. He returned from his shopping with a full carrier bag and said the prices were not too bad. The stores had been full of French people buying up to twenty pounds of butter at a time.

Jean was the first person I had spoken to since landing. Will I ever fully understand the English?

3

When we are young and every new town is a Samarkand, the memory takes photographs, makes sound tapes and records smells that will never dull.

I recall my first arrival in London thirty-six years ago when I stepped from the train at King's Cross and was transported by moving stair-case into the great, primrose-coloured, romantic world of the Underground . . . illuminated machines magically spouting change . . . electric trains like red caterpillars winding through the earth to exotic Monopoly-board stations like Fenchurch Street, Marylebone and King's Cross . . . bright green but empty chocolate machines like cast-iron chapels . . . the smell – the sweet summery metropolitan smell of subterranean London which I have sought in vain many times since. I hear the tall August trees round the Clapham hostel and the perpetual murmur of London through open windows at midnight, far more clearly than the air raids. This will last for ever, it all said. And with the optimism of youth I believed it then, and half believe it still.

It's all wrong, of course. At any other time and in any other weather it would all have been different. So a Frenchman landing at Manchester, Middlesbrough or Plymouth rather than Dover, would carry a different England in his head. But seven million passengers a year pass through this little town. And 300,000 truck crews. For many it is their first sight of England. To some of them it *is* England. For the Dunkirk children on the Sealink ferry, England may always be Canterbury on a blazing day, the warm old walls, the crooked streets. They may never see Dagenham or Hartlepool.

So this morning I've been leaning on the guard-rail outside a newspaper shop at New Bridge – the Piccadilly Circus of Dover – trying to taste their Dover-flavoured England.

Toy London buses, double-decked and red, and dolls dressed as guardsmen among the knick-knacks in the window. In the roadway an obelisk bearing words like distant drums of Empire. 'Rohilcund . . . Oude . . . Delhi . . . in memory of comrades who fell . . . 60th Royal Rifle Brigade . . .' And through the gap between the ranks of Regency houses (so spanking white and uniform, like troopers in white ducks on morning muster, eyes-front out to sea) a glimpse of the great harbour. A man-made lagoon built big enough to parade the whole British fleet from dreadnought to pinnace in the days, just seventy years ago, when the White Ensign ruled the world.

Along the promenade now. Apparently on guard outside the gents, the life-size statue of a man stands on a plinth. He wears a daft little moustache, and he gazes out to France with the pop-eyed and slightly gormless arrogance of an upper-class Edwardian officer. He is, or was, the 'Hon. Chas. H. Rolls', who on 2 June 1910 first flew the Channel and returned non-stop. Near by, the bronze head of Captain Webb who swam the Channel in 1875 – thirty-six years before anyone else, and 'without goggles' boasts the local guidebook.

Beneath the far-flung gaze of these illustrious, and under the butter-yellow towers of the castle on the hill, a scattering of English matrons sit purposefully apart with their clean-limbed litters, thinking their English thoughts – and Dover Beach no more than a bank of painful pebbles, along which a middle-aged man and wife move studiously with an electric machine like a mine-detector. What do they seek? No one can tell. For no one speaks.

> Listen! you can hear the grating roar
> Of pebbles which the waves draw back, and fling,
> At their return, up the high strand,
> Begin, and cease, and then again begin,
> With tremulous cadence slow, and bring
> The eternal note of sadness in. *

A French girl sits on a promenade seat penning postcards. What does she write?

'Chère Maman . . . the weather is fine at Douvres . . . I can almost hear Victoria's soldiers playing in the public gardens . . .'

Perhaps.

4

I was strolling through the Market Square on my way to the bank this morning when I remembered that this was the very site of Julius Caesar's principal British naval base, and perhaps, just here was the forum.

The fact that it was now three blocks from the shingle and more than a mile from the harbour bar; that there had been eight or nine different harbours in Dover, each one a little nearer France; that Calais itself was built out to sea on a swamp; and that silting had bedevilled every Doverian harbourmaster since the Confessor awarded the privilege of sac and soc, and freed them of lastage, tallage, passage, kayage, rivage, pontage, wreck, screwage and lovecope – all this suggested to me that the palaeolithic catastrophe that sundered England from Europe might now be in reverse. It was an attractive theory, and I was engaged on a few mental calculations to arrive at a rough estimate as to when the habitués of the Prince Regent would be shaking hands all round and embracing over their thimblefuls of rosé (and Mary Tudor could rest in her grave at last) when I was accosted from the steps of Barclays by a tubby man of middle height carrying a worn but well-nourished Gladstone bag – a description that would also fit his suit.

* From 'Dover Beach' by Matthew Arnold.

'How are *you* this morning?' he bellowed with aggressive *bonhomie.* 'It's a wonderful day, isn't it? How *are* you?' His accent was not British.

The people standing about waiting for the bank to open gave him swift, nervous glances, edged apart and looked uncomfortable in a choked, English sort of way.

'I'm . . . I'm very well, thank you,' I replied, and though taken by surprise, for I had never seen him in my life, managed a smile. 'But you have me at a disadvantage. Have we met somewhere before?' How we grab for stage-English at such moments!

The woman on his left took off on some suddenly remembered errand. A tall, pale man studied the sky with alarmed concentration. The plump man chuckled. He was obviously enjoying himself.

'When I feel happy,' he announced, 'I like other people to be happy with me . . . Don't *you* think it is a lovely day?'

He stood easily, at home here, though his features and manner suggested an origin in some city between Boulogne and Beirut where plump, cheerful men carry big bags of money to the bank. I think he enjoyed the discomfort he was causing. I have seen English congregations laugh in church. I have seen them smile at funerals. But I have never seen them laughing at the bank. And at opening time! And at Dover of all places! I'm sure he knew it.

I am, of course, aware of the tradition that Englishmen are cold and distant, but I deny it. The so-called 'public' schools are often blamed for the caricature of the emotionally deprived Englishman. But perhaps Dover and its citizens (for centuries the first Englishmen most Europeans met) should take some of the blame too. Not that they don't have a good excuse. Consider their ordeal. The population of their town is 24,000 – about the same as Bognor Regis or Bishop Auckland. It is crammed into its little valley like a Yorkshire mill town. And seven or eight million strangers, almost the equivalent of London's population, surge through its streets and harbour installations every year. No other port in the world takes, and has long taken, such a strain. You don't pause in a stampede to stroke a buffalo. The wonder of Dover is that it stays so calm and that no one shoots the cattle.

My Levantine friend dumped his bundles of pound notes – or pesos, escudos, piastres, drachmas, dongs or lire – on the counter. He gave me a wink then toddled off in the general direction of the forum.

5

I found it hard to drive away from Dover. I felt as though I was leaving unfinished business – as if there was something about the place I had failed to pin down. I walked through the bustling streets where traffic signs were in both French and English ('Tenez la Gauche' reads something like a political slogan). I inspected the medieval Town Hall (it is called the Maison Dieu and was once a hospice for shipwrecked mariners). I strolled along the Esplanade past the stuccoed Yacht Club (very posh). I lingered on the promenade where all day and night the air drums and drones with the sound of marine diesels in a hurry. Every few minutes a vessel passed in and out between the outstretched piers. It is said to be the largest man-made harbour in the world but doesn't look it.

It was all so casual. There was none of the ritual tension of the international airport. If you fancy a trip to Europe you just buy a ticket in the booking hall and catch the next big seaborne bus – to Ostend, Calais, Dunkirk, Boulogne, Zeebrugge – and perhaps get yourself a cup of tea as England slips away astern. Twenty-five thousand ferries and five thousand hovercraft a year – not counting freighters – all orchestrated by a shift of two ex-naval yeomen in the tower at the end of Eastern Pier.

There was a quiet confidence about the place. Was this the essence of Dover, then? The relaxed manipulation of so much power in what is geographically just a country town – her almost casual relationship with France, Europe, the World?

But no: Dover's traffic with the world has not always been so casual. One forgets, on such a sunny day, the young Henry V, returned from France for ever, his mourning queen's procession one league long, and a troop of 500 men-at-arms in black armour, winding up the road to Canterbury; the diplomatic spectacular of the Field of the Cloth of Gold whose gaudy actors passed this way; the burning of Dover by the French; the khaki hordes of World War I and the Dover Patrol droning out to kill in November dawns; Dunkirk and the screaming Stukas.

Dover lies between two hills. The one the traveller sees is the eastern hill crowned by its great, castellated gun platform, the castle itself. The other hill, however, the hollow hill, is for the most part forbidden to the stranger. And this, without doubt, is the strangest hill in England. For a short time, when it was full of soldiers, it was the most lavish, the most terrible and the most warlike hill on earth. Which wasn't very long ago.

When England was at war with France, Spain, Holland and America all at once, whole regiments of miners, masons and bricklayers arrived in Dover to turn this green mound into a vast underground fort. Barracks, barrack squares, married quarters, a hospital – trenches 50 feet deep and 30 feet wide, four miles of them, and all lined with brick at least 18 inches thick. The burrowing and building went on into the nineteenth century and there must have been as many navvies in Dover as there were

Doverians, and later just as many troops. The main entrance from the town, tucked away in Snargate Street behind the main thoroughfares, was known as the 'Grand Military Shaft' – three staircases in a tunnel tipped on end. One was marked 'Officers and *Ladies*', another 'NCOs and *Wives*', and the third 'Other Ranks and *Women*'.

The military thinking was not just to stop Napoleon on Dover Beach. The gamble was he'd land in Romney Marsh and head for London. Then a whole army would pour out of Dover's hollow hill and cut him off from France. But he never came. The rampaging journalist William Cobbett did, though. And he roared:

> Here is a hill containing, probably, a couple of square miles or more, hollowed like a honeycomb . . . line upon line, trench upon trench, cavern upon cavern . . . Either madness the most humiliating, or profligacy the most scandalous have been at work here for years . . . Let the French or the devil take us . . . this is perhaps the only set of fortifications in the world framed for mere *hiding* . . . a parcel of holes made in a hill to hide Englishmen from Frenchmen . . . More brick and stone have been buried in this hill than would go to build a neat new cottage for every labouring man in Kent and Sussex . . . I must from this Dover . . . this anti-Jacobin hill . . . as fast as I can.

Perhaps Cobbett was railing at his enemies in government rather than smiting a hill. But that sober scholar, Professor Nikolaus Pevsner, recorder of all that is notable in English building, came to Dover a few years ago and wrote about 'the maniacal scale and thoroughness of this nineteenth century equivalent of the hydrogen bomb stockpile'.

Well, a little town with a hill like that leaning over its back streets, and half the world using its front street as a doormat, is bound to be different.

I sat in the public library reading about Dover and remembering all the writers from Shakespeare to Dickens who had touched upon her, rented her houses for their characters and taken ship from her harbour, without seeing beyond her cool eyes or even exchanging so much as a slap and tickle. Then I remembered one man who may have come close to understanding her.

He was an American reporter called John Steinbeck. I quote from the *New York Herald Tribune* of July 1943:

> . . . Then Hitler came to the hill above Calais and looked across at the cliffs, and again only the little stretch of water stopped the conquest of the world. It is a very little piece of water . . . With a glass you can see the clock tower of Calais. When the guns of Calais fire you can see the flash . . . From the flash

you must count approximately fifty-nine seconds before the explosion . . . There is a flat blast that rockets back from the cliffs, a cloud of debris rising in the air. People look at their watches. The next one will be in twenty minutes . . . This goes on sometimes all night . . . There is a quality in the people of Dover that may well be the key to the coming German disaster. They are incorrigibly, incorruptibly unimpressed.

Yes – perhaps that's it. Maybe Dover can no longer show surprise.

2

Pleasant thoughts about English skulduggery in a field of
Dutchmen. Compatriots rescue me from foreign devils on
the road to San Francisco. I find solace in the Mermaid,
Normandy in Kent, and peace in a field called Robsack.

1

I HAD SPENT the last three nights in a field alongside a pleasant pub
three miles or so outside Dover. So had about fifty other people with
their caravans and tents. More than half of them were Dutch and there
were a few Norwegians. What pleasant people the Dutch and Norwegians are, and in spite of language difficulties, how well they get on
with the English! There seems to be an instinctive respect, even an
affection, between them. Perhaps it has something to do with the war,
but I would like to think that it runs deeper. There were some Germans
too, keeping themselves to themselves.

The landlord had been saying to me that you can tell the time of year by the arrival and departure of the different nationalities, each having its seasons of flight from home, like various kinds of migratory birds.

'When there is a language problem,' he told me, 'I just say "Go and ask the Dutch to sort it out," and they always do. They're ideal people. Of course, there's no love lost between the Dutch and Germans – or between the Germans and French for that matter. But I don't have any serious trouble. Except when I get the odd mad Irishman or Scotsman.'

That night I sat drinking in the bar with a gentle couple from New Zealand who had just arrived through France. So keen were they to be impressed by everything English that I felt bound to mention the execution of Joan of Arc, and a few other English misdemeanours just to even the score. 'You didn't burn half enough of them,' said the mild-mannered New Zealand fellow with sudden heat. Well, well! So that's the sort of thing they're saying over the tea-cups on the garden-party lawns of Dunedin, is it?

It was all very amusing and cosmopolitan and I could have loafed away a few more days quite happily. But this wasn't seeing England and it was time I moved on. The trouble was, I could not make up my mind which way to go. One day I had a mind to head for Hythe where the town trees are reflected in a still, green canal that has forgotten it was made as part of England's defences against 'Boney', or indeed that it was made for anything but to be a municipal ornament; and where the magnificent locomotives of the Romney, Hythe and Dymchurch Railway puff out of the tiny station and steam across fourteen miles of Romney Marsh to Dungeness, their piston rods going like sewing-machine shuttles. I notice that a lavish guidebook dismisses the railway in twenty-six words as just a holiday attraction whose steam engines are miniature replicas of historic locomotives – as if it were a fairground sideshow. Well, maybe the publishers were short of space. Last time I was there, the R. H. & D. R. was an important local passenger service, and had played an honourable part in the Battle of Normandy. Some trains had been turned into mobile light anti-aircraft batteries. And PLUTO – Pipeline Under the Ocean – the 'secret weapon' that pumped a million gallons of petrol a day to the Allies after D-Day, had been hauled into position by those beautiful toy locos. The railway had been demobbed by the time I got there, but there were still posters in the little carriages forbidding troops to smoke or spit.

There is no stranger quarter in Britain than Romney Marsh with its small grey villages and Martello towers strung along the coast forever waiting for the French who never come. The wind murmurs in the long grass like an old and distant conversation. The Romney sheep with their broad heads, white faces and black noses regard you knowingly. The flat, empty horizon is broken only by some church, crouching under its low broach spire in a clump of trees. No men! 'The human folk of the Marsh,' wrote the poet Richard Church, and no man knew Kent better, 'have a technique of invisibility . . . Do the natives go indoors and barricade themselves against the passing of a stranger?'

To me, it is wonderfully appropriate that among these damp, green meadows the Army tried to teach me how to become invisible. There were rangy sorcerers at large in the Marshes then (their official name was 'snipers') who could move across a patch of turf not thirty yards from the tip of your nose, and all you could see was a few cow pats or a lone whin bush – until there was a puff of smoke from a rifle muzzle. When you looked from cover again, the firer was gone.

Several observers have tried to explain the mystery of Romney Marsh in their different ways. 'The World, according to the best geographers, is divided into Europe, Asia, Africa, America, and Romney Marsh,' wrote a nineteenth-century canon of St Paul's Cathedral. What could he have meant by that? At least that it was different from the rest of England. And indeed for long it was the separate kingdom of Merscwari. I learned that from Richard Church's *Kent*, and also that some of its affairs are still conducted by a body called 'The Lords of the Level of Romney Marsh', who maintain an ancient court consisting of bailiffs and jurats, hold their sessions in old Dymchurch, and levy a local tax to help continue the two-thousand-year-old struggle to keep land and water separate. Or at least they were still doing so in 1948 when Church was writing.

Every reading schoolboy of my generation, and of several others, knew that Romney Marsh was smugglers' country. It was Russell Thorndyke who told us so in those thundering yarns of his about Dr Synn, the eighteenth-century parson who led the Marshland brandy smugglers and knew the paths between every bog by dead of night. If my memory of winter reading and scorched knees by the fireside serves me right, he once escaped from the Revenue Men in mid-sermon by swinging from the pulpit on a chandelier.

It is generally believed that the English are a law-abiding people. But how they love a smuggler or a pirate – so long, of course, as he is English. How they rejoiced in the adventures of fisherman Dodd Osborne when he vanished with the trawler *Girl Pat* before the war, and coastguards and navies hunted for him. How they cheered HMS *Cossack* a few years later when, throwing international law to the winds, she ran up Jösing Fjord under the guns of neutral Norwegian warships to board the German prison ship *Altmark*, release 300 prisoners and pinch the Herr Captain's watch, chronometer and Iron Cross. The great age of English piracy when robbery on the high seas was excused – after the English fashion – by religion and the foreign policy of Elizabeth I, is the best loved and most glamourised chapter of English history. The raid on Zeebrugge during the First World War and the Commando raids of the Second were relished more than most of the great land battles – except perhaps for Alamein which, after all, was executed by one swashbuckler (Montgomery) on the instructions of another (Churchill). It wasn't so much the massive regiments of Europe that fired the English imagination. It was little groups of unshaven men who set out by compass across the brown sea of the North African deserts to singe Rommel's breeches from behind, it was the unconventional exploits of Wingate's 'Chindits' (Long Range Penetration Force), it was the cheek of Arnhem, and the idiotic impertinence of the little boats at Dunkirk. The taste for swashbucklers and swashbuckling, even for a touch of skulduggery, is rarely satisfied in peacetime.

From Hythe and Dymchurch I fancied motoring on to Hastings where the course of history was changed in the piercing of an eye. I had read in the papers in mid-Channel that there was an interesting row brewing over the possible sale of the battlefield and nearby abbey to some developer. But by the next morning I had changed my mind again. Now I was for pointing the radiator towards Kipling's 'wooded, dim, blue goodness of the Weald' where the great oaks for the British fleet were cut, its gunpowder manufactured in little dells, and charcoal made for the smelting of gunmetal. I would lose myself in the deep, twisting lanes of the pre-industrial age as I had done before when, having completed some trivial journalistic mission, I claimed a brief unofficial holiday. Then, perhaps, I would find my way to Horsmonden village for a pint and a round of beef – spit-roasted over apple logs – in the bar of the Gun Inn where, with splendid impartiality, John Browne, gun founder, designed cannon for both Britain and her enemies, for roundheads as well as cavaliers. Then on to royal Tunbridge Wells.

At the same time 'Duty' – that scrawny Pecksniff, was nagging me to seek out that unlikely colony of coal miners towards the north where great, bleak, half-finished estates of National Coal Board houses scar the sweeping countryside, and the mining accents of Durham and Yorkshire are more commonly heard than the soft, Kentish way of speaking English. Socially important! A good, hard industrial story! But a coalfield in the Garden of England has always seemed wrong to me, and though I had passed by there before, I still only half believed in it.

No. To plan my route, to revisit, to talk about productivity and coal – that did not suit my temper. It was not the way to begin such a journey. I was in the mood for a blind date. I was waiting for a sign. And in the end it came.

I was walking down an empty shopping street in Dover quite early in the morning. The stores were not yet open. Someone said 'Frank!'

I looked about me, but seeing not a soul walked on again. 'Frank!' the voice summoned me. It was not until my name had been spoken thrice that I noticed a man standing in the doorway of a sandwich shop with his face half-buried in a hunk of bread. When he lowered his breakfast I saw that he was an old friend, a film cameraman, a bright chip of London whose Cockney gaiety had enlivened many an hour of journalistic boredom between Lapland and the Chinese border. I was delighted to see him. He was now working for Southern Television. 'Come and meet the lads,' he said.

The upshot was that on that day I lunched on roast pork *and* roast beef. And Stilton. And beer, and two colours of wine, in a magnificent old pub standing on the edge of the shingle at the foot of a winding lane that might have been on the coast of Spain rather than La Manche. It was the best of company. A couple of French tourists looked on as they toyed with their chilled soup, apparently confirmed in their worst fears about the heathen English.

Among my new companions was a tall, solid man, who was interested in my journey. He said I should visit his home village of Bishopsbourne. He knew a farmer who would be glad to let me use his land. 'You turn left off the A 2 and down into the valley. See you at seven . . . in the front bar of the Mermaid.'

2

Several million units of the human species pass along the A 2–M 2 between Dover and London each year with their route maps and passports on the seat beside them, heading for some Kensington hotel, or Stratford, or a factory in Stoke, believing themselves to have arrived in England. They have not. The concrete ribbon of the motorway is no more than a continuation of the autobahns of Germany and the auto routes of France and, with a short break of 3,000 Atlantic miles, it resumes in New Jersey then bores along, until it reaches the Pacific. It is no-man's-land. It is everyman's land. It is nothing. The service stations and the petrol pumps are all alike. The food in the snack bars tastes about the same. Only the coins, the accents of the nippies and pump attendants and the side of the road you have to use, vary from zone to zone. Here and there a passing village or town, a hedgerow or a distant spire may signal England, France or Italy, and no doubt some of the travellers are satisfied with that. But they might as well have stayed at home and looked at a picture book. Hamburgers . . . Chips . . . Texaco . . . Total . . . Cola

. . . Shell . . . Milkshakes . . . Service . . . BP . . . Fried Chicken . . . all the way from Salzburg to San Francisco! Unless something momentarily trips the system.

About seven miles out of Dover I felt that disconcerting little tug that usually signifies an empty tank or a bit of muck in the carburettor. I knew I had enough petrol. The traffic was heavy. I was anxious. It happened again a quarter of a mile further on. I looked for a turn-off. There was none. Roadworks narrowed the trunk road. And then it happened. The engine cut.

I stamped on the brake to stop the van rolling backwards. A truck grew huge in the rear-view mirror but stopped in time. Desperately I twisted the ignition key but there was no response. Someone behind began to hoot. The driver of the juggernaut on my tail gesticulated angrily and I had a panic vision of half Europe at a standstill in the blistering heat behind me. I realised I couldn't push the van on to the central reservation without help, for the moment I released the handbrake she would roll backwards, but I got out nonetheless. Seeing this three hefty lorry drivers jumped down on to the concrete, hurling their doors shut in rage and advanced upon me shouting. One was French, another perhaps Polish. They carried on as though I was an idiot who had jumped out for a breath of air. I felt like telling them to bugger off back to Poland or wherever they came from. I was an Englishman and this was an English road and I was entitled to stop where I liked.

I was rescued from this nightmare by a mild chap in an English family car who came bumping up along the grass of the reservation. He and his wife pushed me while I steered through the window. We made for the long grass while the truck drivers looked on sardonically. 'There's a garage at the bottom of the hill,' said my saviour. We waited for a two-way gap in the traffic. Mr and Mrs Englishman gave me a big heave. I lurched out across the road frantically spinning the wheel to the right, slotted myself in between two east-bound lorries, coasted off down the gradient, and my engine picked up. I saw them waving good luck as the big trucks started up and the great procession began to move west again.

The young lad at the garage couldn't undertake an examination so I topped up the tank and drove on. Sweet as a bird she ran after that.

Weeks later I found out the cause. There was nothing wrong with my home on wheels. Nothing that wasn't my own fault anyway. A diligent mechanic found a minute hole in a fuel lead under the tail. I remembered having bumped over a rough boulder in a field while manoeuvring for a level berth during darkness and that had clearly caused the puncture. Every time the petrol sank below a certain level, the engine sucked air. I wondered how many poundsworth of diesel oil and 'essence' that boulder had cost Europe.

I turned off the main trunk road and drifted down a winding way into England.

On my left was a paradise of parkland in which a company of uncurious sheep ambled between tall, well-spaced trees, a scene that had probably not altered – except for the gentle coming and going of the seasons – for hundreds of years. On my right were the poppies, a big field of them.

I cannot say they were red. Nor can I say they were orange. I cannot say either that they were a carpet or a sea of poppies. They were a colour there is no name for and, all there together in their thousands in the warm, vibrating air, they composed a texture I cannot describe and will take some time to forget. During the next few days when I had become absorbed into the everyday life of the valley, I talked with many people. I noticed that their eyes kept turning towards that festival of poppies in the sloping field.

Bishopsbourne was in the bottom of the little valley with the North Downs behind it and the poppies in front. A stream called the Nail-bourne emerged from the parkland of one great mansion, passed between the little houses, gardens and allotments of the village, and disappeared into the grounds of another. It was a very small village, a one-sided main street with a short cul-de-sac called Park Lane running back from the middle and blocked by the steep fields at the foot of the North Downs. Park Lane, I guessed, was the nucleus, the oldest quarter apart from the church along the road. The unpretentious houses of mellow, red brick, tucked up there behind their small gardens, had a Georgian air. But their meandering interiors and heavy beams, I saw later, suggested a sixteenth-century construction. They had probably changed face and shape over the centuries, to suit the size, fortunes and occupations of successive families.

It was a pretty place but not spectacularly so. If the lorry drivers and tourists droning along the A 2 ever look down through the trees and catch sight of its grey church tower and the rosy pantiles of its roofs – Kentish pegs they're called – they might imagine a picturesque community of country people drowsing the centuries away in peaceful isolation. That is the romantic notion of the eternal English village, but there can be few that fit the bill. If the Victorians did not actually devise that bucolic picture they did much to fix the colours. Perhaps it served the purpose of comforting the conceit of newly prosperous town dwellers who liked to believe in a peasantry above which they, of course, were elevated – from which, indeed, many of them had but recently emerged. Or maybe it reassured the less fortunate that there really was an Eden not far from the factories and counting houses, where simple lives were led and where modest virtues still prevailed.

Such visions survived until this century, pervading the pages of H. V. Morton and even later writers. They ignore the poverty that haunted rural England during much of the nineteenth century, and the dilapidation of British agriculture between the two world wars. In the winter of 1830, farm workers of the South – from Kent to Dorset – were so hungry that they wandered the countryside protesting. Ricks were burned and machinery broken. The only violence done to people was the millpond ducking of a few harsh overseers. Yet nine men were hanged. One, a nineteen-year-old, paid that price for knocking off the hat of a member of the great merchant Baring family. Nearly a thousand were imprisoned or transported. So much for the idyll!

The too-romantic view of rural isolation also forgets that it was not until the 1850s that town-dwellers outnumbered country people. And only fifty years before that countrymen exceeded townsmen by more than two to one. It follows, then, that a greater part of the energy that promoted England's nineteenth-century supremacy came from the manor houses, vicarages and small workshops of the countryside than is usually assumed. A look at the memorials of country naves and churchyards shows that English villagers were hardly isolationists. They died in far-off places we have now all but forgotten. It was the English villager who first populated and sustained America. English villagers – from the Stephensons to George Hudson the financier – transformed terrestrial geography by initiating the railways. English villagers stormed the Heights of Abraham and marched across the plains of India. Even Nelson was an English villager.

The doors of the Mermaid on the corner of Park Lane were open to the summer evening. The man I'd feasted with near Dover was waiting for me just inside. We had two pints apiece, during which I must have met almost everyone of drinking age in Bishopsbourne, from carpenter to squire. We then set out for Robsack field.

I am a northerner and more used to wide horizons and distant views than to the lushness of those southern districts where every bend in the road leads to a small new world varying only in disposition of tree, bank and stream; where landmarks are a stump, a gate, a beech bole or a hedgeside rather than a far fell brow or a distant village. In camera terms, one is a long-shot country and the other close-up. In the first you marvel at the changing light on a great slope of heather, or the celestial alchemy that in ten seconds can turn a dun tract of rushes into a plain of blazing gold. In the latter it is the veins on a single leaf, the lichen on a gate post, a ladybird on willow bark – even an abandoned kettle in roadside grass – that invites interest. The south may not inspire Wordsworthian flights of spirit, but it is more human, more manageable: made by men, not gods.

The fragrant lanes we drove along that night were of a southern kind, our two cars climbing between little woods, rounded hillocks and steep sloping meadows crowded close together. Small ranks of oast-houses – like Georgian soldiers with their hats askew – said this was Kent. Yet the farmhouses had an unfamiliar look, with roofs worn like sou'westers, higher from the ground before than aft. Some seemed to be part wind-mills or oast houses, now reclaimed for habitation. And the barns! Those great black roofs as big as upturned steamers resting on their gunnels. I remembered nothing like them. This was England, and at the same time it was not. The coppices and fields were English, but the shapes that men had made, the geometry of their working lives, were not.

Richard Church had written about Kent being 'a child withdrawing from its parent Normandy', and that 'Kent is the daughter who lives next door . . . who has married into England.' 'People who know Normandy,' he said, 'will recognise the relationship.'

'Pretty fanciful,' I had thought when I first read it. I had felt no Frenchness in Bishopsbourne a mile or so back down the road. But here in this small locality I was aware of a foreignness. It did not leave me when we emerged on to a small plateau of hedgeless fields and level, fenceless roads cutting a low, green, unfamiliar crop into straight-sided sections. On the near edge was a new farmhouse beside a burned-out tower mill, and that was where Charles Fagg, our farmer, lived. At the far side, well separated, were two Elizabethan houses of red brick. One, very handsome, stood to attention on the straight roadside. The other, more workaday, lounged alongside a black Kentish barn in a soft bed of cherry trees where the plateau broke and tumbled into a forested valley. And nearby was Robsack, a level field, well-wooded on three sides. The fourth side had an open view across the flat towards the ruined mill. I chose a berth alongside the hedge where the first morning light would waken me. One blackbird pronounced a valedictory to the day, and I must have been asleep before he finished.

3

A Canterbury dream. I hear of the Mystery of the Rings,
learn how Willie chose a pram, mix Elgar with McCartney
and am awakened by doves to witness a miracle in a field of
flax.

1

A S I ATTEMPT to recollect my last few days in Kent, to remember
faces, tastes, feelings, handshakes, and above all to play back
sounds, I feel as though I'm trying to recompose a dream, and only
isolated episodes survive.

Young, supple, adolescent June had grown into sophisticated July as I
had walked among the lanes. They say this county is at its best in spring,
decked out in apple blossom. But I prefer the early summer when swarthy
Kentish brick and tile suit better the strong, green complexion of the
leaves, clapboard façades are warm and dry and silvered, and hop bines
twist up fourteen-foot poles in fields as densely planted as young forests.
But it was time to go and I had allowed myself one last day and night.

In Kingston, the village a few miles to the east, there was to be a fête that day. In Bridge, the village to the west, there was a celebration in which Bishopsbourne would take part. And in Canterbury, first city of the English way of life, there would be an event that evening that could happen nowhere else. Sir Edward Elgar's oratorio *The Dream of Gerontius* was to be performed within the acre where Thomas Becket died. There could not be a more appropriate theatre in which to contemplate the agony of a soul hovering between heaven and hell, and surely none more beautiful.

When I called at the Mermaid for the morning village news I found the place agog. At first I thought it was the mood of festival. Last night the talk had been about the village entry in the pram race which would begin that afternoon outside the Plough and Harrow in High Street, Bridge, 'promptly at 3.15', but this morning there was something else. Some special seriousness, discussed as if it was a family affair. Through the open door, past Heather's general store, I watched people pause and look thoughtfully across the Forty-Acre Field. Then heads would nod, the strollers pause, then look over the valley once again. A man would put down his glass, walk to the Mermaid door, then return pensively to resume his conversation. 'Haven't you heard?' someone said to me at last. 'It's the rings . . . first time they've been seen in living memory.'

Early that morning the first villagers about the street had noticed them and rapidly passed on the word. Four or five large, corn-coloured circles had appeared on the surface of the fields across the Nailbourne stream. Each was twenty or thirty feet across, and this phenomenon was exerting its influence on Bishopsbourne that morning. Someone suggested that the recent heat had dried out the topsoil covering the foundations of ancient buildings. An older Bishopsbourne, perhaps prehistoric, emerging from oblivion and making a communication of some sort? An omen? If these had been days of hardship or ill-tempered weather the signal might have been construed as bad. In that dreamy, summer blaze, the poppies smouldering, and jollity ahead ('By-pass Bonanza,' said the programme. 'The Wantsum Morris Men . . . Church bells . . . Carnival Parade . . .') the omen must be good. Somebody had telephoned an archaeologist who promised to drive out next day and inspect the rings. Meanwhile amateur historians held court. A day to be remembered. The day of the Pram Race . . . the Day of the Rings!

2

I am in the narrow streets of Canterbury, the sun hidden, my view confined by walls and doors and windows, my way impeded by crowds of townsmen and travellers whose faces I do not observe because I am distracted by the presence of the great building that stands behind the houses on my right. I am wondering whether everyone has this awareness – those walking east feeling the Cathedral on their left, those weaving west sensing it on the right like some force unrecognised by science. I enter a small, triangular open space flooded by the sun, a medieval market in which stands a monument, a cross on top, a relief carving of soldier, sailor, airman just below. There is a large pub called the Olive Branch. On the paved area before it and clustered about the monument are seats and tables at which sit crowds of people, mostly young, mostly in jeans, and in the new brightness I see faces from Asia, Africa, Europe. I hear a guitar. A middle-aged man – I think he's English – begins to sing a corny, pre-war song in French. The young smile indulgently and join in.

> J'attendrai,
> Le jour et la nuit,
> J'attendrai toujours,
> Ton retour . . .

As I enter the long bar the song fades beneath the hubbub. The young person who serves my beer is from Sarawak and is called Ranendra Bhattacharrya. There is also a pretty brunette behind the bar from Lake Tahoe, USA. There are Malayans and Italians. I like the place. The landlord – Paul Shingler, an Englishman – tells me there are medieval cowsheds in his backyard and that he believes this is the only pub in England licensed to serve drinks on the Queen's Highway. He says there was trouble in town about the licence. Some citizens objected to people drinking around the war memorial outside. The Mayor, obviously a man of sense, came to the rescue. He said thousands had died to allow others to sit where they wanted. Good Lad! I walk out into the Buttermarket.

'J'attendrai . . .' sing the youth of the earth as I cross towards an ornate, fifteenth-century, gilded gateway which must lead into the Cathedral close. 'J'attendrai . . .' Waiting for what or whom, in such a place?

3

The Cathedral Church of Christ, Canterbury. A row of matrons, line abreast, complexions fissured by a transatlantic sun, expressions earnestly uncomprehending, sinewy necks craned out at forty-five degrees – a row of Lewis Carroll turtles – peer into the chapel known as Becket's Crown and listen to the intoning guide. Facts, dates, stories, desiccated, plucked from history.

> St Augustine founded it.
> Becket died for it.
> Chaucer wrote about it.
> Cromwell shot at it.
> Hitler bombed it.
> Time is destroying it . . .

says the placard in the cathedral close. All true. As neat a selling piece as ever Fifth Avenue devised. But is there something missing? Has not perhaps, along its thousand years, Christ wept for it? How far is it from the shed in Bethlehem, or from Jarrow? How close to Golgotha?

The bones of no Englishman have been more picked over than those of Thomas Becket. No old assassination has been chronicled so well. There were many watchers, and some left eye-witness accounts of the events that led to the murder that December evening in 1170.

The facts are plain enough. Henry II appointed his friend Becket to the archbishopric believing he would promote regal interests. But Becket put Church ambitions first and Henry, in a rage, perhaps unwittingly encouraged four courtiers to go to Canterbury where they hammered on the cathedral door, accused the prelate of eroding royal authority, and felled him in the north transept where he had taken sanctuary. The hair shirt found on his body was alive with vermin. 'He was one of God's saints!' cried the monks when they saw this sign of self-chastisement, then they scraped up some of Becket's brains from the marble floor and with a piece of bloodstained jacket sent the parcel to Santa Maggiore in Rome where the contents were revered as holy relics. Soon Becket was Saint Thomas and Henry came barefoot and hair-shirted to kneel at his tomb and be beaten with a rod. Five strokes from every bishop and abbot, and three from every one of eighty monks. The humiliation echoed clean round Europe and for the next 369 years – until for his own reasons Henry VIII booted them out – the pardoners and summoners and relic-mongers plied their trade among the pilgrims of all Christendom who brought their boils and sores, their heartaches and their money to enrich Canterbury and England.

Now, past a plump statue of Thomas Becket looking not unlike a wily managing director, past the tomb of the Black Prince (who died of dropsy, not in battle), sails the convoy of matrons, line astern. 'I love

England,' I hear one of them say. 'It's so full of history.' Able now to carry Canterbury like a battle honour to their decent Midwest homes.

4

High Street, Bridge. A week ago when I was here, the Plough and Harrow was on the main road between Dover and Canterbury, between Paris and London, between Berlin and Birmingham, between Milan and Manchester, Cracow and Coventry, Moscow and Middlesbrough. The glasses jingled on the shelf. The traffic had, of course, been on the increase since the Emperor Claudius marched with his elephants up through Kent. Chariots then mules, stagecoaches then steam wagons, and charabancs with open tops, tanks, guns. Then all those diesel juggernauts from foreign parts. Thousands a day. Those were the blighters! They were the ones that made people blow their tops and say after two thousand years – enough's enough!

This morning, though, the inhabitants of Bridge awakened to the sound of sparrows on the red rooftops. Pigeons clappered from the tiles between the strings of bunting to peck flower seeds on the road. You could hear the policeman walk down the street. And then the people. There must have been, until this week, people in Bridge who had never heard the silence of their own front street, who had not drowsed abed with some childish sickness, listening to the poetry of footfalls and voices at the two quiet ends of day. The gentle whine of the electric milk cart, United Dairies tip-toeing about the morning, a very English sound . . . The rat-tat of the door-knocker when the insurance man calls three doors away . . . The snip-snip of privet being cut and the whirr of a lawnmower on a summer Sunday morning . . . The starter motor of the old Riley that never goes first time . . . the small world that we suburbans savour but never mention . . . All this had been unknown to High Street, Bridge, as Europe barrelled through its days and nights.

Now the inhabitants stand in little groups looking round in wonder. They gather in the roadway and amble down the crown, bewitched by the experience of a truckless day.

This afternoon they're celebrating the winning of the battle for the by-pass. The only vehicles allowed – carnival floats and prams.

In the back bar of the Plough and Harrow.

Tom: Have you got your pram in the race, Willie?
Willie: No. I've hired it out. Bishopsbourne is racing it.
Tom: You'll have worn out a few prams in your time, Willie.

25

Willie: No. Same one. A good strong 'un. Baby after baby. I said to her right at the start – mind and get good strong axles and bearings, mind. Make sure. So when you push the baby out you can carry half a hundredweight of sheep-feed along. So you're not wasting time. And big wheels mind, to get you through the ruts!

Charlie Hogben and his pram from Bishopsbourne came in last. So much for omens!

5

Canterbury Cathedral. Pier and vault. Summer evening light. Bassoons, clarinets, strings, voices – the words of a medievalist Victorian prelate, foreign to our times.

> *Jesu, Maria – I am near to death,*
> *And thou art calling me; I know it now,*
> *Not by the token of this faltering breath,*
> *This chill at heart, this dampness on my brow, –*
> *Jesu, have mercy! Mary, pray for me!*

Yet we are moved. We weep inside. Music, architecture, poetry, take possession. The hard, uncomfortable chairs forgotten. Time forgotten.

> *Pray for me, O my friends; a visitant*
> *Is knocking his dire summons at my door,*
> *The like of whom, to scare me and to daunt,*
> *Has never, never come to me before . . .*

Time forgotten. Gerontius, who was he? Was he the British general of that name who led the armies of imperial Rome? Or was this old Cardinal Newman himself, listening for his own approaching death?

> *And I hold in veneration,*
> *For the love of Him alone,*
> *Holy Church, as his creation,*
> *And her teachings as His own,*
> *And I take with joy whatever*
> *Now besets me, pain or fear . . .*

I glance along the rows of graven faces near me. At the young man who,

26

before the concert, was swanking to his family – practising the new, fashionable royal accent (Charles on television) in which you bite the vowels out of words and hardly move the teeth. Graven! At the plump military-looking man who was grumbling about inconvenient trains, as if he was writing to the *Telegraph*. Graven!

The tenor voice cuts through the greying air, flies up the columns, lingers for a moment in the curving vaults eighty feet above.

Henry Howell – tenor, I tell myself, looking for a hold on what I call reality . . . Shirley Minty . . . mezzo-soprano . . . John Tranter – bass.

> *Lord, Thou hast been our refuge; in every generation;*
> *Before the hills were born, and the world was, from age*
> *to age Thou art God.*
> *Bring us not, Lord, very low: for Thou hast said,*
> *Come back again, ye sons of Adam.*

6

It is getting near to dusk as I walk towards the van through the small streets rebuilt since the great air raid of 1942 when half the old city was left ruined, including Marlowe's birthplace. I am remembering my only meeting with Richard Church who lived in a converted oast-house beside a cherry orchard in his beloved Kent.

He wrote that when he first entered the great church by the south-west corner he wanted to shout out exultantly with the voice of an army entering in triumph. And he such a mild and gentle man. But *my* first reaction was less extrovert. I had no impulse to claim it as a prize. Mine was to stand in amazement in this building in a country town beside the river Stour and ask How and Why and What? How did fornicating, boozing, sweating men come to summon the towering imagination, the confidence, the courage, the effrontery, even to begin to raise a place like this? Not just to conceive the geometric intricacy, the exquisite thrust and counterthrust, to hang a million tons of stone above a little market town. Not just the grand design – but also to contrive the hundred smaller masterpieces of glass, marble, wood, paint and ink that furnish it. And then to flood it with the sound of angels!

And all over England, from Canterbury to Hexham, they were at it. Hammering and sawing, paring and scoring, building their small cathedrals in every village and little more than plumb lines and set squares to guide them. And all without conscription, by common consent, and despite their foreign wars and plagues. Were there two million souls in England then? And they did all this? I know most of the stock answers, but none of them suffice, not quite.

There are those who come to Canterbury with the right textbooks in their hands, checking capitals, pacing out arcades, as if the stone might have flown away since yesterday. ('Pevsner says the ballflower ornament here is particularly fine . . . Ah, there's the trunch.') God bless 'em . . . corbel counters all! But Canterbury defies such analysis. To me it is more moving than any picture, symphony or poem, perhaps because it is the work of many people, so clearly the willing expression of a whole society, not just the achievement of one entrepreneur or the vision of one artist. It is the signature of an astounding age.

Richard Church wrote of Canterbury – 'Hitherto, man has not made a more perfect civic work of art . . . the Cathedral overshadows everything else. It appears to be uttering some authoritative utterance . . .'

Can we hear?

In which pocket did I put my car keys . . .?

7

Kyrie eleison . . . Christe eleison . . . The sound of angels pursues me past the traffic lights, past suburban laurel and laburnum congealing into roadside woods and then separating to make space for quiet country houses hooded in the black velvet of a warm, moonless night. On such evenings the engine whispers. Headlights search out the silver bends and tyres as soft as slippers transport you surely through the nightscape without effort. A ghost car slithering through Kent.

Down through Bridge again and over the dry ford. A face without a body, like half a Gouda cheese, halts me at the gateway of a meadow and demands a ticket please, then directs me to a parking place across the undulating grass. 'BY-PASS BONANZA BARBECUE!'

A wave of tiredness. Smell of chicken reminds me that I'm hungry. Fragrance of beer. Lights spill across the darkness like a small West End. Kyrie eleison. A marquee. From which comes a roar of voices and a tin noise of music.

> *Sister Suzie . . .*
> *Brother John . . .*
> *Martin Luther . . .*
> *Phil and Don . . .*
> *Uncle Ernie . . .*
> *Auntie Gin . . .*

My name is called. A dozen Goudas round a long wooden table in the open come slowly into focus. Become John, Peggy, Charlie, Susan-from-the-White-Fish-Authority, Robert, Dolly, Jim . . . 'Martin Luther, Brother John'.

Someone has queued for my chicken and beer. Between the little town and the high wood, between sleep and talk, today and tomorrow, Kyrie and McCartney, I listen to Bishopsbourne and Kent. John from Dover says there should be more council houses in the village, and argues well. Someone tells me that the lavatory brush behind the Mermaid bar, wooden back pencilled with a face, bristles for hair, hangs there in memory of a former customer who simply looked that way. Peggy says she thinks the Rings are Roman. Now and again, between trips to the marquee for food or beer, people begin to spill out their secrets. 'So what,' they reckon, 'he'll be gone tomorrow.'

> Sanctus fortis, Sanctus Deus,
> De profundis oro te.
> Miserere, Judex meus,
> Parce mihi, Domine

sing the choristers of Canterbury in my head.

> Someone knockin' at the door,
> Somebody's ringin' the bell,
> Do me a favour, open the door
> And let 'em in . . .
> Sister Suzie, Brother John,
> Martin Luther . . .
> Phil and Don . . . *

> Pray for me, O my friends; a visitant
> Is knocking his dire summons at my door,
> The like of whom, to scare me and to daunt,
> Has never, never come to me before . . .

I park at Robsack for the last time, close up behind the hedge, sometime between one and two o'clock.

* Taken from the song 'Let 'em In' by Paul McCartney.

29

8

I was awakened at first light – sometime between four and five – my head full of a strange pulsating sound, first seeming to come from one direction, then another, undulating, throbbing.

I stepped out into the sultry morning. Someone had splashed black-currant juice across the sky in great big blots. The sun was a blood-red pomegranate. There was unheard thunder in the air.

I walked towards the plateau edge then down through the woods, past sullen cherry orchards, and clapboard houses full of people still asleep. Now the sound seemed to be running through the forest, more musical and haunting, like a half-formed theme hunted by Sibelius. Then reaching a crescendo, gradually it fell apart and became a scattering of small, more familiar voices, that of a multitude of doves and pigeons in dawn chorus, a tide of sound that had swamped the other morning choirs of thrush and blackbird.

A little later, on the plateau, two fields of flax changed from green to burning blue and back to green again all within a minute. Again I was mystified. Walking along a straight, narrow road between unfenced fields, you do not expect the whole landscape to change colour in a twinkling, and with such blazing beauty. You've seen a river bank of meadow cranebills maybe, flaming in July? Well, this blue burned just a little paler but with more intensity. Then I met a woman along the way, standing by an open car, and she explained it to me. The blue flax flowers open only at a certain temperature, which is reached, then passed, as the day's heat mounts. A visitor, she had risen early to watch the little miracle she had not seen since it had moved and astounded her as an evacuee in 1940. I'm glad I met her, or, for fear of disbelief, I might not have dared to tell about Kent's last assault upon my senses. Eventually, I might have disbelieved myself.

Before driving north, I had to go back to Dover to keep an appointment. I parked near the town centre, and when I returned to the car I found someone had left a note under my windscreen wiper.

'Frank,' it read. 'The rings are 1914–18 coal workings!'

4

A new class of Englishman identified, a brief description of my domestic arrangements, and a housekeeping problem encountered.

WHEN Henry Vollam Morton set out on his exploration of England fifty years ago there was no problem for a man of his class about where to lay his head at nights. Like the members of the Pickwick Club a hundred years before, he simply booked in at the best or most interesting hotel in town, and retired each evening to freshly laundered linen, having first left his shoes in the corridor for cleaning. Fifty years of progress, however, have put paid to that.

If, after writing the last lines of *In Search of England* Morton had fallen – Rip van Winkle-like – into a deep sleep for half a century, awakening to begin a rediscovery of England in the 1970s,* the changes and innova-

* In fact Morton lived on into the 1970s but his last years were spent in South Africa where he died at the age of eighty-seven.

tions in the furniture of our lives would have astonished him.

He would have noted that in the matter of goods and gadgets the children of the humble villagers he had interviewed by oil lamp were now as well off – much richer, in fact – than the comfortable middle class of the twenties to which he had belonged. Looking at their motor cars, television sets and washing machines; learning that two English inventions called radar and the jet engine now enabled factory workers to fly safely at 500 miles an hour to holidays in Spain; and being informed that another English device, the fuel cell, had made it possible for men to visit the moon, he might have concluded that the golden age of travel had arrived.

Then setting out in his brand new car (windscreen washer, heated rear window, cigar lighter), with plenty, or so he thought, of the new decimal money in his nylon reinforced pocket, he would have been astounded when he went to pay his first hotel bill. Bed and (perhaps indifferent) breakfast – £12!

Thereafter he would have quickly realised that plain but comfortable hotels were now the exclusive territory of a new aristocracy. No longer could the middling sort of chap, with a decent accent and a clean shirt every day, afford to plan an English tour of any length by fingering through a hotel guide. Cheaper to take a month on the Costa Brava several hundred miles away. Now, you needed a little plastic symbol called a company credit card and, unless unusually well off, you had to be a member of the new salesman-executive class – all expenses paid and a good burgundy for dinner.

All this occurred to *me* as I contemplated my own journey into England. I was not grumbling. I had myself seen a fair part of the world on expenses. But six months' modest hotel accommodation, say, for at least £12 a night, equals £2184. Much more than I could manage. Even six months at pubs and farmhouses would cost well over a thousand.

Now I have slept soundly in some unusual places – from bracken beds on river banks to the iron deck of a bucking tanker. I have spent a night in a crate of strawberries on Liverpool Street Station and another in the casual ward of Dumfries workhouse. And, all in all, I find I have developed a weakness for the luxury hotel. Taking it all round, the amenities are better.

For about half an hour – no more – I considered carrying a lightweight tent, then remembered the fearsome midges in the Cheviots and decided that my Boy Scout days were over.

Someone suggested I should hire a caravan but the drudgery of towing one of those unwieldy monsters and having to seek an 'approved' site each evening, was not congenial. It would limit my freedom and restrict my company. The solution seemed to be a single vehicle in which I could sleep, shave, cook, type and read in reasonable comfort, and, if necessary, invite someone in for a drink. It would be unobtrusive, so that I could park and sleep by the wayside, and visit peer or policeman without bruising the environment or exciting too much curiosity. Something that handled like a family car and used about the same amount of petrol, was what I needed. It was a tall order, but I studied the market. It seemed unlikely that I would find something to suit all my requirements, but I did, and nobly.

There is a small factory on a hill in Devon where they make just such a chariot.[*] Every month or so a number of Morris Marina commercial vans are driven from British Leyland and there they slice off the roof-tops with the nonchalant expertise you or I would devote to a boiled egg. They then remove the seats and refit the vehicle with cooker, wardrobe, sink unit, underfloor water tank, fire extinguisher, shaver point, lighting, reversible seating, fold-away tables, racks, curtains, cupboards – everything, in fact, that an itinerant writer might need, and all apparently without using a nail or a screw. They insert sliding side windows, and put on a tough fibre-glass roof which, by the operation of a simple scissors mechanism, can be raised to room height in a few seconds.

This Devonian box of tricks – it is called the Suntor Marina – seemed to satisfy all my wants. The interior fittings – especially those reversing front seats which with their individual tables enable you to eat in comfort – were ingeniously designed. I have lived in caravans before and wondered why the manufacturers had not employed a marine designer to teach them a rational use of space. But this small vehicle, propelled by a 1300 c.c. engine, had apparently solved all the problems. I went to Devon. I watched them being fitted out. I talked to Ron Webster the designer and I think that now he is a friend for life. I got to know the managing director, Gareth Haylett, and discovered that he could stand at the back door of his local and skim a hat fifteen yards down the bar to cover his own tankard as neat as Kitty's leg. Which isn't a bad recommendation.

I found I could convert my car into living quarters and have tea on the boil in a good deal less than half an hour, and I could take off rapidly each morning after breakfast in less time than I took to leave the house at home. Better still, by arranging things just right the night before, I could have tea in bed each morning for the first time since I left the Army. There was only one problem during that hot summer in which I enjoyed the sensation of awakening in fresh surroundings almost every day. I

[*] Alas, this factory no longer exists.

could not devise a means of keeping butter or margarine from turning into oil. I asked the camping shops for advice. All the managers could suggest was one of those insulated boxes in which you place a bag of cooling chemicals that has to be refrozen every day or so in someone's fridge. Eventually I solved the problem but I had to go back to the country kitchen of Morton's time to find the method. And that did not happen till I reached Stamford market. It is a story for another day.

5

I linger in the haunted fields of Kent, sight a fleet of barns, and learn about a left-handed ghost, the loneliness of Captain Korzeniowski, what the Pope said about Parson Hooker, why Peggy Hogben stitched her way across the world, and how Sir Winston fired bananas at the Wehrmacht.

1

'TO the memory of William Sidney Smith Mulcaster, Major General, late 6th Madras Cavalry. Died January 10th 1910, aged 84. Son of Captain Sir William Howe Mulcaster R.N., A.D.C. to William IV. Died 1837 from wounds in action.' And to the memory of Luther Millwood, village blacksmith, who made the gates of Government House, Sydney, Australia, and told the Squire to bugger off.

Doubtless Saxon, Norman, Dane and Angle-ishman preceded the good soldier into the consecrated earth of Bishopsbourne. They have been planting our ancestors there since 789 at least, and probably there's a healthy, heathen trace of bonemeal in the soil as well. The General's blood was likely to have been as mixed as that of any other modern Englishman. His surname had a Romano-British ring and he also bore the honourable name of Smith, suggesting at least one forebear who wore a leather apron and could bend a shoe. And Master Millwood's imported forename spoke plainly of another theme in English history, that of the protester, hammer of the status quo – a tradition he seemed willing to sustain.

I read the General's memorial tablet in the church early one morning before the dew was off the grass, and heard blacksmith Millwood's testimonial that midday in the Mermaid.

'Sir John . . . that's the father of our present squire . . . the Mermaid on the pub sign is part of his family's coat of arms . . . he wanted Luther Millwood to do some work on the staircase up at the Hall,' said the man in the front bar. 'But Luther was busy. The Squire ranted and raved for above ten minutes, but Luther just worked on, listening but saying nothing. Then at last he picked up his hammer and hit the anvil a great clout . . . and by Christ that can make a noise! . . . then he said . . .

'"Sir John . . . you have had *your* say . . . Now I'll have *mine* . . . Just bugger off out!"

'And so the old Squire did . . .' said my informant reflectively.

Whether the anvil peal symbolised a change in the social order of the village I do not know. But its memory rings down the years. The present Squire is an amiable man, popular in the bar, hailed gladly in the street, and when the Great Equaliser calls him to his ancestors there will be real sorrow in Bishopsbourne and much beer consumed in his jovial memory. But there's no doubt that he knows his place.

The English countryside, every hedge and every village, is haunted by such ghosts, forever telling us who and what we are, how we made and shaped the land. Never does it speak of racial purity. The Kentish fields have heard the tramp of Roman soldiery, men from as far as the Tigris and Euphrates and the northern forests of the old Empire. They have heard the broken shuffle of the pilgrims' feet, and whispering in the orchards, as the lame and lusty pious of all Christendom travelled to and from the shrine of St Thomas of Canterbury.

For four years, women and old men worked in the fields and listened to the murmur of the guns as Europe tore her sons to pieces not thirty miles away. And for another four *their* children looked up and saw the summer sky scored by Messerschmidts and Hurricanes, then watching west from bedroom windows, observed the glow of burning London. I mention these events in order of chronology, distancing centurion from squadron

36

leader, thus to the stranger perhaps making time-distant men less real. But to those with eyes and ears and hearts for England, the years are just convenient labels and all the ghosts have substance.

Charles Fagg, my temporary landlord, was such a man, farming his little plateau on the Downs in such company. I called on him one morning to get water and he introduced me to his ghosts. He sat me down in his living room with a bowl of fresh-picked cherries and brought out two shoe-boxes full of little objects wrapped in tissue paper – arrowheads and tools of flint and bronze left in the fields by men four thousand years ago, and turned up by his plough. 'Look,' he said, 'this man was left-handed. You can tell by the marks . . .' He took me out across the fields, explaining that the fine brick farmhouses of the first Elizabeth's days were made of clay from the land on which they stood, and that if we looked about among the outbuildings and gardens, we'd likely find the pits from which they came.

Farmer Fagg was a practical man, and as such appraised the work of other craftsmen. We stood in black Kentish barns that looked like Viking halls. They rested unanchored on the earth, and yet they were so strong in post and truss and purlin that they could be inched along by tractor. He pointed out the tool marks of the old foresters and shipwrights, reading every cut . . . 'They cut these timbers over a trench,' he said, 'the oversawyer working the saw from above, and the undersawyer down below with his hair full of sawdust.'

Those big baulks had once been the main timbers of men-o'-war and like as not had first been felled in Kent. Having served their imperial purpose they had been sailed back to England, used for barn-building, and still looked as though (if they were conscripted once again) they would serve as stoutly as two hundred years before. I left Charles sailing his barns to Coromandel and went down to Bishopsbourne.

I crossed a small embowered bridge on the edge of the village, and looking over the parapet into an abandoned railway cutting, now over-grown with sycamore and bramble that hid the entrance to a tunnel, reflected that all ghosts could not be solemn, that all great men were capable of folly, and that – thank God! – all soldiers were not called to heroic action.

It seems that Winston Churchill, on taking office as Prime Minister in World War II, remembered that two 18-inch guns – bigger than anything in the modern Navy – had been used in France during the previous conflict.

Each shell was 6 feet 7 inches long and weighed one and a quarter tons. One gun had last been fired in 1916 when it demolished Arras railway station with three rounds. Both pieces had since been outlawed by international treaty and should perhaps have been destroyed. Mr Churchill, however, ordered a search for them. They were rediscovered somewhere in Nottingham, renovated at Darlington railway works, then transported by rail, disguised as banana wagons, to Bourne Park Tunnel, just behind the Squire's house, though the movement of some 250 tons so labelled must have seemed a curious transaction in those fruitless times.

The guns were hidden in the tunnel and manned by a hundred gunners and Royal Engineers who lived in railway sleeping coaches at a nearby station. They were called the 11th Super Heavy Battery, though surely there were not another ten such elephantine outfits.

The sappers were necessary, for although the gunners could elevate and depress the barrels they could not traverse them from side to side. Thus every time they were brought out for firing, the guns had to be hauled by loco to a bend and new track laid to point them at their targets – at once expensive and inaccurate. Even the dullest military advisers must have questioned the cost-effectiveness of this Churchillian gesture. But the great man in the siren-suit had spoken. And so it had to be.

At any rate, a hundred men, spared the perils of a more intimate encounter with the Boche, were privileged to earn their Defence Medals in the fair fields of Kent. Doubtless their presence proved a boon to local publicans and provided exercise for Kentish maids, a not ignoble consequence. As for the *military* havoc they achieved, the only evidence of this I could discover was that the Lickpot Inn – or was it the World's Wonder Bridge, somewhere down the track? – lost its windows once or twice on firing days.

2

As I continued my morning stroll – on the way to taking tea with Peggy Hogben, the postman's wife – I was reminded of two other unsettled spirits who walked down this village street and still turn up in village talk.

In the large white house just past the church lived Teodor Josef Konrad Nalecz Korzeniowski, born in the Ukraine of Polish parents exiled by the Russians for too openly expressing a taste for national freedom. His second language was French, but he learned English at twenty when he became a seaman, and later Master, on a British ship – so thoroughly indeed that, as Joseph Conrad, he stirred our English imaginations, and enhanced our literature, for all time to come.

Conrad spent his last days in Bishopsbourne – five years of poor health, financial worry and that 'indestructible loneliness that surrounds, envelops, clothes every human soul from the cradle to the grave . . .'

'English,' he once wrote, 'was for me neither a matter of choice nor adoption. The merest idea of choice had not entered my head. And as to adoption – well, yes, there was adoption; but it was I who was adopted by the genius of the language, which directly I came out of the stammering stage made me its own so completely that its very idioms, I truly believed, had a direct action on my temperament and fashioned my still plastic character.'

He left us a record of his first encounter with the language. It seemed an insignificant event at the time, but it was to be the beginning of his greatest, and ultimately tragic, love.

A few strokes brought us alongside, and it was then that, for the very first time in my life, I heard myself addressed in English – the speech of my . . . future, of long friendships, of the deepest affections, of hours of toil and hours of ease, and of solitary hours too, of books read, of thoughts pursued, or remembered emotions – of my very dreams! And if (after having been thus fashioned by it in that part of me which cannot decay) I dare not claim it aloud as my own then, at any rate, the speech of my children. Thus small events grow memorable by the passage of time. As to the quality of the address itself I cannot say it was very striking. Too short for eloquence and devoid of all charm of tone, it consisted precisely of three words, 'Look out there,' growled out huskily above my head.

In 1924, at sixty-five, the fashioned fashioner of English died, his last years darkened by a belief that he would never be its master.

Three hundred and thirty years before – it must have been about the time the farmhouse near Robsack meadow was being built and there was much hammering and hauling of new timbers in Park Lane – another stranger had arrived in Bishopsbourne with luggage, books and wife, to become parson at the little church. His name was Richard Hooker. He was forty-one, a gentle, studious man, and already an author of international repute. He had been a fellow of Corpus Christi, Oxford, and Master of the Temple, but had asked for a country parish so that he could have peace to complete his most important work. Queen Elizabeth had granted him the living. She could not, however, relieve him of his wife, referred to by one commentator as 'a virago and a slut', and who is unlikely to have been much help to him in his writing of that monument of theological literature, the *Laws of Ecclesiastical Politie*.

Though rarely read these days by anyone but scholars (William Rees-Mogg, formerly editor of *The Times*, is the only journalist I know to have read it), in its time and for long afterwards the *Politie* caused quite a stir. It was a defence of the *via media* – the middle way between the extremes of Puritanism and the claims of Rome – and by all accounts it had some lasting things to say about statecraft and the role of monarchy. Even Pope Clement VIII got quite excited about this document from an heretical realm: 'There is no learning that this man hath not searched into; nothing too hard for his understanding: this man indeed deserves the name of Author; his books will get reverence by Age, for there is in them such seeds of Eternity that if the rest be like this they shall last till the last fire shall consume all learning.' From His Holiness to an Anglican vicar being nagged to death in Bishopsbourne, it was praise indeed.

Richard Hooker, too, died within five years of arriving in the village, and only five volumes had been published. The rest came out years later. And Izaak Walton, draper, angler, and Hooker's first biographer, blamed Mrs H. for that.

3

The kettle was on the hob by the time I knocked on Peggy's door. But first she would show me round the house to see the alterations of four hundred years – me tapping plaster walls and touching beams big enough for battleships, pausing at unexpected windows to see the rose-filled garden. Peggy in her sixties was an attractive woman whose qualities one comes across in many English places. Blue eyes. Straight back. Energy, intelligence, curiosity and artless charm.

I had already heard in the village how she had befriended two New Zealanders who happened upon Bishopsbourne, then how she'd taken in sewing till she had earned enough to visit them. Afterwards, someone counted up the bobbins. Thirteen miles of thread she'd sewn – or was it twenty-one?

In the bright front room with the tea and sunshine, and whisky if I wanted it, Peggy talked about her life – father a soldier, mother in domestic service – about her garden flowers, and about the two American botanists she had guided to rare plants in the chalklands. Then from her shelves she brought down her treasure, one small, thin volume with a faded blue cover – *December Spring* by Jocelyn Brooke – 'to Peggy Hogben from the author'. She said, 'He was gentle and humble. He taught me how to appreciate the French composers . . .' I opened it and read these lines by the war-tortured poet who died in 1966.

> In the copse behind the village
> In days of early June,
> I found the white helleborine –
> Its ivory demi-lune

Erect amid the green
And close-springing ivy . . .

. . . But walking home to the village,
Hand clutching helleborine
And pale spotted orchis
In the drenching mist and rain –
How tender the rain-washed green
Of that tumbled and twilit lane,
How bright the vision of that country.

'He lived just down the road. I used to visit him on Thursdays,' Peggy said.

When I left, the lane was drenched in sunshine and there was a fragrance from the great limes in the copse. I went to the Mermaid and bought a pint from the landlord, brother of Richard Aldington, that other poet whose soul was maimed by war. The poppy field, ahead, shimmered in the heat.

Village ghosts.

6

In praise of Essex, hemlaths, tempenheads and prick posts.
I arrive at Thaxted and find myself with Gustav Holst,
Lansbury's Lambs and H. G. Wells at the barricades
where the English revolution faltered.

1

THE LITTLE LANES that meander through the heart of Essex, so
close to the tourist Babels of the West End, are yet undiscovered by
the charabancs of America and the Continent, and are even neglected by
the lemmings of London. One observer has blamed this happy circumstance on the squalor of Liverpool Street station, the east London railway
terminal that serves the county. But that is nonsense. Tourists use cars
and coaches. Anyway, the man who hates Liverpool Street is insensitive
to history and spectacle.

No. I think the chief reason for the unpopularity of central and upper
Essex – among the English anyway – is that when they think of Essex they
think of Dagenham, Romford, and Chingford and all the once-pleasant
villages that got swamped by Henry Ford and the overslop of London.
Speculators in the twenties offered free chicken-and-champagne train
trips to entice London home-hunters to their ramshackle townships built

on swamp. Elderly East-Enders, ready for retirement, thought they were spending their savings on nine bean rows and a hive. In places like Pitsea and Laindon they got cess pits, communal standpipes and unpaved streets that looked liked Flanders when winter came.

Later, the sales pitch became less brazen, the houses more weather-proof. But I cannot think kindly of the builders and estate agents of the last thirty years. Or the planning committees who gave them licence to spill their mess all the way to Southend. Even the bright young bureau-crats in the municipal planning offices served Essex ill when they devised huge council estates with such disregard for the tribal needs of Cockneys that many of the new tenants slung their hooks, and trekked back to the warm slums of Bethnal Green.

South Essex is a pox that is still spreading. Hornchurch, for example, where H. V. Morton paused for tea, has swelled from 39,000 inhabitants to 104,000 in twenty years. How could that be happy? But south Essex is not Essex.

I did not mean to mention London on this trip – London is another story – but it got in my way.

I crossed from Kent to Essex beneath the Thames by way of Dartford Tunnel. I was bound for Cambridge but became confused by what seemed to be contradictory road signs, and found myself in Dagenham outside the Ford factories at knocking-off time. It took me an hour of driving and map-reading through the tawdry streets of a dozen murdered hamlets before I reached the palings of suburbia.

Then London ends abruptly. One minute you are halted by cross-traffic on a main road outside a concrete road house of the thirties – and the next moment the lights change, the traffic thins, the woods begin, you round a bend and come face to face with the tremendous timbered façade of an inn that was probably doing good road-house business when the first Elizabeth was plaguing England with her tours.

After that the road is tree-lined and there are glimpses of small spires and those decent Essex villages that were strung along the highway long before 'ribbon-building' got a bad reputation. Nice places, they look, with modest names you've never heard of, the occasional colour-washed cottage under thatch, and people who have lost – or perhaps never had – that set metropolitan scowl.

At five past six I stopped at a pub called the Chequers, and after my first swallow, asked the landlord, Nobby Clark, the name of the village I was in.

'Ugly,' I thought he said. 'And I'm the Ugly landlord.'

He looked round the bar then leaned confidentially towards me. 'And I'll tell you what,' he said, 'there's a lot of Ugly people round here.'

43

Nobody seemed to take offence. But nobody smiled either. Not just then, anyway. And it took me another few swallows before I realised that I was in the village of Ugley which, after a glance at the map a mile or two back, I had assumed would be pronounced Yewjley.

I liked that. I once knew a seaside place with a pleasant main street called Fish Walk. An honest name. But the people of the town, corrupted a little by respectability, had persuaded the local authority to rename it Marine Parade, because it sounded posher. There are lots of Midden Lanes that have become Maiden Lanes. There's even one alongside King's Cross Station, but the smell lingered in the syllables and they changed it to York Way.

And here was a whole village, not only disdaining a change that could have been insinuated over a century or two, but waylaying the casual traveller with its puckish humour.

2

Aythorpe Roding, High Roding, Leaden Roding, Margaret Roding, Berners Roding, Beauchamp Roding, Abbess Roding, White Roding; Wyvenhoe, Bardfield Saling, Howlett End, Wimbish, High Easter, Good Easter, Thaxted and Saffron Walden. The sounds of Essex.

I didn't press on to Cambridge that day. Or for many more. I was drugged by the sweetness of this country. I got lost in wayward lanes, and was redirected in a village I cannot name by a woman on horseback with a face like old Spanish leather. When she leaned down and smiled it was like a burst of moonlight. So off I went again and got lost again – in an archipelago of hamlets with long ponds by the roadside and signs saying 'Goatsmilk'. I could have been in Tolkien's Shire. Come to think of it, the man who taught me the difference between a wallower and a hemlath, and told me about poll ends, uplongs, tempenheads, prick posts and cottered bridle irons as he showed me round a windmill, could have been Bilbo Baggins of Bag End.

There is not much stone to be seen in the streets of *this* Essex, but much timber and plaster. The plaster and wattle panels fill in the squares and triangles between uprights and braces, and they are washed in pinks and greens and ochres and siennas. Some of the plaster is pargetted – given a surface of rings, bullseyes, fruit or foliage. The high street of such a town is a pattern of rectangles, broad and narrow, that could not have come off a drawing board. Apparently haphazard, it has a liveliness, a fitness for warm, varied, human habitation, whose secret we seem unable to rediscover.

The timbers are not nailed on. They are the skeletons of the houses. They hold the roofs on and the walls together, and you can see it. They are not neat planks cut yesterday to standard dimensions by machines. You wouldn't have to tell a child that they were once trees. He would see the shape of the trunk or the bough that lived in the forest six hundred years ago. Of course the carpenter, knowing the size of the plot on which he was building, or the kind of family that would inhabit the house, would choose the tree for the beam, or the limb for the big, bent cruck. And he hadn't dictated the shape and girth of the plant, like a man from the Forestry Commission. So, to some extent, the tree designed the house. The builder's working life was a partnership with forest, terrain and climate. The result was lively streets of timber and plaster houses, not one a repetition of another, yet all within the discipline imposed by material and vernacular techniques, each become part of its immediate neighbours.

I felt, during those few days in Essex, that when exiled Englishmen dream of home – even if they were born in a London suburb, or like me in a gritty northern town – such is the England they imagine.

3

Wherever your journey begins – north, south, east or west – if you ever go to Thaxted you should contrive to arrive from the south which is the old approach from Dover and from London. To do otherwise would be like beginning a play with the final scene, or hearing a story back to front. You might understand the message, but you would lose the sense of drama. Thaxted, and its part of Roman Watling Street, lead north.

I entered the town in late afternoon on foot. I turned into Town Street and there stood before one of the great scenes of England. I hesitate over that word 'great' for it can suggest grandeur – grandeur like the view of Durham from the railway or Manhattan's skyline, places which make their initial impact through mere size. But this is Essex. Thaxted was made slowly, and by tradesmen, not by giants. It is an essay in harmony, not scale. But great all the same.

A green, cast-iron water pump stands next to a round, red pillar box on the pavement opposite the Co-op. Barclays Bank is lime-green, bow-fronted, Georgian. The wide street tilts, curves and narrows up the hill past colour-washed shops and houses – some timbered, some faced with stucco, some medieval, some classical – until, where the road forks, the timber-framed fifteenth-century Moot Hall sits on oaken stilts with its two overhanging storeys and two hipped roofs, marking the secular centre of the community. It was the guildhall of the cutlers when Thaxted was a little Sheffield. It was recently restored for £70,000 and sold to the County Council for a pound. There, the lane that forks left is narrow, and cobbled with pink and brown rubble. To the right, Watling Street steepens, then swings round behind and out of sight. A swell of big treetops appears above the Moot Hall, and from the foliage springs the delicate spire of St John the Baptist on its hidden hill.

And that's just about it. It doesn't fire salutes. It just sits and smiles. An amiable English country town, population 1,830, early closing day Wednesday, market day Friday. A place of simple country people with simple interests, you might think. A mirror of English stability. A far cry from the politics of revolution, of strikes and barricades – all the nonsense that fevers the minds of city people.

Well now! Many people have found Thaxted and been bewitched. Some have stayed. Especially in the days when William Morris was wallpapering the drawing-rooms of the rich, and broadcasting seeds of revolt against their very world of stocks and shares and steam, and making those dreams of Merrie England that still haunt some Englishmen. Handmade Thaxted beckoned such middle-class dreamers – potters, parsons, poets, folk-dancers, handloom weavers. One of them was Gustav Holst who first saw Thaxted on a walking tour in 1913. He bought a house and stayed to play the church organ till 1925. When I walked up Town Street on the left, I passed the window of the room in which he wrestled with *The Planets*. There's thunder for you!

Street posters announced an exhibition of art at such-and-such a farm. The annual flower festival would include organ recitals and baroque chamber music. A fine Georgian house was devoted to 'residential courses in Liberal Studies, Social Science, Drama, Art'. A bookshop window displayed *Les Misérables*, *The Old Churches of London*, Edmund Gosse, Hilaire Belloc . . . Among the publications on sale in the magnificent pewless church I found *Folk Dancing and Religion*, *The Church and Party Politics*, *Learning to Live with Modern Architecture*, *The Blessed John Huss of Bohemia*, *Gustav Holst and Thaxted* and *Conrad Noel – Prophet and Priest*. All had been written in this little town.

As I zipped myself into my sleeping bag in someone's paddock I decided not to move on next day. There was more to Thaxted than a pretty face – something recent enough and powerful enough still to influence the present. I had to find out what. I fell asleep till a barking dog wakened me for breakfast.

The manager of the Co-op where I called for supplies next morning gave me my first lead. And Harry Lowe the corn merchant across the road confirmed it. *They* knew what had happened all those years ago, and their faces lit up with the memory and the mischief of it all. They had been schoolboys at the time. The handloom weaver at the top of the town hard by the Swan – a charming man with a Mosaic beard – confirmed it in his own way too. He refused to say a word. He got me out of his shop courteously, but swiftly. It all had to do with that man Conrad Noel, 'Prophet and Priest', whose name I had seen in the church, and it wasn't too far removed from the dreams of William Morris after all. Or from revolution.

The Reverend Conrad Noel became vicar of Thaxted in 1910. He had been born in a Grace and Favour house. His grandmother, Lady Gainsborough, had been lady-in-waiting to Queen Victoria. He was appointed to this living by the socialist Countess of Warwick. Those were days – difficult to imagine it now – when there was some concern that the Church of England might be turning 'red'. A bishop had recently declared of the scriptures, at a conference in Caxton Hall: 'I dare any of you to say this is not a revolutionary doctrine'.

'The Battle of the Flags' – which is how Thaxted's little revolution became known, and which has its partisans to this day – was really a war between two Christs. There was the Christ of the Thaxted carriage folk who was, of course, an honorary member of the Conservative Party and supporter of Empire, a Saviour who knew his place, and was rewarded with middle-class pew rents and straight-faced Protestant worship each Sunday morning. Then there was the Christ of Conrad Noel. In Noel's own words He was 'the Divine Outlaw who founded a Red Army to turn the world upside down and prepare for the coming in Glory of the international Commonwealth of God'. It was Christian duty, he believed, to destroy the capitalist system and the British Empire, and to return the English to the old Catholic faith.

On his first Sunday in Thaxted he threw the pews into the street. He filled the lovely building on the hill with ordinary people, and he led a strike of confectionery workers. He reintroduced incense and dramatic medieval church ceremonial, religious processions with bright vestments, flowers, torches and banners. Gustav Holst not only played the organ. He conducted the masses of Byrd and Bach and wrote works specially for performance in Thaxted church.

Our church bells at Thaxted at Whitsuntide say,
Come all you good people and put care away . . .

To Noel and his disciples it must have seemed a lovely dawn. And what sweeter place than Thaxted for the springtime of the socialist millennium? What greener fields than Essex fields? What dearer land than England? He brought Morris men to perform the dances thought to have been imported from Spain by John of Gaunt after watching Moorish festivals – Morris equalling Moorish, and no connection with William. And in 1918 he founded the Catholic Crusade which was '. . . to break up the present world and make a new, in the power of the outlaw of Galilee . . . in which . . . the mighty shall be dragged from their seats, the hungry filled, the rich sent empty away . . . in which . . . the traffickers in oil and wheat and cattle and the bodies and souls of men shall lament as the smoke of their cities ascends to the heavens . . .'

It was heady, patriotic stuff and the old saints were his allies. 'If while you know the most deadly tyrants are not kings, but financiers and speculators, captains of industry, you would also, with St. Thomas of Canterbury, destroy that nest of flunkeys, the Court . . .'

Ah, what waterfalls of words! What inspired name-dropping! What days they must have been in Town Street! What a setting for the English revolution! Perhaps Moscow, where the goings-on at Thaxted were reported to the hungry comrades, really thought it might be about to happen when the Red Flag was hoisted in Thaxted Church.

Noel and his followers flew three flags: the Red Flag, the banner of St George of England (Noel and his partisans regarded the Union Jack as a symbol of imperialist exploitation), and the tricolour of Ireland, for those were Black and Tan days. The pewless local establishment protested to the War Office, the Home Secretary and the Prime Minister, all of whom were legally powerless in the matter. A gang of students from Cambridge tore down Noel's flags and hoisted the Union Jack. Then the fat was really in the fire.

The Conrad Noel faction tore down the Union Jack. They burned it in the street and re-hoisted the banner of revolt. The undergraduates returned, took them down again, and, scaling the steeple (it is 181 feet high) affixed the Union Jack where they believed no one could retrieve it. But they did. And so it went on. Noel boasted that every time his colours were removed, they flew again within the day.

The Cambridge brigade were now thoroughly aroused. Newspaper readers, from the Athenaeum to the miners' lodge at Hetton-le-Hole, must have been united in the delight with which they read – in the

London *Times* and Lansbury's* *Herald* – that the 'insurgents' had now established a headquarters at the Cock Inn, and that they were parading the town crying insults and slogans at the 'reds'. On Empire Day thousands of sympathisers poured into Thaxted to join them. Blows were exchanged. Hats were knocked off. Army cadets joined in and it was even reported that shots were fired.

The Cambridge faction had hidden a lorry-load of stones in the backyard of the Swan, and they threatened to break the windows of the vicarage and every house in town that failed to fly the Union Jack. But a body of ex-policemen known as Lansbury's Lambs (I swear it's true: they had been sacked for going on strike) discovered the cache of missiles, drove it out of town, and immobilised the vehicle by slashing its tyres.

Then the Cambridge rioters swarmed up Town Street to the handsome old vicarage where parishioners were taking refuge – just as H. G. Wells arrived in a Rolls-Royce.

I ask you to pause, and relish the scene. It is surely one of the great comic moments in English social history. The background of timbered houses. The mob. The undergrads. The flags. The angry voices. Then the little genius with the small moustache, squeaky voice, wing collar, and probably spats as well, emerging from the cavernous limousine in the nick of time, and appealing to the crowd not to attack. And it worked, by heavens! They went away.

Eventually the cause of the flags came before an ecclesiastical court whose Chancellor ruled against Noel's banners, not (so said the court) because of the ideology they represented, but because they threatened a breach of the peace. And so, with that touch of sweet English hypocrisy, ended Thaxted's days of fame.

Conrad Noel died in 1942 and was buried under the great east window of the parish church. Poor, dear man, he was a saint in his way, and in other times might have been recognised as such. He was succeeded by a Marxist priest, and then a campaigner for 'Gay Lib'.

I've been sitting in the sun like a Peruvian peasant this afternoon, warming my behind on Gustav Holst's back doorstep. The house is empty. I've been watching the willowherb weed poke through the paving of the small terrace in the overgrown garden, grateful to the genius of England for the existence of such places, and ever so reluctantly, making up my mind that it is time now to move on.

---

* George Lansbury, beloved leader of the Labour Party (1931–5), editor of the *Daily Herald* and *Lansbury's Labour Weekly*.

I would have gone to Saffron Walden for the music of the name alone. How could anyone resist it? Saffron: that expensive dye that English housewives use in minute quantity to tint rice, with which Cornish women flavour saffron cake, which the Romans used for perfume, the Irish and the Greeks to colour royal garments, and with which Buddhist monks still stain their robes. Walden: the name of a lake in the woods of New England, which once belonged to the poet Emerson and where Henry Thoreau lived in his cabin, trying to make his solitary Eden.

The substance saffron comes from a glowing crocus which is neither yellow, nor orange nor gold but is all three just the same. And this Essex town is so called, they tell me, because in other days the saffron crocus crop (imagine it, a saffron crop!) was brought here from the fields. That puzzles and pleases me. For a little saffron goes a long way. And it is difficult to think of a town's economy, let alone its name, being supported by the heart of a crocus.

I know a city street in Asia with the lovely name of Lalezar. It means 'where the tulips grow' but there's not a flower in sight. It is full of money dealers, cheap tailors and radio shops that blast out oriental 'pop'.

Saffron Walden does not disappoint. I have walked the narrow streets and the broad, I have supped at its inns, taken shade under its trees, read in its library, jostled with its shoppers, talked to its people, enquired of the housing business from its estate agents, and scratched my back at its street corners against age-silvered oak. I have found nothing, absolutely nothing, to offend me. It seems incapable of bad taste. A town that has survived at a point on the way to perfection – a shrewd balance between past and present – beyond which it would be dangerous to pass. A town where I could live contentedly for ever.

Saffron Walden – whether by good sense or the dictation of topography, I do not know – has acquired its cheerful personality without draughty, continental pomposity, wide open spaces and monumental buildings. The busy little shopping streets are informally disposed, and just broad enough for a couple of wagonloads of crocuses to pass in each direction. In the small market square there is a public library – an eccentric, baroque building with little stone towers and modest flourishes. At one time it might have been a corn exchange. Quite recently it must have become too small for the press of readers (I am just guessing: I did not stay to ask) and they have modernised the interior with such self-assurance, charm and good manners that the most hidebound conservationist could not cavil.

In my youth most towns, however poor, could support at least one secondhand bookshop. You could feel the purpose and the grain of a place in its bookshop, in the kind of building it occupied, the proprietor himself, the specialist subjects (seamanship and marine engineering in Sunderland, theology in Durham), and the customers. But now there are considerable towns that could hardly support a decent row of shelves. Well, at Saffron Walden you walk up a little hill from the market stalls, past a number of town shops – a grocer's, a delicatessen, and the kind of general store I thought had disappeared – and there, beginning on a corner, is as fine a bookshop as I've seen anywhere.

It is not one shop. It is a labyrinth. It used to be the Sun Inn, and Cromwell used it as a headquarters. But you don't let such dismal associations bother you as you burrow and sample your way past the Nelson Classics, the Everymans, the Left Wing Book Club issues, the old Pears Cyclopedias, and the Thinkers Library, in search of dusty treasures.

But I am just a traveller, and I cannot stay anywhere for long. I see what I see, meet whom I meet and read only what I have time to read – in local newspapers in libraries – before I move on. In the places I visit, there must be important issues I have no inkling of, even secrets. Something was teasing me now about Saffron Walden. A town has to have a reason to exist. Even Saffron Walden could not survive just to warm the heart. There must, I thought, be some little rat race somewhere to maintain this appearance of prosperity.

So I went into the Cross Keys intending to enquire about such realities. But all the landlord told me was that Dick Turpin had been a local lad, and that it was the highwayman's old schoolmarm who recognised his handwriting on a letter and secured his last arraignment.

I asked a young woman in an estate agent's office about the town's principal industries.

Oh yes, she said, there were some factories.

What did they make?

Shuttlecocks, she said.

And that was that.

7

*What the 'Likely Lads' did in Trumpington . . . how the
atom was split with a biscuit tin . . . and concerning the
outrageous price of ham pie in Cambridge.*

1

I WOKE at sunrise next day in the paddock on the northern edge of
Thaxted to which I had returned at nightfall. The dog that had
barked the morning before had now discovered my encampment and
resented the intrusion. He was a big fellow of unfathomable ancestry but
with much of the wolf about his jaws. He growled and prowled behind the
chickenwire that separated us. I have learned to expect a respectful
comradeship among habitual early risers, but when I sat down to breakfast on my back doorstep, pretending nonchalance, he flew into a rage
and kept hurling himself against the wire, showing his fangs and shaking
the fenceposts in a most unfriendly manner. I would gladly have shared
my meal with any creature, on four legs or two, who had given me a

decent Good morning, but this one ignored the bacon rind I flung him and gave alarming intimations that he preferred his meat uncooked. So I stowed my gear with more than usual alacrity and skedaddled. I was through Saffron Walden before the milkmen, and running down the hill out of town I heard a rattling above my head, and realising that in my haste I had not secured the roof, was obliged to stop and make fast.

The day was still young. My breakfast companion was far behind. I decided to dawdle. Such a morning, after all, was made for dawdling. It was dawdling weather and dawdling country. Nothing looked more important than the wide East Anglian sky, and nothing seemed to move more purposefully than the mountains of summer cumulus that dawdled across it. I resolved not to drive directly into Cambridge where I would have to pit my wits against other motorists for a parking space. I would, I thought, go to Grantchester, by way of Trumpington, and taking the path across the fields, arrive on foot in Cambridge at the same point as the river Cam.

And of course, when I thought of Grantchester I thought of Rupert Brooke. And thinking of Brooke I thought of the Old Vicarage where he had rooms, and how that modest building had survived in the imaginations of millions of English people who grew up between the two world wars.

Perhaps no two lines have been written this century more powerfully nostalgic, and more redolent of the pre-1914 England for which the readers of H. V. Morton so clearly yearned, than the couplet that ends Brooke's poem 'The Old Vicarage, Grantchester':

> *Stands the Church clock at ten to three?*
> *And is there honey still for tea? . . .*

Those lines, together with the fourteen written four months before his death on the way to Gallipoli in 1915 ('If I should die, think only this of me: That there's some corner of a foreign field . . . that is forever England . . .') were part of the emotional furniture of the England into which I was born. It even cast its spell on people, imprisoned in gaunt northern townscapes, who would never know that 'holy land' and for whom the idea of lying day-long 'to watch the Cambridge sky' and 'flower-lulled in sleepy grass, hear the cool lapse of hours pass, until the centuries blend and blur' was beyond possibility. Patriotic sentiment, and the romantic acceptance of war, have been mocked by cleversides through subsequent decades. I struck such intolerant attitudes myself in adolescence. But people – a people, a society – react to the tragedies of their times in the ways of their times. To expect otherwise is a failure of imagination. What other generation needed comfort more than that of Brooke?

I had been re-reading 'Grantchester' on my way through Essex – the first time for twenty years or more – and found it a more complicated piece than I remembered. At the beginning it is a grumble of the kind that many Englishmen express when they find themselves in surroundings too well-ordered, in this case pre-war Germany.

'Here tulips bloom as they are told . . .' he writes. And then recalling his Cambridgeshire village . . .

> Unkempt about those hedges blows
> An English unofficial rose;
> And there the unregulated sun
> Slopes down to rest when day is done,
> And wakes a vague unpunctual star,
> A slippered Hesper; and there are
> Meads towards Haslingfield and Coton
> Where das Betreten's not verboten.

Later, there are twenty lines of joyous English mick-taking about the Cambridge neighbourhood – irrational, or at least out of place, a foreigner might think, in a context of such lyricism. But by Gum it works!

> For Cambridge people rarely smile,
> Being urban squat and packed with guile . . .
>
> At Over they fling oaths at one,
> And worse than oaths at Trumpington . . .
>
> But Grantchester! ah, Grantchester!

Before Grantchester is Trumpington. And there I did indeed find worse than oaths. The twentieth century has dealt meanly with that village. It would be less offensive to the eye and less depressing to the spirit if it stood by the North Circular among the gimcrack suburbs of north London, not on the edge of Cambridge. I hadn't the stomach to stop and look at the Church of St Mary and St Michael (Pevsner calls it 'sumptuous') and the famous life-size brass memorial to Sir Roger de Trumpington. Had I been travelling in Morton's day, however, I would have paused to visit Trumpington Mill. It stood on the river above Byron's Pool till it was burned down in 1928.

How bureaucrats have changed, I thought as I turned left off the A 10. One such came to Trumpington and may have seen St Mary's and Sir

Roger. We know he saw the mill for he wrote a story about it. It concerns two Geordie lads, Alan and John – at least I take them to be Geordies by their speech – who came to Trinity as students. It tells how they were cheated in a business matter by the miller of Trumpington and how they had their revenge, the one rogering the miller's daughter and the other plumbing the miller's wife, not once but 'till the third morning cock began to sing'. You may have read the story. It begins:

> At Trompyngtoun, nat fer fro Cantebrigge,
> There goth a brook, and over that a bridge,
> Upon the whiche brook ther stant a melle:
> And this is verray sothe that I you telle . . .

It is, of course, 'The Reeve's Tale' but it might as well as have been called 'The Likely Lads', beating the BBC by six hundred years. The itinerant clerk was Geoffrey Chaucer, the man who first got hold of the English language and shook it till the French fell out. He wrote it – and the rest of the *Canterbury Tales* – just about the time Henry Yevelle was replacing the Norman-French of Canterbury Cathedral with that great nave, and England was in her Aprille.

I stood in the middle of Grantchester and was pleased to see that, unlike Trumpington, it was still a village. At least outwardly. It seemed so far to have escaped those gentlemen who have some grudge against the curve and must forever be sending out young men with theodolites to obliterate all ancient bends, for the convenience of the motor car and the discomfort of pedestrians. The main street of Grantchester, winding up a gentle rise, probably follows the byreward path of some untidy herd of cattle that preceded even Chaucer.

I could see why the word-masters had been coming out from Cambridge colleges for centuries, on foot, on horseback or by river. Wordsworth came and Tennyson, Brooke and Chaucer. Surely, too, Holinshed and Marlowe. Spenser, Bacon, Marvell, Macaulay, Pepys and Herrick – even Erasmus – a cavalcade of writers who belong to the world as much as England. Byron's Pool, close by on the river, is so called because the poet – more interested in boxing, swimming and his pet bear than serious study – used to bathe there. He would be an unusual Cambridge scholar who did not walk across the fields to Grantchester at some time during his academic term. For though millers' daughters may not always be available and willing, there is honey still for tea – sold with brown bread and butter in the orchard next to the Old Vicarage (1683 and dark red brick). The church of St Mary and St Andrew has a fine chancel. There is a pub. And although there are many places more picturesque, its position near to the river, its unassuming aspect, and the thought of all the actors in the English story who have trodden the same dust, invest it with a special charm.

I did not stay to enquire what sort of people occupied the pleasant houses in the street these days, though I guessed they would not be the country folk and minor gentry of Chaucer's or even Brooke's time. (Since then I've learned that a nearby house was part of an international LSD network. Its occupant got ten years for peddling hallucinations.) But I did meet a man out walking who pointed through the gates of a large house, now a place of agricultural research, and told me that that was where the 'Green Revolution' had begun. He was referring to the development of the multi-harvest grain that was – or so the newspapers had said – about to fill the bellies of the hungry world. I had half a mind to walk in and ask what had become of that bright dream and whether it might still come to pass, but it was still early in the day. So I took the path that leads between Grantchester's lush back gardens and out into the fields.

2

The track approaches Cambridge from the south-west, at first along the tops of fields that slope gradually towards the river on the right. The horizon on the left being therefore close at hand, the eyes are drawn along the stream towards the city just a mile or two ahead.

This prospect was quite the most emphatic and most memorable that I had looked upon since I approached the cliffs of Dover from the sea. Maybe hidden somewhere out in Russia beyond Omsk, Tomsk and Nizhni-Novgorod there is such another statement printed on the sky – an old city of towers, spires and pinnacles; complete in one glance, apparently without suburbs, isolated, independent, as if enclosed entirely within walls or behind a boundary moat. Until two hundred years ago, perhaps even in the last century, it must have been a common experience for the traveller on horseback or on foot to have stood with feelings of relief and expectation at such a point of promise where his destination first came unambiguously in sight. There he must have paused to look on spires, roofs and chimneys, reading the signs as one reads the face of a stranger with whom one must spend some time. So must travellers from the north have stood with the ghost of Whittington on Highgate Hill, looking down into the reeking bowl of London; or arriving from the Channel, halted on the edge of Blackheath to watch the world's traffic sailing up past Greenwich and between all the spires of

Wren. So indeed must voyagers across the Great Salt Desert have stood in awe before the turquoise gates and domes of Isfahan.

Today we have lost the drama of arrival. The airport terminal, the railway terminus, the airport bus, the imperceptible transition from half-hearted countryside into the spiritual dilapidation of Trumpingtonia, then ingestion by a hotel lobby approved by the Diners' Club – these are poor ways to meet a city. The path from Grantchester reimposes the forgotten pace of all the arrivals in the earlier history of man. And furthermore it leads directly into the heart of a city of such wonders as could not have been imagined by Marco Polo or any of the old travellers.

I doubt whether there is a more complex settlement of 100,000 people anywhere on earth. I wonder whether any other city could claim so confidently that what has been thought and wrought within its bounds has so entirely changed the world. And, leaving aside London, I doubt if there is another city in the kingdom that contains so many clearly discernible ingredients of the national broth. Here are representatives of England's brilliance, her hypocrisy, her lofty liberalism, her astounding conservatism, her special talent for self-deception and her appalling sense of superiority. In that glorious high street (variously known as King's Parade, Trinity and St John's Streets) they pedal to and fro with their long college scarves and their long English faces as if they still owned the world. Only an Englishman – or perhaps an anglicised Indian railway superintendent – could ride a bicycle as if it were a ceremonial howdah.

It was, however, down that street that in 1932 a sober thirty-five-year-old Yorkshireman called Cockcroft cycled at more than his accustomed speed, shouting at any passer-by he recognised. The words he shouted were – 'We've split the atom! We've split the atom!'

I walked down through the long grass to the little river Cam and took the towpath beneath pollarded willows. An early rower passed. His cargo was a transistor set and a freckled girl. The broadcast voices I heard above the splash of oars were from another England beside a dirtier, bigger river – the voices of the Beatles. I envied the rower for a passing moment, then strolled on towards Cambridge, experiencing that combination of affection and diffidence with which I usually approach this lovely city.

3

The names of Cambridge are like a peal of bells. The traveller walks in from Grantchester by way of Lammas Land, and Sheep's Green lies across the water. The river broadens at Mill Pond, narrows again, runs on behind Queen's, then Cat's and King's, and Trinity and Clare, and disappears between the buildings of St John's before swinging right – once more into the open – to skirt Jesus Green and Midsummer Common.

South of St John's the walker makes a choice. He may cross by one of six or seven bridges – Silver Street, the Mathematical Bridge, the Bridge of Sighs and so on – and then proceed towards Trinity Street by whatever tintinnabulation of alleyway, court, lawn, arcade and fountain his fancy chooses, having first of all traversed that hallowed strip of land known as the Backs.

No city anywhere has a more enchanting front garden than the Backs. It lies between the colleges and the Cam, a few hundred yards wide, much as Victoria Gardens lies like a green foreshore between the Savoy–Adelphi cliffs and the Thames. But the similarity is only in the disposition. Scale, texture and the variety and lightness are altogether different.

I have known the Backs in every season, from crocus-speckled spring, through gaudy June alight with summer frocks, to November evenings when mist advances from the fenlands diluting lamplight and confining scholars. It always says the same to me. It speaks of innocence.

On the Victoria Embankment – Westminster on the left, Temple Gardens to the right, the Foreign Office and Downing Street beyond the roofline, and all those tall hotels bustling with important clients – one hears the rumble of power. Here live the manipulators, men who can afford to have no doubts. But in Cambridge they ask questions. And even when they find an answer, they do so only to ask something else.

That taciturn farmer's son, Newton – 'with his prism and silent face' – who came to Trinity with his brain full of figures and his mind full of questions, for whom the moon was an apple that did not fall to earth – he did not know that he would change the world. At Trinity, with his 'causes and affects', he invented what we now call common sense. Having looked into his prism, dissected light and divined the mystery of colour, having extended mathematics with his calculus, he sat down in the year plague ravaged England (while other men read signs and portents all around) and thinking of his principle of universal gravitation while London burned, he set a course for man's discovery for the next quarter of a millennium. Then he went to his tomb believing his vast writings on the Book of Revelation were as important as his great scientific work, the *Principia*. There's innocence!

Charles Darwin's father sent him to Cambridge hoping he would become a parson. But young Darwin was more interested in beetles, and his professor of botany arranged his celebrated trip to the southern hemisphere aboard the *Beagle*. He was reluctant to publish the conclusions of his studies. But when he was at last persuaded, men could never again look at their world as they had done before.

There is a group of unpretentious buildings to the west of Cambridge. When the first part was built in 1873 at the Duke of Devonshire's expense it bust the budget by £2,000 and still cost less than ten thousand. No one would take a bus ride to view the architecture. At least half the population of England have never heard of it. But if it were a practical proposition I would write a whole book about the men who have worked there with their bits of string and tin and bicycles and inexpensive apparatus to make the twentieth century, and the men who are still busy there upon the twenty-first. Beside this hamlet, the White House and the Kremlin are but igloos and the Tower of London a vulgar peep-show. It has been called 'the nursery of genius'. It is, in fact, the Cavendish Laboratory. In its rooms some of the most awesome discoveries of history have been made. Yet I would call my book *The Seat of Innocence*.

Here worked Ernest Rutherford, son of a New Zealand farmer. Rutherford never earned more than £1,600 as a professor. But before they made him a lord and buried him in Westminster Abbey alongside Newton, he had split the atom. When asked 'Where do we go from here?' he answered with 'Who knows?' and then returned to his work of asking questions of the cosmos. He did not live to see the bomb.

Before that, at the Cavendish, J. J. Thompson had discovered the electron (1897), showing that the atom was not an irreducible speck of matter but a complex system. James Clerk-Maxwell had advanced the theory of electromagnetic waves, clearing the ground for radio. F. W. Aston first separated isotopes here in the twenties. Charles Wilson made artificial clouds in a 'cloud chamber' (he blew the glass himself), developments of which made P. M. S. Blackett an international authority on cosmic rays, and led to the Cavendish discoveries of positron and neutron. Sir Edward Appleton discovered his 'ceiling' in the sky, making long-distance radio communication possible and demonstrating the feasibility of radar. And so it snowballed. One could go on adding to the list of intangible continents discovered – cathedrals built behind closed doors – up to the 1930s when Sir John Cockcroft built his atom smasher of biscuit tins and plasticine . . . or until 1940 when, with England bombed and under siege, the 'Cavendish boys' reported that the most fearsome firework in history could be made . . . or until 1943 when the atomic research team was evacuated, lock, stock and innocence, to the USA. At which point it could be said that the humility of science began to live in sin with the arrogance of technology, and innocence perished.

But did it?

Certainly in 1885 when research facilities for forty Cavendish students cost £500 a year atomic fission was undreamed of. When, in the thirties, the accidental breakage of a ten-bob piece of apparatus held up research for weeks, and a Nobel Prizewinner worked his equipment by hand, turning the pedal of an upturned bike, no one thought of Hiroshima. When the particle accelerator of Cockcroft's atom smasher was, at £500, the most expensive device the Cavendish had ever owned, nobody could foresee obliteration.

But when World War II had ended with The Bang two Cambridge men discovered the pulsar – that weird, dense spinning star – and Sir Martin Ryle, professor of a new branch of pure science called radio astronomy, could sit in Rutherford's old room and lightly tell a visiting reporter that if the coffee spoon he held contained, instead of coffee, part of a pulsar, it would weigh about the same as one hundred and fifty giant ocean liners.

The US Navy tried to build a radio telescope to observe events ten thousand million light years ago for £60 million, which had to be abandoned because it did not work. Cavendish devised a new system for half a million, and it did.

Radio astronomy, solid-state physics, super-conductivity, X-ray crystallography, molecular biology, a new geology, questions, questions . . . the names of new sciences, the news of new discoveries pour out of the Cavendish, and in proportion to her population, Britain wins more scientific Nobel Prizes than any other country.

Where do we go from here? Who knows?

I walked up through the sweet irregularity of Trinity Great Court, past the huge octagonal fountain with its Elizabethan bonnet, passing the apple tree supposed to be descended from the one that inspired Newton. I made my way to the alleyway that conceals David's, my favourite bookshop in all England. Actually I was seeking something that would tell me the name of the pub where Cranmer, Latimer and Ridley (Jesus, Clare and Pembroke) are said to have supped in the days before they were burned for heresy at Oxford. I never did find out.

I walked across Market Hill (only a fenman could call such a level square a hill) and stood beside Great St Mary's and read a sign inviting tourists to see Cambridge from the tower for tenpence. Coachloads were disembarking, hanging cameras round their necks, wiping their stale faces with little perfumed pads, stroking straight the backs of dresses bought in some C&A in Hamburg, Rheims, Rotterdam, Chicago, then fanning out across the road towards King's, Trinity and St John's, like so many Swan Hunter men let loose five minutes before the hooter. Opposite stood Gibbs's classical Senate House streaked with rain-rust, tucked in its corner, saved from being monumental by the architectural activity around. I could see the silvered stone cage of King's Chapel and knew that such a building could exist in no other country. The market clamoured behind me. And I was happy that Nicholas Hawksmoor's grand baroque design of 1713 for sweeping vista, colonnades, forum, and the straightening of Trinity Street (inspired by an Italian plan for the Vatican) had got no further than the paper it was drawn on.

I called for a half at the Rose in Rose Crescent just around the corner, to listen to the chat and to watch that cheerful dark girl filling pints behind the bar.

I sat on the terrace of a riverside pub and observed a cocksure punter with a cut-glass accent almost come to grief among the swans before the overhanging balconies of a house once occupied by the Darwin family. And torn from this spectator sport by the outrageous price of ham and egg pie I adjourned for an excellent pub lunch at the Baron of Beef which is run by a former SAS man of most hospitable demeanour.

4

I had been in Cambridge for three days. Someone had been saying that our notion of linear time was mere convention and about to be exploded by the new physicists. I was attracted by that. It seemed particularly apposite in this time-crowded island where one could 'hear the cool lapse of hours pass, until the centuries blend and blur . . .'

But now here I was, lugging a plastic carrier bag half full of notebooks, tape recordings, booklets and brochures (enough material for half a book about the silver city on the plain) and beginning to worry about my *time*table . . . whether I had *time* to find a caravanserai that night . . . how *long* it would be before I reached the North . . . if there was *time* to visit Cornwall. The first stormclouds of summer were gathering as I walked towards the University Library where in spite of regulations restricting it to scholars (and no one had ever called me that) I had left my van.

It is easy to be so infatuated by the physical beauty of Cambridge and so awed by its intellectual reputation that one overlooks the warts. The Library is one of those. It was completed in 1934 and looks as though its creator set out to build an electricity sub-station, but taking leave of his senses of humour and proportion, had multiplied the specifications five hundredfold and stuck a tower in the middle. Still, it has the charm of period idiocy these days and is decently hidden by a screen of trees. Its designer was Sir Giles Gilbert Scott, the man who gave London the bold innovative beauty of Battersea Power Station, who skimmed the graceful

61

arches of Waterloo Bridge across the Thames during World War II, and who planted in Liverpool that enormous Anglican cathedral. Such versatility – from Battersea and twentieth-century grand Gothic to this static hunk of bricklaying – and such a demonstration of the fallibility of genius, warmed me. It seemed to me appropriate, even satisfying, that after my communion with the Cantabrian saints and flirtation with quasars and pulsars, I should be brought to earth by this architectural bathos.

It was going to rain. Ordinary, wet, window-steaming English rain was about to fall on roofs and pinnacles, to drip off mortar boards and drench academic gowns after all those shimmering, dream-like weeks. Godlings from King's College would complain of soggy trouser legs in 'The Whim' along Trinity Street where generations of England's golden youth had feasted on ambrosia and the tongues of nightingales in the form of hot buttered toast and much-burnished epigrams. There would be an odour of wet raincoats in Heffer's bookshop. The shoes of Extraordinary Fellows would be streaked with clay. And I had to cross the Fens.

8

Pursued by stair rods, I navigate the Black Fen, hail the islands of carrots, celery, yellow-bellies and tigers, then having been fed, watered and steamed at St Ives, I make my peace with the Lord Protector.

1

AT THE END of Queen's Road I turned left at the traffic lights and headed west. I passed signs to Girton on my right and to the American Military Cemetery on my left, both part of the suburban furniture of Cambridge, both punctuation marks in the English story, however recent. Generation by generation the husks of history fall, in the fields and streets and by the roadside, so that it is barely possible to traverse a mile – in some places not a hundred yards – without treading upon someone's memory. I had not been to either place. But today I wanted to push on and race the storm.

I can enjoy rain in some situations. I like to hear it pattering in a broad-leaf wood. There is no light like that of a wet day in late summer for bringing out the colours of an English garden. Every shade of green becomes distinct – every leaf an individual. Pirouetting fuchsia flowers draw a more intense magenta from the damp, grey air. On clifftops among the short, fine grasses there are secret forests of unseen herbs that offer incense only to celebrate a day of rain. And there are Pennine places, especially in the west (I think of Kendal), that seem to have been made for rain. Lethargic in hot sun as if afflicted, in wet weather they come alive. The beer-brown river takes to capering and dancing through the heart of town and hurling itself against cutwaters and plunging through dark arches, shouting at bookshops and warehouses as it prances by. Shop lights come on as Saturday shoppers walk more swiftly and more lightly, broadcasting smiles and greetings as if they shared an ancient northern joke that no lowlander would understand. Oh yes, rain can be a pleasure. But not, I thought, in Cambridgeshire.

My intention therefore was to drive without pause across that raft of peat known as the Black Fen which lies between Cambridge and Peterborough. Then I would rejoin England where the Great Limestone Belt runs beneath the fields and woods, diagonally across country from Dorset to North Yorkshire, surfacing every mile or so in villages and small towns of stone, of almost unbelievable loveliness. Of these the market town of Stamford with its six churches, river-island meadows and pitching limestone roofs had been dear to me for three decades and, putting northern thoughts out of my head a while, this was the bourne that I appointed to sustain me on my passage through the flatlands.

Fenland has a poor reputation with the English. Even for the fields around Spalding in the silt fens near the Wash, which become a counterpane of daffodils and tulips in the spring, the praise is faint and brief. It is as if we would like to forget those 2,700 square miles of Cambridgeshire, Huntingdonshire, Lincolnshire and west Norfolk, and as though their inhabitants were a breed apart. Perhaps my own remark that I would cross the Black Fen and 'rejoin England' was the unconscious echo of an ancient prejudice.

A mild aversion to the fenscape seen from the unnatural isolation of a scudding car is understandable. England is a crowded place, and the English eye expects that round every other bend it will light upon a huddled village – pubs, corner shops and perhaps a St Michael's on a hill. But here there are not even bends. Those dead-straight roads, accompanied for miles by the high escarpments of dead-straight drainage channels (like railway embankments deserted by the trains), that ruler-drawn horizon broken barely by a few wind-warped trees which lean west instead of east, fill the motorist with unease. If people live here in this inhospitable landscape – what sort of people can they be?

An understandable reaction, but not valid. And I owe it to memory and past hospitality to deny it. Fenland has delights, but they do not come pre-packaged in familiar stone. To find them one must adjust one's temper to a different key and change to an old rhythm whose metronome is the arrival and departure of the roving wildfowl. The landscape, though tortured by our recent ancestors, has a story just as full of incident and effort as any in the kingdom. The fields are now the most fruitful in Britain and managed by the most efficient food farmers. And out round Willingham there's a whole prairie of chrysanthemums to gild the autumn evening.

And as for people – well, is there another place in Britain outside Wales whose men in mid-conversation may move suddenly into home-made rhyme, and like the Welsh are half in love with words, echoing the notes of some language now forgotten by our mongrel breed?

I would have lingered. I had a mind to swing to starboard and sail once more across the fields where Ely, beneath her stately Gothic crown, still queens it over miles of flatlands. Ely, the isle of eels, which, like all the other Fenland places with names ending in the Anglo-Saxon 'ig' sound meaning island – Stuntney, Coveney, Thorney, Whittlesey, Ramsey, Southery, Eastrea, Manea – is now surrounded principally by land.

If it had been May and a morning of low-lying mist, then perhaps I would have mounted some small eminence and, looking out across the drifting surface, recalled what Charles Kingsley was still able to describe in the last century as 'a paradise of golden reed beds, countless waterfowl, strange gaudy insects, wild nature, majesty and mystery'. In my imagination I might have glimpsed that race apart, descendants of those Celtic refugees who had there taken refuge from the Roman legions. Ingenious hunters. Wily traders of crane, heron, snipe and lark. Anglers of the mysterious burbot found only in the Rhine and her former tributaries. Men who moved quietly by boat to tend their cattle, who stalked across the marshes upon stilts, took to pole-vaulting as a means of locomotion, and in winter could move more swiftly than marching men or horses on ice skates made of bone. Drinkers of brandy and poppy-seed tea against the cough. Eaters of opium against rheumatism and malaria. Called 'yellow bellies' for their froggish habitat, and 'tigers' for their ferocity in defending it.

I was tempted to call on old acquaintances and argue over beers about the price of carrots or the watery art of growing celery. Or about the Earl of Bedford's thieves who came with spades and pumps and the Dutch engineer Vermuyden to drain the fens and rob their ancestors of their reedy Eden. Or about Oliver Cromwell, 'Lord of the Fens', who promised to support Fenland's fierce resistance, then having decapitated a tyrant king on principle, joined up with the drainers and pinched two hundred acres for himself.

I *would* have lingered. But time was at my heels and the sky was darkening. So I drove on towards St Ives and Huntingdon, towards a softer and more populated countryside. Suddenly I was hungry. I thought about cheese and lettuce sandwiches. And a pint or two of beer, if I could avoid a Watney's house. I parked somewhere near the fire station in the village of St Ives and walked into the market-place, and there found the pubs were not yet open. Then the rain came. It was not ordinary, gentle English rain.

2

I do not like St Ives. I like Fenland Chatteris with its windswept streets where one grey morning I wandered – trespassed I suppose – into a farm-yard outbuilding opposite the church, and instead of being upbraided by the cheerful woman who discovered me, emerged ten minutes later with several cartons of the herb-laden cheese she dug out from pans as wide as millstones. I am not averse to Spalding, and I admire Wisbech with its impeccable platoon of Georgian houses at ease along the Nene. Boston, to the north, is a splendid little Dutch town gone to seed, and no less amiable for that. Ely I love.

But St Ives! It has all the makings of a pleasant English town . . . A leafy little waterfront on the Great Ouse and a wide horizon out beyond . . . pretty church and some timbered houses . . . an extra-ordinary bridge, humpbacked and with a stone chapel in the middle . . . a well-used market-place. And yet I cannot warm to it.

Is that because on my first visit I had found one of those honest, rambling inns there, full of farmers arguing in unexpected nooks – then, returning some years later, found it had been re-equipped with concealed lights, plastic bars and a polished barman? Or was it that man Cromwell lowering on a plinth at the top end of the square with his preacher's face and ridiculously rakish hat, seeming to preside over all the town's affairs? He came from nearby Huntingdon and moved on to Ely before ruling England and farming here – where he was said to have suffered from religious melancholia.

As the pubs were closed, I took shelter in the disused railway station. I chose the driest spot, beneath a broken platform canopy, and looked across the weedy track at wrecked waiting rooms and the rotting im-pedimenta of what once must have been a prosperous and busy line. People who could allow their railway station to fester thus could not be of

66

much account, I thought, as the rain came down like stair rods.

Ten minutes later I tried the pubs again. Yes, they served sandwiches, they said, but not, of course, on Sunday. It *was* Sunday. St Ives was running true to form. Why not? I asked. Was there some religious ban? Raised eyebrows. A suffering glance around the company. Quite clearly I was mad. I tried another pub, with similar result.

It was not until I was completely soaked that I found my oasis in a narrow street down near the river. I walked in dripping water on the floor and was at once guided to a glowing fire. A chair was found and I was ordered to dry off and make myself comfortable. A delightful woman who looked like Millicent Martin the singer – the same intelligent vivacity, the smile, the mouth that looked as though it was about to lisp – told me there were no sandwiches prepared but she would gladly make some. What would I like – cheese, beef, salad? And meanwhile would I care to have a drink? And what a storm! And had I far to go, Sir? Even the other customers, who must have lived close by, to judge by their dry clothes, were solicitous and friendly.

So I was fed, steamed, watered, waited on with gaiety and shaking curls and competence, half expecting that the proprietress would burst into song.

I stepped out at last thinking a little better of St Ives. I glanced at the pub name above the door. It was the Oliver Cromwell – and there was his picture. He was not exactly smiling. But he looked a little less like a Sunday School superintendent with a gumboil all the same . . .

9

*I recall a Himalayan night in Fenland, find a miracle
among the chain stores, tell how Chad hung his jacket on a
sunbeam, and am disturbed by a smell of tomorrow.*

1

ANYONE who has checked British Rail punctuality against his watch
one hour out of London en route for Edinburgh will know that the
city of Peterborough is a horizon of uninteresting buildings beyond a belt
of seedy car parks. No spire lances the horizon as at Grantham further up
the line. There is no lattice of Victorian glass and steel as at Darlington
and York. No castle on a cliff like that greatest of all railway views at
Durham. Peterborough is a pause without exclamation, flat and uninvit-
ing, and no voyager would willingly break his journey there. Unless, of
course, to see the miracle.

The motorist heading north who finds Peterborough in his path would be well advised to take the by-pass. If he does not he crosses the river Nene by a small forest of stunted pylons, passes the Marital Aids Centre (sex shop), the Turf Accountants (betting shop) and finds himself in as addled a collection of second-rate twentieth-century buildings as may be seen anywhere north of London. There is nothing monumentally bad. Nothing so vulgar as to engender awe, affection, laughter. It is just a jumble of all that is tawdry and tired of imagination from all the works of all the mothball users who man the planning committees of provincial England. Oh yes, they left the pleasant seventeenth-century Guildhall standing on its open arches in what used to be the market square. And of course there is the miracle.

'The late 1920s and early 30s will be memorable in the City and Soke of Peterborough for the gigantic and far-seeing schemes which completed the transformation of a congested, old-fashioned market town into a spacious modern city', boasted the local paper on the occasion of its own centenary.

To be sure, Thursday 26 October 1933 is a date that should be remembered in Peterborough as 1066 is recalled elsewhere. That was when they opened the new town hall – or Municipal Buildings as they titled it – the façade of which incorporated a battery of chain stores flanking the ceremonial entrance. Despite the confluence of four railway routes within the boundaries, Peterborough had possessed some of the variety and warmth of a decent country town. Two coaching inns, for instance, and a pleasant main street called 'Narrow'. All this had fallen before civic ambition. Where the Golden Lion and 'Webb & Webb High Class Provisions' had once traded, the Municipal Buildings stood now in a charmless street.

'The architect has paid tribute to the great master . . . Sir Christopher Wren, and the design is frankly of his period. It is essentially English,' trumpeted a book brought out to celebrate the opening. It was entitled *The Municipal Buildings – Story of a Great Enterprise Price Sixpence* and it carried the portrait of a mayor looking like a dormouse in a cocked hat. 'The occasion crowns a scheme of great courage and faith . . . There can be few towns, if indeed there is any other, where . . . a scheme has achieved such large purposes as are combined in the widening of Narrow Street and the erection of the Municipal Buildings.'

The councillors and their guests danced till 2 a.m. and sang, not inappropriately, 'Oh God Our Help in Ages Past'.

There must be half a million men in England still – and I am one of them – who had the good fortune to be stationed in wartime East Anglia but whose leave journeys brought them to this limbo on the edge of Fenland. One delayed return to duty till the latest hour. Trains were slow and crowded. Timetables seemed to have been abandoned. Thus through the night crowds of strangers, tired and bored, were stranded on the platforms of Peterborough North waiting for the next train east.

We then had something of a choice. We could walk down into the city centre, where pubs and cinemas were shut, to seek a 'Y.M.' bed in a converted shop. Or we could sit in the squalid station waiting room – which many preferred, for there was a coal fire sometimes. Even when an eastbound train turned up there was still the long, jerky journey across the plain with odd, unscheduled halts at which a man with a lamp cried out of the steam and the gaslight such melancholy words as Whittlesea! . . . March! . . . Ely! . . . Brandon! . . . On such a night – just once – this journey was brushed by enchantment of a kind, and for that memory I can think of Peterborough with some affection.

I don't know where the episode began – at Peterborough East perhaps, or Whittlesea. At any rate we had all settled after the ritual ill-tempered scramble for best seats, when at an unnamed halt the train was boarded by a hundred or so oriental soldiers in khaki turbans, perhaps Gurkhas. They did not enter the compartments. They padded the length of the whole train and sat in the corridors side-by-side, backs to the outer walls. Off we went again, and at first the only sound was the slow clacking of the wheels and an occasional cough.

Then from somewhere – the next coach I think – there came a diffident but rhythmic chant, a soft drumming of fingers on floor and woodwork. Then one raised voice. Then a dozen voices. The lolling British servicemen sat up. They cocked their heads. Doors were rolled open to let in the unfamiliar sound. English ammunition boots, built in Northampton, began to tap. The Gurkhas grinned, grew confident, sang louder. And when the song was finished, a train creeping through the East Anglian night poured out applause across the dark, flat fields. Another lay from Nepal, then the Tommies obliged with 'Blaydon Races', 'Ilkla Moor' and 'The End o' Me Ole Cigar'. So it went on until, somewhere short of Norwich, the train stopped again and the brown-faced men slipped, grinning, back into the dark. But we all went on singing to Norwich Thorpe, a trainload of disgruntled troops transformed on the Wensum banks with a song from the Himalayas.

Which brings me back to Peterborough again, and to the miracle.

There are miracles and miracles. Water into wine – yes, I would call that a miracle, and welcome! If modern Peterborough and its 90,000 people were to produce just one picture, symphony or poem that all admired, that would be one too. If someone hung his coat on a sunbeam – well, more of sunbeams later.

My understanding of the miraculous is of a great manifestation of the human spirit with the power to move the hearts of men for ever, a power greater often than the sum of its, ingredients – bricks, timber, notes, words, pigment. Peterborough contains a miracle. To see it you walk up Bridge Street, with Mothercare, Millets and the Municipal Buildings on your right, then turn under an arch by the National Provincial Bank.

There is nothing – nothing in England, perhaps nothing anywhere – more poised and eloquent than the three great portals that compose the whole west front of Peterborough Cathedral.

Many great buildings owe something of their effect to situation. Durham and Lincoln cathedrals, for example, stand upon hills and reign over cities. Peterborough lies apart in its modest precinct. Others are costumed with stone figures or veils of glass – Exeter, King's College Chapel, Cambridge. Stripped of all ornament, Peterborough's great west front would lose no grandeur. Gothic façades are usually two-dimensional – or at best bas-reliefs providing shelves and niches for statuettes. Each of the three great portals that compose Peterborough's front is like a separate creation – with its own high-vaulted interior, depth, mystery and invitation – and yet part of the greater whole. The receding rows of slim Early English columns that outline each arch leap skyward, then bend together to take the strain from one another at each apex, seeming to bear the three gables and two towers above them without effort.

Of all the façades of Gothic Europe, Peterborough's great triple portico is the one that speaks most clearly to the engineer. Here the spirit of man soars toward some destination still unachieved. It has been called 'the architecture of adventure'.

There are other wonders. Beyond that west front of 1233 is the longest, highest, widest Norman nave in England. Congregations sit beneath a timber ceiling – 204 feet by 35 – still darkly glowing with the painted patterns of the Early English. In the east is the fan vaulting of the so-called New Building, constructed in the fifteenth century when Englishmen – alone in Europe – tried to turn stone to gossamer and came very close.

Peterborough was an abbey church and it was not till 1541 that Henry

VIII raised it to cathedral rank. Its founders chose the site in 665. Nine feet below the flagstones lies the roof of the great limestone belt that runs diagonally across England and has furnished material for many of her greatest buildings. A few yards east, though underground, is the abrupt edge of that stone shelf. Here too was the forest edge, and here began the great, wild fen across which came Danish pirates. Thus travellers who wished to avoid the dangers of both kinds of wilderness were bound to pass this way. Were these the reasons for this choice of site? So we are persuaded. There is another story though. It emerges from the shadows of a past when men still believed in miracles of the old, magic kind, and it is worth the telling.

4

Once upon a time, when the island was divided between several rulers and people worshipped more than one god, there lived in Northumbria a beautiful princess who was loved by two kings. The first was her father, the saintly Oswald who followed the cross of Christ. The second was Peada, King of South Mercia, a worshipper of the old northern deities. Alfreda would marry no pagan, but when Peada, for the sake of love, accepted the Christian faith the two were wed. And Peada, in his gratitude, ordered the building of churches and monasteries.

Time passed – four years, in fact – and with it the love of Alfreda for Peada. She betrayed him to his enemies and he was killed. Peada's brother, Wolfere, confusing the faithlessness of Alfreda with the worth of her religion, stopped all church building, forbade his sons Wulfade and Rufine, on pain of death, to kneel before Christ, and banished all Christians.

One day, as the missionary St Chad prayed in a secret part of the woods for some miracle to stem the pagan advance, an exhausted hart in flight from pursuers fell at his feet. He tried to comfort the beast and covered it with ferns, but Prince Wolfade rode up and roughly tried to claim his quarry. Chad spoke softly and persuasively, telling the young man that God had led him to the spring of true faith. He and his brother were converted and often prayed together in a chapel hidden in the forest.

But there lived at court a royal adviser, Webode, who spied on the princes and informed their father who, surprising them at prayer, killed both. Webode went mad, tearing the flesh from his arms with his own teeth until he died. And Wolfere in horror and remorse sought out St Chad, confessing to the murder of his sons.

'Give me a sign', he cried, 'that Christ is king.' And Chad took off his cloak and hung it on a sunbeam.

King Wolfere prayed, was received into the Church, and ordered the resumption of the abbey building at Medehamestead – the homestead in the meadow between fen and forest – which was dedicated to St Peter.

As centuries passed, men came from many lands to worship there. Peterborough rivalled Rome and Canterbury as a place of pilgrimage. Its holy relics were revered throughout Christendom. For here were treasured a piece of the swaddling clothes of the Holy Child, a splinter from the True Cross, a sliver from the manger of Bethlehem, a morsel from the feeding of the five thousand, a fragment from the veil of Christ's mother, the shoulder blade of one of the holy innocents, a scrap of sackcloth from the robe of St Wenceslas, part of the hand of the murdered St Magnus, the jaws and teeth of St George and St Christopher, a finger of St Leofridus, sinews from the hand of St Athelard, and relics of St Peter, St Paul, Mary Magdalen and St Thomas of Canterbury.

But most famous of all to Englishmen was the 'imperishable arm of St Oswald', father of the faithless Alfreda.

Which, like all the rest, has perished.

5

I walked past the plain, black slab that covers the remains of Catherine, the girl from Aragon who married England's Defender of the Faith, who jilted her and Rome as well. It was placed there by the Catherines of England, Ireland, Scotland and America in 1895. I left the precincts by the western gateway near the King's Lodging, and emerged into the Peterborough of chain stores. Fourteen miles ahead of me was Stamford, this city's ancient rival, where grace and beauty won and 'progress' lost. But Peterborough pursued me up the valley of the Nene, past the Victorian courthouse built like a Norman castle and towards the fields of Castor, once one of the great potteries of the Roman Empire.

Peterborough has designs on that countryside. It plans to increase its population from 84,000 to 185,000 (by immigration rather than pro-creation, one hopes), to spend £400 million, provide 50,000 new jobs, construct 34 miles of urban motorway complete with 6 miles of car park, plant 7 million trees, build 40 schools, raise an air-conditioned shop-office-and-leisure centre to serve 400,000 consumers, and weave a 110-acre artificial lake through the three new townships of which it will all consist. I hope, of course, that the new Peterborough will succeed. I realise that twentieth-century problems require twentieth-century solutions. But like many Englishmen I instinctively mistrust grand social (or political) panaceas conceived in town halls (or beer cellars, or the

Reading Room of the British Museum for that matter) and wish this new way of life, blueprinted for the many by the few, had first been tried in Alice Springs.

In the hot evening I drove past some of the new 'dwelling units'. Men who call houses 'dwelling units' should themselves be labelled 'breathing modules' and be made to dwell in them. I approached a 50,000 square foot Sainsbury–Boots superstore among the trees. The big, yellow, diesel-driven JCBs had been carving trenches out of the living earth for the foundations of the Cresset – a shopping, sports and social complex which will include a centre for the handicapped. The layers of soil, full of severed roots, were black, then brown, orange and grey down the walls of each incision, and there was an ageless smell.

Inside the hypermarket the well-dressed factory workers of Peterborough's future thronged the indoor streets between avenues of goods, waited for one another with their trolleys loaded in the enclosed 'open spaces', gazing through plate-glass walls with uninterested eyes at the coloured Fords and Datsuns ranked against a border of dark conifers. The pace of life seemed regulated by a sweet, slow beat of unmemorable Muzak. And here there was the clean, new smell – Deodorant? Air conditioning? Pizza pie? Incense? Chloroform?

Was this tomorrow's England? How well behaved it seemed to be. How convenient. How well controlled.

Presently I found a field and went uneasily to sleep.

10

*In which beer and plumstones, spires and haycocks,
bicycles and torpedo boats, Mary Stuart and Charles
Dickens, delay me on the limestone way to Stamford.*

1

THE OLD ROAD to Leicester bisects the Edinburgh–London line just
south of Peterborough Station, and when I passed at daybreak a
yellow-nosed Deltic called *The King's Own Scottish Borderers* was working
itself up into a rage beneath the bridge having just hauled the night train
from Newcastle down through Darlington, York, Doncaster, Retford,
Grantham. A few sun-burned men – newsagents' loaders waiting for the
London papers – sat on a low wall under wan electric floodlights. A
trickle of dishevelled travellers emerged from that well-remembered

portico and sleep-walked down pale morning streets. I paused to listen to 3,300 horse power rev up and assault the morning before it growled out through a forest of brickwork chimneys for the 100-mile-an-hour lope through Beds and Herts and Middx towards the capital.

I know that there are people who are not in sympathy with engines – among them those light sleepers who do not properly esteem the music of a pair of 18-cylinder opposed-piston two-stroke diesels driving six electric traction motors and auxiliary equipment through their pre-breakfast dreams. Well, their consolation could be that the Deltic is one of the world's most powerful diesel locomotives, that the engines were adapted from the power units of fast naval craft, and thus that the morning thunder is the equivalent of two motor torpedo boats roaring through the fields and woods. But some people just can't be comforted!

I never cross that ugly iron bridge at Peterborough without a sense of homecoming. It delivers me into a land of pleasant roads that wind past woods, mills and churches to villages and pubs where I have met contentment many times.

It is limestone country. And for that silvery material – so obedient to the skilful hand, so ready to absorb the colours of the English landscape, responsive to the weather – men have paid fortunes, taken it by barge down the Welland and the Nene and by oxcart along turnpikes, to build their manors, palaces and temples. The monks of Romsey Abbey in the Fens had a contract to pay 3,000 eels a year for building stone quarried at nearby Barnack. But here in this countryside men have used it to make a serene environment of homes, barns, churches and graceful towns and villages.

It is also a country of fine beers and no national beer factory holds sway. Sam Smith's 'Old Brewery' bitter comes down from Tadcaster in Yorkshire and is well-kept in such ancient hostelries as the Bull and Swan at Stamford. In the tiny Dolphin across town you may order a Stone's bitter at one end of the bar – a decent working drink to go with conversation – and just along the counter Suffolk's majestic Greene King Abbot. There is Home's Ales of Nottingham, Bateman's of Lincolnshire, and Tolly Cobbold draught is cheerful in such company. Alas, Melbourne's, the town brew, has passed away though the handsome brewery still stands in Scotgate, Stamford, now a beer museum and a club for connoisseurs. I once put down the names of fifteen brews available in this small town and I'm sure I missed some out. But monarch of them all, a beer whose first swallow stills the conversation of wise men with important things to say about sprouts and vegetable marrows, is Ruddle's 'County'. This regal brew is raised lovingly near Oakham, the old capital of Rutland. It should be regarded with respect. It is no ale for callow children in their twenties.

And ah, the places where these liquors are consumed! I think of slithering across ice in the coachyard of the White Hart, Ufford, to reach a new-lit fire and a pint of Home's Ale alive and kicking in the pot. Of May mornings in the Millstone down at Barnack and choosing between 'County' and 'Old Brewery' – a sweet dilemma before Sunday Yorkshire pudding. Of the Marsh Harrier in Stamford and a giant's breakfast served there one Sunday morning in a room above Red Lion Square, the bells of St Mary's competing with All Saints. And of cold lunch on a hot day in St Mary's vaults. Now there's a skirmish for you! I bet there's no better value in the land. You turn right from the coachyard out of sunlight and walk beneath the dark, bent beams to a large serving table and survey the field of battle. Beef, ham, turkey, pork – these are your main adversaries – supported by platoons of pickled onions, companies of crimson beetroot, hordes of chutney, battalions of potato salad, eggs, fish, rice, an aristocracy of cheeses in reserve. You pause and name your foe en route to collect your pint.

'Beef it is.'

'Yes, *Sir!*'

Your plate is charged with slices, rim-to-rim. You take on a whole squadron of sweet-corn kernels, streak the potato salad with blood-red cabbage just to frighten 'em. You choose your weapons and withdraw to your table and to inevitable victory.

2

West of Peterborough I stopped near a wood to brew a cup of tea and glancing across a nearby hedge saw a low modern building of glass, brick and concrete. Care had been taken by a well-mannered architect and it was not intrusive, but it lay below me in an English meadow on an English summer morning with its electric lights ablaze looking like a hotel transported from a Bahamian pleasure beach. Instead of tea I thought of palm trees, hot rolls, cool butter and pungent coffee served bitter-black among ornamental vines. But along the roofline the letters of dull red said not Hotel Miramar but Thomas Cook.

Now Mr Cook was the secretary of a temperance society in Leicester just up the road. One day he hired a brass band and a train and took 580 teetotallers on a day trip to Loughborough twelve miles away. It was such a novel event that thousands went down to the railway station to see them off. That was in 1841. And from that early day-excursion grew the first, the biggest and the most successful travel business in the world. Soon Mr Cook was conducting expeditions up the Nile by luxury yacht, and ultimately his bright idea changed the seacoasts and economies of whole countries, bringing Everest within tourist reach of Surbiton.

Thomas Cook's was nationalised in World War II and is now owned by the Midland Bank, Trust House Forte and the Automobile Association. But I remember when it wore a more romantic face – for me, the pale, rather worried face of a certain Mr Taylor. I speak now of days when people carried 'travelling rugs'. The Inverness cape had not been long put by and cabin trunks still bore the labels of the Cunard White Star Line and the Peninsular & Oriental Steam Navigation Company in full. Mr Taylor's station in life was behind a long, brass rail on the counter of Thomas Cook & Son, Fawcett Street, Sunderland. From maps and directories he could tell you the exact time of the next train through Petropavlovsk, the next BI boat out of Shanghai or the price of a ticket from Kraj to Ljubljana. Mr Taylor was not tall. He had a heavy and mysterious limp. Maybe he had never travelled beyond Calais, and in middle age – now I come to think of it – had perhaps earned no more than four-pounds-ten a week. But as far as I was concerned, he was a giant standing at the gates of the world. When my father returned from Chicago smelling of Chicago, or from Riga in gigantic snow boots with stories of night sleigh rides full of fleas to Daugavpils, it was Mr Taylor who had arranged it all and brought him safely home. With his racks of pasteboard railway tickets for exotic destinations, Mr Taylor was for a time my boyhood hero, and my secret collaborator with school essays. I was not quite tall enough to see across Cook's counter, and when I composed an imaginary trip to Bombay, Mr T. heaved his heavy foot across bare boards and round into the shop to load me up with maps and pictures, to discuss the possibility of a night out in Lourenço Marques, or to advise me about buying presents from the bumboats of Port Said.

An electronic thingummy for measuring the brightness of the day switched off the lights in the meadow all at once. Soon 1,500 clerks, typists and Telex operators would be arriving to resume communications with 672 Cook's offices in 137 countries. I washed my dishes and trundled down to Castor – from which the Romans supplied their empire with crockery and where men still turn up bits of bowls and plates in village gardens – and was swallowed by the limestone country.

Along the way I did a favour for a fellow who was suffering an embarrassment of roses. I did not actually meet him. He lived in some fine mansion beyond an estate wall of thin limestone slabs about the size of Roman bricks. But one bush in particular had topped the parapet, was leaning out towards the A 47 and clearly needed thinning. Petals were falling on the grassy bank and traffic skirled them in the air. I stopped – the road was empty now – took out my jack-knife and made the cull. The red and pink flowers transformed the interior of the van and looked handsome in the top buttonhole of my faded denims.

Now, with Stamford as my goal, which way should I choose? Should I turn right here with my load of roses, entering a maze of roads and hamlets? Through Helpston, for example, where John Clare the peasant poet laboured in the fields . . .

> Sweet flowers that in the still hours grew –
> We'll take them home, nor shake off the bright dew.

. . . and was buried in the churchyard, believing in his last sad insanity that he had become Lord Byron?

Or should I stay with the A 47 – passing the thatched Royal Oak, the Fitzwilliam Arms, the Wheatsheaf, the Prince of Wales, and the spire of the church founded by St Kyneburga, daughter of Peada King of Mercia – then reaching the A 1, turn right and cross the Welland by St Mary's, Stamford, in time for lunch at the Lincolnshire Poacher?

I sat on a bridge wall and spat plumstones on to an abandoned railway track known for some reason, lost to local memory, as the 'Bread and Onion Line'. A Victorian railway station had been turned into a secluded home and I envied its habitants. My problem was not simplified by local knowledge. So many memories and places called. To do justice to this paradise I would need a bike, and a month cut off from bank managers and telephones. That's the way to travel in those parts, moving on from spire to spire without map or guidebook. You can stand at one steeple and see the next. Each indicates a church, a village and at least one public house below – sometimes a signal box, a white-painted level crossing, or a bridge across a small section of shaded river that appears and disappears in the gentle English jungle. Many are broach spires. They're the thirteenth-century kind that spring directly from the tower walls without an intervening parapet, and so – unlike their younger, slimmer sisters – without the aid of stabilising pinnacles or little flying buttresses. Why they should be so common here I do not know, but the way they stand – placid, blunt and broad of base – suits this mellow countryside.

The sun had already warmed the stones beneath me. I pondered lazily. Should I run north to Tickencote (Saxon for goat-pen) which for eight or nine hundred years has stood just beyond sight of what we call the Great North Road? The church there is an ornate little box encrusted with half shafts and intersecting arcs, devices reminiscent of the Normans though actually a restoration of 1792. Inside, though, the chancel arch astounds. Six genuinely Norman arches, one within the other, progressively receding, and madly out of scale with their surroundings. Time and sheer weight have forced the supporting shafts from the vertical, turning the whole thing bandy. Dr Pevsner calls it a 'tour de force . . . wildly overdone . . . incompetently constructed'. Incompetent or not, it has stood there since about 1160. And anyway, age, bulk and deformity do not entirely explain its power. Here the mind of some long-dead sculptor stirs the veils of time. Upon the concentric orders of the arch he chiselled the fashionable zig-zags and billets of his time, and journalistically he marked a royal quarrel with the heads of a king and queen facing outwards in a huff. But among the foliage and mouldings there are other things – cats' heads, bears, half-human monsters with protruding tongues, a fox devouring the head of a decapitated monk.

But which way? To Duddington in its happy hollow just up the road? Or mysterious King's Cliffe with its dancing limestone roofs? Both film-set villages almost too photogenic to be real but one made for a Merrie England feature and the other for some tale of the sinister and secret. Or should I go back again to Fotheringhay beside the meandering Nene whose happy English name and proud lantern church tower forget that here the administrators of Tudor England beheaded Mary Queen of Scots for reasons convenient to Church and Crown? The English did their best to mislay the memory of that dismal day. They carted the body to Peterborough at dead of night and buried the Stuart heart in some field corner now forgotten, in case it should be stolen as a martyr's relic. They let the castle crumble and disappear, and now Fotheringhay – once a royal birthplace – is but a drowsy hamlet.

The marks of history are seldom erased so easily, in England anyway. As I sat on my warm railway bridge – itself now a monument to another age – I had to remind myself again that the landscape all about me – walls, hedges, field-shapes – was the product of a fairly recent revolution, the great enclosure movement of the eighteenth and nineteenth centuries when the medieval fields and common pastures were taken over by private landlords. John Clare was still complaining in his journal of 1824 about the disappearance of beloved landmarks uprooted in this vast planning operation that created the hedged chequerboard of England which we think of as timeless.* Yet in the meandering of a by-road, the situation of a river bridge, the ridge and furrow of the medieval peasant farming still visible in many a meadow, the old England is still discernible.

* The lust for profit that enclosed the fields and changed the face of England is now working in reverse. Conservationists protest (and with good reason, for such recklessness causes land erosion and inhibits wildlife) at the grubbing out of hedges to create huge fields more amenable to machine agriculture. In many cases, though, such farming may restore the landscape to its pre-Enclosure Act appearance.

Even serene old Stamford with its limestone streets and five pre-Reformation churches – towards which I was making progress in my fashion – was timber-built and had seventeen churches and six religious houses till Queen Margaret arrived with an incendiary Lancastrian army in 1461. With the torch, she did the stonemasons a great favour, and later many surviving timber buildings were given a stone shell to keep them up with the fashion. But the street-plan of today's Stamford was laid down in the ninth century. The former A 1 dog-legs up from the river, first left then right then left again, so as not to breach the vanished walls, contributing a great deal to the town's delightful, wayward character. In the alleyways connecting the main business streets you find the projecting beams of overhanging storeys, proclaiming to the observant that there are old timber buildings masquerading as stone shops and dwellings. A year or two ago I tried to buy a house in Stamford. The agents advertised it as a town house of the eighteenth century, and sure enough, its windows, architraves and plaster were of that period. But in the living-room there were two late Norman piers, half a medieval arch was embedded in the lavatory wall and investigation showed the building was a twelfth-century hall-house with eighteenth-century cosmetics. The heavy limestone roof was carried by the original oak timbers, and, hardened by time, they were as sound as when originally cut.

3

I did not reach Stamford that night after all. I lay among the buttercups in the 'Hills and Holes' of Barnack, which is where, until the fifteenth century, armies of dusty yokels – men for whom Crécy and Acre were contemporary battle honours – quarried the famous stone for Peterborough Cathedral, for Cambridge and the great buildings of East Anglia. And I hung over the churchyard wall in the village, where Saxon builders, emerging from the dark timber age as from a summer haze, raised their first church of stone then decorated the tower with crude imitations of wooden beams. (Thus our suburban fathers nailed spurious Tudor beams on plaster gables in Acacia Avenue.) No good spoiling a tower for a ha'porth of Saxon kitsch!

So by such meandering ways and with such idle thoughts this indolent fellow crossed the Great North Road at last, and passing over the ten arches of a sixteenth-century bridge that spanned the Nene, he entered the broad and empty high street of Wansford-in-England.

I am only guessing when I say that Wansford must once have been a considerable market centre. But why else should there be such a main street and three public houses (until the 1930s there were four)? If you called the present population (350) out of doors they would hardly fill the garden of the Haycock Inn. It is also remarkable that the handsome but extremely narrow bridge formed part of the main London–Edinburgh road within my lifetime. There is width for one machine alone, and foot passengers must wait in stone refuges till it passes. And as for Wansford's Sunday name – well, that has been a cherished joke, at least in Wans-ford, for the last two hundred years.

The alleged explanation is that in the eighteenth century there lived a mile or two upstream a farm labourer called Barnaby with more thirst than sense. Having taken his fill of ale one day he fell asleep upon a haycock which was washed away by a sudden flood, and the simpleton did not awake until the Nene had swept him close to Wansford Bridge. He gazed around, bewildered.

'Where am I?' called out Barnaby to curious villagers peering down.

'Why, Wansford!' called back the delighted onlookers.

'Wansford? . . . what . . . Wansford in England?' the simple soul is said to have cried in amazement, believing that he had been transposed to foreign parts.

Poor Barnaby! I have sympathy for those who fall asleep in haycocks – a more civilised form of inactivity than many other practised more commonly today. At any rate, the story stuck, and is commemorated in the name of the inn and on its signboard which depicts a countryman, pitchfork in hand, reclining on a haycock.

The Haycock is a seventeenth-century hostelry with more than an acre of Collyweston slate – that's limestone – on its roof. I was told that it changed hands once in a game of cards, that it was visited by Princess Victoria before she became Queen and that it was an ammunition factory during World War I. But its chief virtue is that it serves Ruddle's County, and it was over a pint of this that I gave some thought to the history of Barnaby. It is a good general principle not to question stories of that sort. It is a spoilsport game, and one which I would not have played had I not scented a more intriguing possibility. Leaving aside the ultimate fate of Barnaby (did the jeering bumpkins rescue him, or let him float off through the Fenlands to the Wash?), the tale had a familiar ring. Was it a coincidence that another famous simpleton bore that unusual name? Had not the creator of *Barnaby Rudge* travelled up and down the Great North Road to visit his friends at the nearby great house of Rockingham which he turned into Chesney Wold? Was it not possible – even likely – that the great scavenger stood in this same back room, beard tilted, listening to bar-talk, while a Dickensian storm hurled the Nene against the bridge outside? And hearing the old story would he not have retired to his room beneath the rattling Collywestons to note down Barnaby for a role in the Gordon Riots? Or was it maybe the other way round? After the publication of *Barnaby Rudge* in 1841, did Barnaby become a synonym for rustic fool, and was it borrowed by an astute nineteenth-century landlord to give glamour and publicity to his hotel? Historians have based theories on less evidence than that.

I was intrigued, too, by the name of the pub across the road – the Papermills. Eventually I found out that a nineteenth-century owner of the *Stamford Mercury* newspaper (about which more later) had a country mansion here, and that he ensured a constant, cheap supply of newsprint by shipping bargeloads of old rags up the Nene to make it in a mill at the bottom of his garden. Alas, such days of direct enterprise are past. Some big-circulation newspapers are in the newsprint-making business sure enough, but it is all stocks and shares now, and international transactions by men who may never have seen a reel of paper made. And they don't even get their newsprint cheap.

And so to Elton by the evening. This lovely, rambling village used to make a famous bicycle. I like the thought. Newsprint at Wansford, and the most civilised of all forms of transport made not in a hole like Birmingham, but within bellsound of a fourteenth-century church and the whisper of a mill race.

Almost opposite the old blacksmith's shop on the A 605 a by-road dips down invitingly through trees and wide green verges, between well-spaced, well-founded houses. It levels on an open space – Stocks Green – which is overlooked by Duck Street and one of those handsome, heavily timbered butcher's shops with wide open fronts – alas, now used only as a storehouse. Beyond the Green the once-busy Nene flows quietly from old quaysides in Northampton. A great, square, abandoned watermill stands near the locks. And at the foot of Duck Street, the Crown Inn – thatched, low and broad, warm and cheerful with an immense chestnut overspreading.

The hymn that was being played there that evening hung on the wall beside the bar where Greene King Abbot was being served. It began with veg. or chicken soup and then continued . . .

Soused mackerel . . . Avocado and Walnut Mousse.
Home-made chicken-and-liver pâté . . . Fresh Crab Mornay.
Fresh Norway Lobsters Grilled in Garlic Butter.
Roast Duckling à l'Orange . . . Breast of Chicken Kiev.
Loin of Pork Ardennaise . . . Lamb Cutlets in Shrewsbury Sauce.
Fillet en Croute with Mayonnaise . . . and so on.

Glory, hallelujah and Amen!

11

Awakened by Phantoms, I meet beauty in a poke bonnet,
talk to a man who has mislaid a Danish borough and hear
how the aristocracy saved Stamford.

1

PHANTOMS awakened me soon after dawn. I had stolen into the field
beside the watermill the night before, too late to seek permission, and
had fallen asleep to the sound of rushing water. Cambridgeshire, Northamptonshire, the Soke of Peterborough, Hunts, Lincolnshire or Rutland? I was not sure which county I was in when daylight came. I knew
that Cambs had advanced to Stamford in the great local government
jumble sale and that Leicestershire had swallowed Rutland. I thought
perhaps that Elton was still in Hunts. But I knew a Phantom when I saw
one. It banked overhead and sheered off towards Alconbury.

This was aeroplane country: Gladiators, Harts, Hotspurs – Whitleys,

Blenheims, Wellingtons – Hampdens like tramcars droning through the sky, even the short-lived Defiant. Then Lancasters and Stirlings before the Meteors, Hunters and Vulcans. Studded with military aerodromes these fields and woods had seen them all. When, a hundred years from now, social historians describe what it was like to live in East Anglia and the eastern Midland counties from the 1930s onwards, I wonder whether they will say how the airmen came, sometimes taking over whole villages, many remaining when their service ended, marrying local girls or importing families from Scotland, Ireland, even Portugal and Poland, the biggest change of population since the Vikings.

Another pair came over. Lovely, they were. As fine as sailing ships and, I suppose, just as doomed. People sleep soundly in these parts. I left before the village was astir and no one noticed me.

I had an appointment to meet a young historian at the Bull and Swan in Stamford and it was another golden summer morning so I thought I'd walk. Well, to tell the truth I didn't have to think about it. I would have walked into town by that southern route – the old A1 – if it had been blowing half a gale. For that is the way to see one of the most wholesome sights in England – Stamford running down towards the river Welland, then ranging up beyond the northern bank like an old dream of what England ought to be. It is not a well-known view now. The new by-pass conducts its columns of long-distance travellers round to the west, affording but a glimpse of distant towers. Drivers who, at the George Farm roundabout, detach themselves from the trunk road, have hardly time to adjust to the real world before they are down the hill and into town. Even in slower coaching days, when Stamford was an important stage on the long journey north, inside passengers had no forward view, and 'outsiders' perhaps had only thought for the celebrated hospitality of the George Hotel.

But Sir Walter Scott contrived to notice it, and declared it the finest scene between Edinburgh and London. Why Sir Walter of all people, preferred it to York Minster or towering Durham, is a mystery. He was a man of broad and stormy canvases, and Stamford is a miniature of domesticity. Soft, mellow English domesticity at that, whispering its small household confidences from attic casements, from bar-parlour bays and in the subtle concealments of the winding high street as it drops gently towards Town Bridge.

I had left the van beneath trees close to the dilapidated splendour of a long-abandoned racecourse beyond which a family of Harrier VTOL jets rose and fell and hovered in the shimmering air with the humped backs and drooping wings of monstrous insects. I struck the path to Stamford and a mature plantation intervened, cutting off the last small sound of the arterial road. An eight-foot limestone wall, laced here and there with orange lichens, marched with me on my right, girdling the park of Burghley House with a seven-mile band of silver. In front, the density of trees and the winding road concealed the nearer part of Stamford and foreshortened what was visible beyond the Welland. The illusion thus created was of a thickly wooded valley still a mile or two ahead, from which protruded the spires of a small town with a superfluity of churches. Then suddenly – without preamble: no straggle of mortgage-conscious semis – the abrupt revelation of High Street St Martin! A country road – then all at once this handsome town!

Small mansion alongside amiable cottage. Seventeenth century, with stone mullions and canted bays. Eighteenth-century town houses put up by prosperous tradesmen to elevate their wives. Nineteenth century, with little flights of front door steps, curving iron handrails, bell knobs, brass plates, footscrapers enough to illustrate a history of the subject. The square tower of St Martin's Church with its four corner pinnacles. Diversity; but submitting to a discipline of scale which has more to do with local materials (limestone of a dozen shades and colours), man-size economics, and an instinctive understanding of its station in the world than with any kind of art or planning. A scene not to be exchanged for half a dozen Bath crescents or the whole parade of Nash terraces round Regent's Park.

I dare say there are men – imaginations bounded by next year's balance sheet or natural stupidity – who would erect high-rise blocks in such a place. One tower intruding on the Collyweston skyline would destroy something beyond the calculation of computers, something not merely picturesque, but the sum of centuries of comparative contentment and modest sensitivity such as few other towns are privileged to know. It has been put in jeopardy before by the railway builders. I'm told that it is in peril once again from a 'by-pass' that would not quite pass by.

However, on this lovely morning, High Street St Martin, Stamford, seemed safe enough, and rather in a 1920s mood. Morton – with his weakness for a pretty leg – would have liked the three young ladies descending the steps of the High School for Girls in their long summer frocks and coloured boaters.

Had he run short of pipe tobacco he might have tried for cigarettes at the large machine made of some forgotten alloy and mounted in the wall of an eighteenth-century garage halfway down the hill . . .

HARPER DELUXE AUTOMATIC
CROYDON ENGLAND
Packets and refused coins
delivered here

. . . and inserted his 'two pennies' or his 'sixpence'.

He would have read the sign outside Number 52 that says: 'Here lived Lady Frances Wingfield, who claiming relationship with Oliver Cromwell, persuaded him in 1643 not to level the town.'

Then coming to the hill foot he would certainly have paused at the corner of the George Hotel near Town Bridge. There a sign says that this was the House of the Holy Sepulchre, that the Knights of St John of Jerusalem were entertained here, that the mulberry tree in the back garden dates from James I, and that three kings and 'many other famous people' had lodged here. On the other hand, he might not have noticed for the spectacle ahead.

If I have given the impression that the southern entrance of St Martin's is the finest sight in Stamford, I amend it here. There is another equal to it – and that is the northern exit. Here one does not look downhill, but upwards to the tower and great broach spire of St Mary's Church. The narrowing perspective of the stone bridge parapets continued by the five or six hundred yards of St Mary's Hill curving left between the limestone frontages, the tall domestic chimney stacks, the finials on the inward facing dormers, the lancet openings of the belfry – all these enhance the verticality of the 162-foot spire. It is a powerful composition made the more so by the glimpse of St Mary's Street running from right to left beyond the tower and forming a T-junction with St Mary's Hill. This crossing also declares that Stamford has changed its axis and become an east-west orientated town. I have often wondered if the view would have been so exciting if this portion of the old A1 had continued the line of St Martin's and run straight on north. Perhaps not. The picture needs that small argument.

I stood outside the George with time to spare. It is a glorious hodge-podge of a building, which has acquired numerous extra limbs and organs through its history. It may bewilder visitors more used to the drab predictabilities of the international style, but there is no more animated place in Stamford on a summer Sunday morning when the main yard is hung with foliage and brilliant flowers. The cobbles are strewn with little tables, the tables are loaded with cakes and ale, the cakes and ale are being consumed by pilgrims from many quarters, and it could be in no other place than England. Even the Germans look relaxed and the Americans less earnest.

I turned to the front door and glancing through the lobby towards the courtyard I saw a burnished mailcoach at the exit. There were four horses in the shafts and a group of people in late Georgian dress stood by as if waiting to embark. Stepping into the front bar, I asked the barmaid for an explanation. She had no idea, Sir, and by her apparent lack of interest suggested that such things happened every day. I moved towards the courtyard doors and observed that the centre of attraction was a youngish man of great elegance in lilac trousers and a pale top hot who, when he saw me, whipped his topper off, broke into a grin and called out – 'For Pete's sake, Frank – what on earth are you doing here!'

Such encounters – like the one in Dover that led me to Bishopsbourne and Robsack Meadow – are a delight, and thank goodness are still possible in England. There are, of course, too many of us – but being crowded cheek by jowl in a somewhat smaller space that Arkansas or North Carolina, means that accidental, village-high-street meetings can still happen. I had not seen the cocky, cheerful Martin Young for years, so this unexpected apparition, and him all togged up like Sam Weller come into money, called for celebration. Which took place forthwith in the bar that used to be the booking office for the Edinburgh–London coaches.

He balanced his props-department hat on a nearby stool, explained that he was making a series about coaching days for Christmas viewing (such are the small deceptions of the media), then began to sing a hymn of praise to Stamford. He told me his expectations had been dismal. They were based on memories of what seems to be not long ago when we were all much poorer and rare trips to London were made by cheap, night-travelling motor bus. In those days Stamford was a halt on the A1 a hundred miles short of the capital. You jolted into town in darkness. The street lamps had long been extinguished. You stumbled into the one patch of light and temporary ease – the Willow Cafe – for a cup of tea, seeing nothing else of Stamford except the noisome, often unlit public lavatories. And so, for thousands of northern people, Stamford is remembered. A heart of darkness. It is a grossly slanderous recollection.

'Have you looked at the view outside?' he asked. 'That church . . . that bridge . . . the meadows by the river . . . It's marvellous!'

But soon the coach was ready. The horses were thumping the cobbles and jingling in the shafts. The other passengers – who included a young lady of most agreeable aspect in ribbons and poke bonnet – were eager to be off. I watched through the front curtains as the whole equipage rumbled out into the High Street and took the London road with a glimpse of silk and braid and a bright eye through the offside window. I felt a strong desire to go with them. But then I recalled a coachman who might well have visited this room beneath his habitual mountain of scarves and wraps, and who once, in not dissimilar circumstances, delivered himself of the following observations:

'Wot's the good,' he asked, 'o' callin' a young 'ooman a Wenus or a angel?'

'Ah, what indeed?' replied his companion.

'You might jist as well call her a griffin, or a unicorn, or a King's arms at once, which is werry well known to be a col-lection o' fabulous animals.'

'Just as well,' the other agreed.

'Drive on, Sammy,' said Mr Weller.

And so I did.

2

Young David, the historian, was already in an armchair in the bay window of the Bull and Swan. He was tall and thin. He wore a beard and spectacles, behind which articles of furniture there resided the kind of analytical intelligence that would do credit to a Holmes or Maigret. This morning, for example, his mind was exercised by the disappearance of a complete Danish town. And furthermore, it could be argued that he'd lost the place himself.

I should explain that Stamford has two High Streets – High Street St Martin which we already know, and the east-west orientated High Street across the Welland. The last had long been recognised as the axis of the planned Viking settlement – one of the five boroughs of the Danelaw* – and all neighbouring streets as a map of that ancient town. Upon these assumptions all notions of the shape and growth of Stamford had been based.

But David told me that yesterday, while strolling down that High Street, he had stopped for a chat with workmen laying gas mains in a trench, and noticed a dark layer three feet down. Being a historian and not an archaeologist, he had immediately called in the Director of the South Lincolnshire Archaeological Unit, a Miss Christine Mahany, who identified the coloration as iron-smelting slag.

Now, iron-smelting was brought here by the Vikings who arrived about 870. But people don't build ironworks down the centre of their main street. Therefore generations of historians must have been mistaken about the location or alignment of the borough . . . or their dates were up the spout . . . or both.

'At first,' said David, 'we were confused. We were reluctant to abandon the conception upon which all our understanding had been built. We thrashed about for another explanation.'

Instead, they recalled other clues which severally had seemed insigni-

* Danelaw – the eastern part of England ceded to the Vikings by Alfred the Great. The five boroughs were Lincoln, Nottingham, Derby, Leicester and Stamford.

ficant, but which now pointed in the same direction and deepened their sudden sense of loss. The Viking town must still be there somewhere, but they had reached the uncomfortable conclusion that this part of Stamford was not planned by eighth-century invaders but by Anglo-Danes in the late ninth century. History had that day been nudged over a century or more.

I am never bored by Stamford. In thirty years I have not entered that town of 14,670 inhabitants without discovering some fresh delight, falling into some bizarre conversation, having some small adventure.

Somewhere along the road I had met a man whose face lit up at mention of the place. He described how he awakened there one war-time night in the town mortuary having been brought in as dead from the wreckage of his Hampden bomber. Later I encountered a middle-aged clerk wearing a top coat of outmoded length, a trilby that had seen far jauntier days and an expression of deep melancholy. When Stamford came up in conversation, however, he was transformed into a likeness of the man in the advertisement who has taken Kruschen Salts. 'Ah, what a town! What memories!' Why, it was on that aerodrome just outside the borough that he'd crashed into a hangar while taxi-ing a Lancaster! For half an hour he was almost debonair. When he picked up his worn attache case and toddled off with a bronchitic wheeze, I was almost moved. He not only admired the town I love – but that man had once driven a Lanc, however carelessly!

In St Leonard's Street where Stamford suddenly sprouted a small Victorian working-class suburb on priory land and where – but for the odd sixteenth-century cottage – one could be in Blackburn or Accrington at dusk, I bought fish and chips from the corner shop with a Union Jack on the back wall, and ate them from a newspaper in the street. Which, as any northern connoisseur will tell you, is the only circumstance in which that noble dish will render up the flavour that chefs may imitate in vain.

What I cannot remember, though, is whether it was in the George Tap or the Poacher that I was told about the sixteen-hole lavatory seat that had been discovered on the site of a medieval convent. 'A thunder of nuns!' some wag commented. And there was the story of the Stamford Prioress who offered notorious hospitality in a private house in St Martin's High Street. And that of the nun who, when hauled before Bishop Alnwick on suspicion of sexual transgression, told him blandly that she'd had a child last Michaelmas but had managed to avoid conception since. Her seducer's punishment – noted in the record of a fifteenth-century episcopal visitation – was sixteen circumnavigations of St Mary's church in sackcloth and ashes while being thumped by monks. 'A sad story,' said the teller, as though describing the misfortunes of a neighbour, which indeed he was.

It was, however, in the Stamford Arts Club – a brightly furnished cellar under the Assembly Rooms where the only work of art I can recall was hung in the urinal – that I heard the story of the Stamford Bull Running. It took place every thirteenth of November for six hundred years and was not unlike the tourist spectacle at Pamplona. But it so shocked London reformers that dragoons were sent to stop it. The soldiers simply joined the frolics till – in 1839 – a combination of troops, police and fiscal pressure spoilt the sport. They have a song about it in Stamford still.

The day after my arrival I walked up St Martin's to Burghley Park where Capability Brown made a kind of English Eden to contain the vast, fantastic palace with which the Cecils proved that we are as proficient as any other nation at vainglorious ostentation. The pepperpot domes, bays, oriels and tall clustered chimneys were confected by William Cecil to show that he was more fit to lodge the Virgin Queen for a night or two than any rival magnate. What fun he must have had chucking his money at the sky and astounding all his neighbours. Time and a romantic reverence for the old-fangled have invested this gallimaufry, more like a town than a house, according to Defoe, with charm and dignity and made of it a special English pleasure, and why not! Certainly no other country celebrated the rediscovery of ancient Greece and Rome with such a fine abandonment of classical calm.

There, in a sunbaked courtyard, I met an American architect, a cultivated, modest man. He seemed overwhelmed by the architectural acrobatics of the Elizabethans. It emerged in conversation that he was from California and had gone to school with John Steinbeck. Now I was overwhelmed.

We joined a small party of tourists and trailed off through the Black and Yellow Bedchamber, the Green Damask Room, the Pagoda Room (all mother of pearl), the Purple Satin Bedroom, the Jewel Closet, the First, Second, Third, Fourth, Fifth (or Heaven) Rooms. Our guide was a tiny Scottish member of the household who recited daintily like a wee lass at the Sabbath School . . . 'Near the window hangs the sword presented to the Third Marquess of Exeter, then Lord Burghley, by the officers of the Northamptonshire Militia of which regiment he was colonel . . .' Through the bedroom furnished for the Virgin Queen herself, her bed hung with velvet, green and gold. Through the less virginal apartments where Victoria and Albert occupied themselves with the business of restocking the royal courts of Europe while cherubs charged across the ceiling and eagles grabbed at thunderbolts. Past the

Rembrandts, the Velasquez, a Rubens, a Dürer, the Van Dycks, a Holbein of Mary, Queen of England, Verrios, Lawrences, Kauffmanns, and *Lord Burghley Pulling Fortune by the Hair* by a P. Liberi. But I had not quite recovered from my vicarious encounter with John Steinbeck. Beside a picture of *The Flight into Egypt* I saw the Oakies migrating along Highway 66 to the promised land of California:

> Noah and Uncle John and the preacher began to unload the truck. They helped Grampa down and sat him on the ground and he sat limply, staring ahead of him. 'You sick, Grampa?' Noah asked. 'You goddam right,' said Grampa weakly. 'Sicker'n hell . . .' Without warning Grampa began to cry . . .

Deer ruminated in the Park outside, a peacock cried, and modest, decent Stamford quietly went about its business a mile down the road. It was Friday. At the market that marches down from Broad Street on that day I solved my problem over melting butter (see p. 34). On a stall in Red Lion Square I saw a red earthenware container between *The Boys' Wonder Book of Empire* and a huge chamber pot price £1.50. The red pot had an inner glass compartment and a lid with a pleasant moulded decoration. It looked good, and I remembered my grandmother used to have one. You filled the space between the inner vessels with water, which slowly evaporated through the porous sides, keeping the interior cold. With an elastic band to stop the lid rattling off along the road, I had cool butter for the rest of my journey. So much for chemical freezers and the rest of the impractical technology that camping shop salesmen had tried to sell me all the way along the road from Dover.

3

Sunday morning now. A few early walkers taking exercise on the Town Meadow – a large island in the Welland joined to the two halves of Stamford by footbridges and surrounded by one of the most serene townscapes in England. Sunday morning, and in such a summer, is when all Stamford's citizens might be abroad and marvelling at the survival of their exquisite town.

After Queen Margaret's flaming torches it was rebuilt on wool, but then the river silted and the town could not keep up with new technology in textiles. Houses stood empty and roofs collapsed as the Cecils were raising Burghley House. The saviour was a canal to transport the goods of the merchants, carpenters, leather workers, brewers, masons and shopkeepers who built contemporary Stamford, patronised the seventy mail and stage coaches that called each day and attended functions at the theatre and new Assembly Rooms.

When all was set for expansion by the new capitalists of steam and steel Stamford had the good fortune to be a 'rotten borough' controlled by powerful landlords who resisted an Enclosure Act that would have freed land for factories and suburbs.

The greatest threat of all came from George Hudson, the 'Railway King', who planned to bring his Scottish line into the heart of Stamford with a marshalling yard between St Mary's and the George and put the Town Meadow beneath the cinder. Had he succeeded Stamford would have suffered the dingy fate of Peterborough. But the Marquess of Exeter up at Burghley House would have none of it. The contest between aristocrat and tycoon was waged in the lobbies and committee rooms of Westminster, the counting houses of the City and no doubt the clubs of both. It was echoed in the streets of Stamford and in the pages of the *Mercury*. Burghley House was the victor, and when at length a branch line came through town it was put underground in a tunnel almost directly beneath the alabaster tomb of Elizabeth's chief minister in St Martin's Church.

Luck and lack of capital saved Stamford from gross industrialisation between the wars. That rare creature, an inspired planning officer, helped by an energetic Civic Society, spared Stamford from the high-rise boom of the 1950s–60s. A timely by-pass saved it from traffic strangulation a few years ago, and now that same cure – an east-west by-pass to speed traffic from booming East Anglian ports and industrialised argriculture to the shop counters of the Midlands – has itself become a threat to Stamford's spectacular southern entrance.

Sunday morning. From the Meadow I emerged from a crooked alley by way of a Norman arch on to St Mary's Hill opposite the Georgian town hall. Five cherubs clasped swags of fruit across their private parts above Lamb's the ironmonger's, its windows full of spades, cake tins and Swan Brand kettles. In Scotgate, over from Snowden's Hospital (almshouses rebuilt 1820), the new-swept pavement was still wet outside Pauley's shop (open Sundays) and the irises and potplants were still dripping.

The rams' heads above F. Dickinson and Sons (licensed game dealers) gazed blindly into an empty High Street where 87 per cent of the shops now belong to national multiples but which is not bad for all that. The Millstone (Courage) announced 'Good Stabling and Loose Boxes' in handsome Roman lettering above a projecting bay, and even Curry's – of all emporia – shrank reticently behind Corinthian columns of salmon pink.

Ah, but Barn Hill! Now there's a street. Queen Anne and Georgian – and something somewhat earlier, for in one house Charles I spent his last night of freedom. Small mansions with clean steps, fanlights and polished knockers, each standing a little out of line like churchgoers of some puritan persuasion gossiping on the pavement after Sunday service. And there was their very chapel, prim and ugly, apparently put up to hide a little darling of a meeting house in the back yard which no stern nonconformist would wish to be seen consorting with on Sundays. Such daintiness, such vanity!

But then Barn Hill backslides gently downwards past the Crown and the Marsh Harrier to the small-town worldliness of Red Lion Square – tea rooms, shoe shops, chemists, painted stucco – all overlooked by All Saints' Church with her handsome steeple, her frivolous thirteenth-century arcade, her brazen fifteenth-century windows, sure of herself in her pre-Reformation Romishness.

NELSON'S
HOME MADE
SAUSAGES
AND PIES

. . . declared the wooden signboard above a small colonnade, beneath which stood a solitary newsvendor among his stacks of *Sunday Peoples*, *News of the Worlds* and *Mirrors*. And then the bells began to ring.

What is it on such Stamford mornings that lifts the heart, that seems to put it on a level, if not with heaven, at least with the rouged and gilded angels with earthy, knowing faces, who for five hundred years of Sunday sermons have peered down from the rafters of St John's at the hats and pates and purses of its parishioners? I am not sure at all. I only know that I am filled with pleasure.

12

*Concerning Baha-is in Ruddle's County, gypsies on the
Great North Road and the quest for a yellow garter in
King's Lynn.*

1

BEFORE I set out from Stamford on Monday morning I glanced
through an old copy of the *Stamford Mercury* someone had left
behind. I am fond of local papers and I feel that in some respects the
editors have a more difficult task than their Fleet Street colleagues. Such
men have no time for frills. Nor can they deploy a team of hard-nosed
'firemen' who clean up a story, then leave town, a trail of damaged
reputations or smoking tempers in their wake. Unshielded by well-paid

secretaries, uncushioned by metropolitan remoteness, the country editor has to observe every current at close quarters, and report as comprehensively as possible to a readership ready to pounce upon the tiniest inaccuracy. He must give space to each public voice whether the speaker is a genius or an idiot, and yet maintain a tone of wisdom and authority.

I truly think that the small local newspapers of England together present a more accurate and profound account of the country's health than any of their London rivals. And the *Stamford Mercury* accomplishes this task as well as most. It is a broadsheet, heavy in the hand, it even smells good. It plies its honourable trade under an old-fashioned Gothic masthead (*Lincoln, Rutland* and *Stamford Mercury*, Established 1695), and believes itself to be Britain's oldest newspaper. It carries such headings as – Twenty-four Thousand Visit Library – Forgotten Bride Celebrates 50 Years Later – and – Disturbing Events in Argentina. But what turned this issue into a purveyor of pure magic for me was a letter from a professional man – I think his dart was aimed at blood sports protesters – complaining of the 'creeping sovietisation of Stamford'.

I pulled out of town by way of the Sheep Market and past the tall, narrow sixteenth-century house which, if approached from the bus station at the rear, turns out to be a public lavatory. The shops on St Peter's Hill were busy. The end house was for sale in Rutland Terrace, a confident row of Regency houses upon whose crackled stucco the sun shone, and from whose cast-iron balconies there is a splendid view of Stamford and the wooded valley. The mixed economy seemed to be pursuing its ramshackle course with ease, and there was not a commissar in sight.

Presently I saw a roadside sign which indicated I was entering Rutland.

2

I now have it on the best and most congenial authority – namely a brochure put out by G. Ruddle and Company Ltd, The Brewery, Langham, Oakham – that Rutland is as alive and well as can be expected under alien occupation.

The booklet – entitled *Much in Little* – is 'a guide for the Beer Drinker who cares' and by way of text and diagram treats of the mysteries of making Ruddle's Barley Wine (original gravity 1.080 which is pretty powerful stuff), Ruddle's County (1.050), Ruddle's Mild and Bob Brown (1.033) and Ruddle's Bitter and Light Ale (1.032 which comparatively speaking is on the nursery slopes). 'The wort, with some added sugar, is vigorously boiled in the copper with hops for one or two hours. The golden dust at the bottom of the petals . . . contains certain resins . . .'

Now all this looks fairly innocent, and near enough to poetry for some. However, it is the date of publication that speaks to the observant. Rutland was incorporated into Leicestershire under the Local Government Act of 1974. 'Why "Much in Little"?' asks the author, in 1976. 'Because it is the motto of Rutland, a county of great individuality with which Ruddle's has been proud to be associated for over a hundred years.' And on the back page under the banner 'Rutland Lives!' comes the real defiant stuff:

> Many people are under the impression that . . . the County of Rutland has disappeared . . . Nothing could be further from the truth . . . England is more than just a collection of Administrative Areas answerable to some central authority in Whitehall – England is a patchwork of diverse pieces of country-side and towns and cities all with their own distinctive characteristics and all giving rise to staunch loyalties . . . It is in this sense that Rutland lives on; certainly she has her own District Council and retains the parliamentary constituency of Rutland & Stamford; but more than all these things, she exists in people's minds as a peaceful and charming little bit of England which is the home of 30,000 people (and one brewery!), who regard Rutland as 'their' county.

Perhaps fifty or a hundred years from now historians will not, after all, be enquiring into the causes of England's industrial decline in the mid-twentieth century. It will then be clear that Britain's manufacturing and marketing supremacy was but a brief episode which began to flicker out a whole century before. There are other and more admirable reasons for English repute, among which have been the comparatively peaceful development and excellence of her humane and democratic institutions and the gradual erosion of unmerited privilege. These were, of course, partly inspired by the social dislocation of rapid industrial development. But, contrary to fashionable sentiment, they were fashioned and sustained largely by an enlightened and flexible section of the profit-making classes.

No: a more interesting area of study will be the failure of the English, from 1914 onwards, to recognise or understand her peculiar assets and so fail to protect them against expanding industrial, governmental and trade-union bureaucracy.

When Morton was a lad, the Englishman and any foreigner who cared to come, enjoyed freedoms now forgotten, and lived without restrictions he now accepts as normal. 'Until August 1914 a sensible, law-abiding Englishman could pass through life and hardly notice the existence of the state, beyond the post office and the policeman,' writes the socialist historian, A. J. P. Taylor.* Today, however, the state may change an ancient currency, alter our accustomed ways of measuring and weighing, give legal protection to a system that can deny a man the right to work, and empty a whole cartload of stumbling blocks in the path of enterprise and excellence. Of course most of us accept that legislation to protect the defenceless is not only prudent but just. But so used have we become to Regulation that we permit government – both national and local – to bleed us of our native vigour and strip us of our identity. No more arrogant assault on justice, Englishness and indeed common sense has been committed than by that Local Government Act of 1974 which abolished Rutland County.

Rutland – as every schoolboy used to know – was the smallest English county. It measured no more than seventeen miles across in any direction, encompassing only 150 square miles. Yet it was rich and had been so for long. You can measure the historic wealth of any English district by the number and size of its churches. So prosperous were the peasants and masters of Rutland in the fourteenth century that they had fifty churches, which is one for every 250 people. And they were no mean churches either.

Rutland had no mountains, no waterfalls, none of the great set-pieces of nature. But it was pretty, fit to be given as a trinket to a queen. Ethelred gave it to his Emma, the Confessor to his Edith and John to Isabella. A trinket studded with fine buildings upon an emerald background, marbled with rivers and a lacework of green lanes. Rutland did not manufacture. Its riches came in crops and wool and that oolitic limestone (from Ketton and Clipsham) which has been shipped as far as London and graces the colleges of Oxbridge.

The county had no strategic value and the only war ever fought on Rutland soil has been the one against Whitehall. That future historian, sitting in Oakham public library as I did, will be able to read among the news cuttings of how, when county boundary signs were taken down, Rutland men stole out at night and erected new ones made in garages and sheds. And of how some post office Bumble decreed that all letters on which the word Rutland appeared would be deliberately delayed. He will see the cartoon depicting two civil servants, one of whom is saying, 'Why should you be afraid of Rutlanders, Pennywhistle? They will easily be outnumbered by your administrative staff.' And he will study the survey of villagers in which 85 per cent of those questioned wanted Rutland to remain.

And then the headlines – Last Ditch Stand for Rutland – Rutland

* *History of England 1914–1945.*

98

Tells Government: There's a Feeling of Outrage – Melton Tells Rutland: We'll Fight For You – *Cry, God For Rutland, Ruddle's and St Bride!* And sadly – Rutland Sold Down the River. And finally – Goodbye Rutland.

3

When Morton went to Oakham, there was still thatch in the main street and the population was 3,500. Now it is nearer 7,000. He was served beer and beef by a blushing wench and says the inn walls were hung with fox masks and sporting prints, this being Cottesmore Hunt country. I have never cared much for the kind of girl who blushes and am – well – indifferent to fox-hunters. I was therefore happy to be served by an engaging lady from Hamelin town who did not turn pink even when I uncovered her ignorance on the subject of rats and pipers . . .

It is a respectable enough town, with stocks still standing beneath an oaken butter cross in a tiny market square. It has a splendid fourteenth-century church and an excellent museum, in a barny sort of building, full of kitchen implements and farming gear. But having said this much, I have exhausted my enthusiasm. I like brick. But in limestone country and with golden ironstone villages just to the west, there was too much brick about. Furthermore I could not find a pot of Mrs Love's celebrated horseradish sauce. I used to go to Oakham just to buy it years ago.

Whoa! says some architectural student, you have not mentioned the famous Norman courthouse whose walls are covered with horseshoes. All right, I will! And I'd best mention, too, that this former castle hall is said to be the best of its kind in England. Well, I'm afraid that Norman architecture – which is just a debasement of the Roman that got lost in the dark ages – leaves me unmoved, unless like little Tickencote or the great nave of Durham which have a poetry of their own. And the fact that Oakham castle enjoys the ancient right to levy a tax of one horseshoe from every passing noble – that even Queen Bess 'stood and delivered' and there is one horseshoe seven feet high and made of solid bronze (a gift of George IV) – that is no more than a curiosity.

I was about to leave the town when someone – I've forgotten who – told me that Oakham was a centre for the Baha-i faith. I stopped in my tracks. If I had been asked to find an assembly of Baha-is I might have gone to Shush or Khoi or Yazdikwhast, but hardly Oakham . . .

Baha-is believe that the appearance of great spiritual teachers – Krishna, Zoroaster, Moses, Christ, Mohammed – continues to occur as world conditions change – 'whenever mankind needs a kick in the pants', as a Baha-i once put it to me. They believe that the latest of the line was the

99

son of a Persian court minister who after 1852 became known as the Baha'u'lah (Glory of God). In prison and later exile in the Levant he taught a gentle discipline without ritual or dogma, the aim of which was to promote the unity of nations, the establishment of universal justice, the reconciliation of science and religion and the equality of men and women. When he died in 1892 he was succeeded by his son Abdu'l-Baha who became *Sir* Abdu'l-Baha Abbas, KBE, when the British chucked the Turks out of the Middle East during the Great War.

Unexceptionable as were these Utopian dreams, to find them in this oriental guise in a sleepy country town plumb in the middle of England was an incongruity precisely to my taste. So I knocked on the door of a neat bungalow in South Street and was invited in to sit down for coffee and biscuits with the chief Baha-i of Britain – a Mr John Long who had retired from his job as head of the Department of Boot and Shoe Manufacture at Leicester Polytechnic. He was an intelligent and courteous man and I enjoyed listening to him. ('Beware! Lest ye offend any heart!' says the Baha'u'lah. 'Beware! Lest ye hurt any soul! Beware! Lest ye deal unkindly with any person!')

When he had first arrived in Oakham he told me he went to Barclays and asked if he could open an account for the Baha-i funds that he was handling. (There are 140 Baha-i assemblies in Britain alone, and a considerable intercontinental publishing section operates from Rutland.) The branch manager agreed without much enthusiasm, then found that the new customer from the bungalow round the corner was talking about sums seven digits long. There can be few Rutland industries with turnovers like that!

4

I think we were all a little 'touched' that year. When I look back through the heat-haze of that fabulous summer I see an England where, for me at least, the days and occasionally the nights were infinitely elastic. I could stretch them out and fill them full of miles, or chance engagements with grave, important men, or loafers like myself, or just with villages and towns, streams and woods, hills, farms, fairs and fetes. Or I could cut them short and go to sleep in some convenient hedgeside. I could stay up all the short night long and go to bed at the morning rush hour in some northern city. I could talk to anyone I pleased, ask any question that came into my head regardless of convention. And on the whole the English seemed to be the most relaxed, uninhibited and hospitable of people.

Maybe this was the effect of months of sunshine on a people who get more than their fair share of February. Or maybe my new way of life had so unsettled my professional pessimism that I was able to see what was always there for the first time since I was a cub reporter counting wreaths at funerals. At any rate, the day that I left Stamford by way of Rutland and ended up in Norfolk, was one of the long ones. But of course it included the incident with the gypsy . . .

I struck the A 1 south of Grantham at a place called Stretton and had not been travelling north for many miles when I saw a gypsy camp on a large ring of grass which seemed to have been set aside for a future round-about and then forgotten. There were three vehicles. Two old-fashioned caravans and a four-wheel cart. A group of horses cropped nearby.

In the clock-ruled world to which I have since returned, most people, and that includes myself, might have glanced at this Borrovian group, and sped on. In my new role of vagabond, however, I parked the van in a lane and set out through the long grass. Two figures I had seen near the wagon quietly vanished. But I suspected I was still being watched.

Thirty yards short of the nearest van I was challenged by two snarling dogs and would have gone full speed astern had I not noticed that each was tethered by a long steel chain. Retreat would have been humiliating. I passed between them with a foot to spare on either side and, arriving at the first vehicle, there was nothing left to do but shout 'Good morning'. No reply. I sat down on the step, then, hearing a slight movement, I half turned and tried again.

'Yes?'

Now in the half-dark interior I made out a man of middle age, seated on a chair with his hands crossed in his lap.

'Lovely morning,' I tried again.

'Is it?' said the man.

Fencing continued till my adversary seemed satisfied that I was not from the Council or any other agency and gradually, giving a little ground here and there, we established a rapport. For an inkling of my occupation he traded the news that he was not a tinker, tinkler, traveller, potter or bloody mender – he was, he said, a true Romany.

It was hard going, though, till I reached into my pocket and asked him if he smoked. He leaned towards a shelf and produced a clay stump much darkened by tobacco juice. He held it towards me and replied . . . 'when I can get terbaccer!'

It was not the two-ounce envelope of flake that did the trick. I believe it was the fact that the pipe I happened to be using was also made of clay and it too was almost black with use. From then on, the duel was conducted between cautious equals.

101

He asked me if I had been to Appleby that year, by which he meant the great horse-trading gypsy meeting that takes place every June in Cumbria and which, alas, I'd missed. Then, after the pipes, he offered me dark tea from a pot singing on a stove, and produced a son of nine or ten. He said there must be a few quid in the book-writing business and I was obliged to explain that it was possible to write without attaining riches. That seemed to give him satisfaction, not because he wished me poor, I think, but because he thought I lied well.

In turn I asked him about caravans and how much they cost and where he got these two and whether they could still be made. But it was when we got into the subject of interior decoration that he threw out all his native reticence. On the rear wall, glittering like a reredos in a dark Spanish church, was a large sheet of expensive mirror glass on which had been engraved a great, capering horse. It was a magnificent, unearthly creature with streaming mane and rippling muscles and it gave light, luxury and drama to the small habitation. On the other walls were smaller samples of the same artist's work. The gipsy not only told me who the artist was but how he had bargained with him and how much they cost. He may have exaggerated a bit and I don't intend to break his confidence. But I can tell you that many a well-lacquered housewife in her suburban villa would not spend as much to furnish her front lounge.

Before I left I offered to share the rest of my tobacco, and so we went outside to the four-wheel cart and he took some time shifting tarpaulins and layers of utensils, till he found an old tin in which to keep it.

As I began to walk away he suggested I should bring my son to spend a day with his, and he forecast his movements for the next few weeks. He hinted at a network of long-established routes beneath which our Gorgio geography of motorways and cities was of marginal importance.

The dogs meanwhile had shrunk. They wagged their tails and looked almost amiable as I went on my way.

5

I have no grudge against motorways and trunk roads. Indeed, I respect them. The M 62, for instance, which vaults across the Pennines from the great concrete bobbins of Ferrybridge power station to the warm, dirty, sprawling vestibule of Manchester, is quite splendid. It dips and soars and sideslips from east to west, from wool to cotton, across hags and mosses that a few years ago were the territory of the peewit and the shepherd. And far below is the slow-moving pageant of the Industrial Revolution . . . Leeds, Morley, Batley, Brighouse, Rochdale . . . once-famous mills – handsome, square and Georgian – that sustained the capital of the world and raised a special, pre-supermarket kind of man and woman as different from the English of Middlesex and Surrey as Londoners from Patagonians . . .

The M 6. That too is a noble road as it scores the multicoloured flank of the Cumbrian mountains, and overcomes the high desert of Shap Fell. The M 5, once it has shaken free from the tangle of Spaghetti Junction and is on its way to Exeter, through the Cotswold, Mendip, Quantock and Blackdown Hills, is a happy road in any company.

In my own lifetime the A 1 – the old Great North Road – shared this companionable trait, taking sustenance, as it did, from the Wansfords and Stamfords through which it passed between Edinburgh and London. But now, with its by-passes and roundabouts, it is the dreariest 400 miles in Britain, touching little and inspiring nothing – only a desperate desire to arrive at journey's end.

Yet there is one stretch of the A 1 where a stranger new-landed at Heathrow could, for a mile or two, think that he was in the England he'd read about in travel brochures. For here the Department of Transport signposts speak in poetry.

O, signboard, point me along the primrose path to *Melton Mowbray* by way of *Burton Lazars*! Does *Old Somerby* still await for me, glass ready filled, beneath some shady chestnut? How fares *Burton Coggles*? And *Boothby Pagnell*? Does *Dry Doddington* still hone his wit on gouty old *Stoke Rochford*? Do *Braceby* and *Haceby* still go *Horbling* at *Bassingthorpe* with young *Newton Walcot*? And is *Carlton Scroop*, that wily old solicitor still in practice?

Many times have I travelled that road and as many times been tempted. This afternoon, I was at last seduced. I turned off right and followed the sign to Boothby Pagnell. At Great Ponton I had passed a handsome church with a viol for a weathervane. I crossed a brook called Witham, then passed over Ermine Street – on its way to what the IX Legion knew as Lindum and we call Lincoln – coasted into the Lincolnshire of Newton's bereaved boyhood and drew up near a vast village green. At the gates of a large house I said Good day to the only human being in sight – he turned out to be the father of the owner.

The name Boothby Pagnell was ringing a faint bell. When I was fifteen and much more afraid of arithmetic than of Heinkels, I took refuge – at algebra time – in a large tome with the forbidding title *A History of Architecture on the Comparative Method* by Sir Banister Fletcher. Equilateral equations and quadratic triangles are still a mystery to me. On the other hand, Sir Banister has been a stout companion. In a sense he taught me who I was. Whether it was the soft southern sound of the name that had stuck in my head or the small drawing (one of 2,000) at the top right-hand corner of page 396 – it is hard to say. Anyway, it suddenly came back to me, and I said to the old man in Boothby Pagnell: 'Isn't there a Norman manor house round here?' 'Yes,' he replied. 'Would you like to see it? It's at the bottom of our garden.' And so it was.

There is something pretty superior about having a Norman manor down the garden, but my guide was nonchalant. Although it was not much bigger than a modern semi, and built of stone, of course, it had accommodation for cattle on the ground floor and an outside stairway leading to the upper, in which the lord of the manor, his family and servants lived. There was also a solar – that is a small retiring room to which Monsieur et Madame could withdraw from the common gaze when they had private things to do. That would have been quite a status symbol at the time when it was built. I was more impressed by this small building than by the great hall at Oakham for I could picture real people living here, with babies being changed and the sweet smell of cow dung drifting through the glassless windows.

But it was time to leave Boothby Pagnell. I turned south and taking a by-road-of-the-by-road came to Burton Coggles. Swinging east to find out whether Corby Glen lived up to its name I found a grey stone village once a market town that would not have looked out of place in a Yorkshire dale. It was also distinguished by a pub where you could lean your elbow on the bar and watch the next few gallons being brewed in vessels of stainless steel. Thence east through Bourne (once a sanctuary of Hereward the Wake and now famous for watercress and racing cars and as the birthplace of the man called Fred who founded Worth of Paris); through Spalding (where Newton and Alexander Pope were once members of the still extant Gentlemen's Society, where seven bridges span the Welland, and where every spring half Britain's tulip crop blazes in the fields) and out into another kind of countryside. This was the northern Fens and I would have turned towards Boston had I not noticed a sign pointing to King's Lynn and remembered the last evenings I had spent there in the Woolpack – how long ago? – and the song we used to sing.

AYE-round – her hair . . . the song began . . .
She wore a YELLow ribbon.
SHE wore it in the Springtime,
And IN the month of May . . .

6

King's Lynn . . . Lynn Regis . . . once Lynn Episcopi! Lynn where the flatlands end and the lanes of north Norfolk begin their rolling and their pitching between high hedges from church to round-towered church, hamlet to hamlet, mill to mill. Lynn the small capital of the Wash, all rich brown brick and flint and stucco. Two great market squares. Rows and curves of Stuart and Georgian houses built for well-breeched Stuart and Georgian merchants with as much good taste as money. Commercial Lynn with its wharves and medieval warehouses. That small, square Custom House on the quay designed by a seventeenth-century mayor and perhaps the happiest building of such purpose in the world. Cosmopolitan Lynn – an English country town swept for centuries by the human eddies of the short seas – Hollanders, Lithuanians, Norwegians, Finns and Frenchmen. But especially Hollanders, bringing their money and leaving their bricks and gables to enhance English streets so that from across the Ouse you might be looking at a painting of a Flemish seaport. The sharp smell of Lincolnshire tomatoes in the Tuesday Market. Cabbage leaves underfoot. Parading girls. Brown legs and cheeky eyes. Lounging airmen from Milwaukee and Nebraska. Gusts of song from an open fanlight.

> AYE-round her hair,
> She wore a yellow ribbon . . .

A cavalier's town. A trader's town. A wenching town. A carousing town. A broth of a town. A lovely, lovely, lusty town.

I slackened speed after the big roundabout on its outskirts, rumbled through the medieval South Gate, coasted down to the Saturday Market and pulled in alongside St Margaret's. What a church! In many towns it would do for a cathedral. The bells said it was seven-thirty. Just right! A pub door stood open across the way. I strolled across, walked in and found . . . not even a barman!

There was nobody in the market-place outside either. I walked up through empty streets on clean, bare pavements between handsome houses. My footsteps made sharp echoes. A solitary pigeon rose steeply from the roadway, clapping over the pantiles and away, with a sound like mock applause. A lone couple leaned together in the recessed plate-glass doorway of a locked radio shop, watching a TV programme they could not hear. When I emerged on to the vast Tuesday Market there were only two old ladies trying to park an 1100.

Lynn's Tuesday Market Square is square all right, and surrounded by well-shaped, solid houses, showing it was all thought out in prosperous post-medieval days by men who knew the price of a bag of beans and how to draw up a bill of lading. Ambitious men, self-conscious, sensitive to Continental fashion and a little bit up-tight. The handsomest building – the one that dominates the square – is the Duke's Head. When it was built in 1689,* and for a long time after that, it was sunny Norfolk brick. Then along came the style for stucco, and they turned the Duke's Head into a flaming iced cake. I crossed the empty square, climbed the steps and walked in. A receptionist sat staring straight ahead and my passing did not break the beam. I moved across soft carpet, past red-faced men filling their armchairs with their large behinds and bellies. Businessmen? Visiting aldermen? The bar looked more like a place for cocktails than quenching thirst. It wasn't my night for Martinis and lemon peel, so I left without deflecting the electronic stare of the woman at the door.

Across the square again to a place I remembered through a haze of Camel-smoke . . . *Dee-dum, dee-dum . . . She wore a yellow garter . . .* But that had been changed too – been given a smart, new Dickensian theme. I headed for the Woolpack corner. Closed! And closed for many a month to judge by the dusty windows.

Through the deserted streets listening for voices where there were no voices . . . *she wore it in the Springtime and IN the month of May . . .* Then footsteps – the only human sound in King's Lynn on that summer evening – and in a while their owner ambled round a bend. A young copper with a limp moustache and a little radio clipped to his lapel.

'Can you tell me where I can find a pub?' I asked. 'An ordinary pub.'

'Arr . . . that depends what you mean,' he replied after some reflection.

'An ordinary, straightforward pub. Last time I was here there were lots of pubs.'

'Arr . . . I've heard about those days . . . Can't remember that far back, but I've been told. One on every corner then, they say.'

I felt a little old. 'Not so long ago really!'

'Well, there's a place up by the South Gate that sells real-ale. You turn left then right and up past . . .'

I gave up. It was too complicated. Even for draught beer. 'Thanks,' I said, and walked away before he'd finished. Suddenly I wanted to leave Lynn. I drove out of town – or what was left of it, for the developers had been up to their gimcrack tricks – and was soon healed by the lilac and oak and ash and poppies and tall grass of Norfolk.

A few miles on where the trees fall back and the sky widens I saw a

* By Henry Bell, the mayor who designed the Custom House.

long, high, wire fence and a sign that read *Sculthorpe*. RAF SCUL-
THORPE! But that had always been a kind of lie. For the word
Sculthorpe not long ago meant America. Ten thousand Yanks there were
at Sculthorpe once, and for fifteen or twenty years they colonised this
part of Norfolk. Seaside Hunstanton was almost part of the Union. And
Lynn too. Now the Sculthorpe runways were cracked. Hutments empty.
Rabbits on the tarmac.

I cooked my dinner that night on Fakenham Racecourse, and drank
half a bottle of Beaujolais sitting on the back step. It was a lovely
hawthorn-scented evening and there was one of those wide Norfolk
skies. This evening it was painted lilac over to the west, with brush
strokes of lime green.

> *AYE-round the town,*
> *She pushed a p'rambulator . . .*

That was what had happened of course. They'd gone. And Lynn was a
quieter, poorer, sadder place for their going.

> *SHE pushed it in the Springtime and in the month of May.*
> *And WHEN they asked her-why-the-hell-she-pushed-it,*
> *She pushed it for that Yankee who was far, far away . . .*
> *Far away,*
> *Far away,*
> *She pushed it for that Yankee who was far, far away.*

The Romans had departed!

13

A chapter composed in a Norfolk carrot house due south of the North Pole and telling of a one-eyed admiral, a one-clawed lobster, a thundering parson, and a bountiful Canadian.

1

FOR THE NEXT WEEK I lived in an empty carrot house in Norfolk and I swear I never occupied a more congenial billet. It stood on a hill behind a town called Wells-next-the-Sea, and from the open door I could look out over the roof-tops, across salt marshes and beyond a beach curiously known as Abraham's Bosom, then on towards the North Pole with not an island between me and the eternal ice. I was informed by an old man out for a walk, who woke me up as I lay beneath a hawthorn bush one afternoon, that this geographical position – where England sticks its backside out into the cold North Sea – made it a hard place when the wind blew from the Arctic. But by all the saints of Norfolk it was hot that week. Wonderfully, delightfully, stupendously hot. The sea below was a dazzling blue that hurt the eyes. The fields were as dry and yellow as the Arizona plains. It was so hot that farmers who had prodded the stone-hard earth for weeks, miraculously forgot to grouse and went out in Land Rovers to fetch barrels of beer. It was rumoured that an extreme case in Suffolk so far forgot himself that he came back with a new hat for his wife. Normally taciturn men of the land grew garrulous. One leaned against my caravan and actually admitted that he had to find £31,000 that year for Mr Healey. He wasn't grumbling. Another, in a pub, said there was nothing to worry about really. 'We farmers expect one bad year in five, and . . . well . . . this is it.'

So what did I care? My carrot house had a washroom with running h. & c., and the decor was what would be called nowadays 'way out'. The social climate was perfect too. The cuisine was exactly to my taste and some pin-striped Ariel in Portland Place had so arranged the music on the Third that it was not only an answer to my best pleasure but seemed also to excite the owls at night, and once – I think, I think – a nightingale. I drank like a man, slept like a baby, and in between pursued my leisurely vocation as a student of the English race.

It may well be asked how I came by the tenancy of such an unusual residence. The reply must be that I knew an admiral's son called Tom, who introduced me to a publican called Les, whose customers sang a song about a one-clawed lobster, and among whom one evening there happened to be a farmer called John (buying a barrel of beer) who grew carrots and invited me to go to church. It fell out thus.

2

The day after my night on Fakenham Racecourse I was trundling along the coast road between Lynn and Wells. I call it the coast road, but only because it is the main highway nearest to the sea, which indeed it touches now and then. But the coastline of north Norfolk is a fickle and elusive boundary, changing so often that I wonder how the map-makers keep track of its wide marshes of sea lavender and marram grass, its shifting dunes and roving spits. It is a serpent that slithers silently round unwitting sunbathers, encircling them with a maze of creeks and mudbanks in ten stealthy minutes. It is a thief, a devourer of whole villages now marked only by a sea rock or a legend. A deceiver that in one night of 1695 lured two hundred vessels (mostly Geordie colliers) on to its travelling sands and claimed a thousand sailors. A deserter of fishing villages and a runaway from harbours. (Wells-next-the-Sea is now an upstream port despite its name, and Castle Rising, now four miles inland, not even that.) It is a ravenous tiger that savages soft Norfolk cliffs, and a rampage of lions in time of tempest. Every schoolboy learned his first historical joke when he heard how King John lost his baggage in the Wash, and maybe future schoolboys – at least in Norfolk – will be taught a hundred years from now how on the last night of January 1953, 26,000 acres of farmland were covered by the sea, eighty people died, and fish swam in the aisles of St Margaret's Church, King's Lynn.

However, this Norfolk coastline is a seductress too. And in the summer sun when you can pause where the coastline used to be and look north across the marram where some sailing craft is drifting along a hidden watercourse like a ghost vessel on a prairie, when there is lavender in the air and the smell of wild garlic from the woods at Onion Corner, when there are Holkham pots for sale to Birmingham families at the pottery by Holkham Hall, when Wells puts out striped awnings, opens pub doors wide, sells tons of pink, sticky rock and pretends – successfully – to be an Edwardian seaside resort, then there is a special gaiety and colour about the place which forgets winter, and I am a devoted and most willing victim.

Anyway, I was cruising along the road to Wells on such a day – and wondering why so many spireless Norfolk churches had round towers instead of square – when I spotted Tom standing by his cottage wall at a place called Overy Staithe. He had long ago cast off from the quarter-deck of his youth and become a journalist, but had retained an interest in the life of Nelson, about whom he'd written a book. His was a welcome face I had not seen for years. It was another of those happy village-high-street meetings, and the upshot was that he proposed to take me to a certain pub.

Now there is a small, unspectacular patch of England – perhaps no bigger than ten miles by ten – to reach the heart of which it is necessary to navigate a reeling, swerving, undulating maze of byways where in summer visibility is limited by high hedgerows, and in late spring by barricades of may blossom. And there, within a small building that serves as post office, village store and public house, men in fishing smocks and seaboots sing the moon down the sky while drinking the best beer in England (which of course means the best beer in the world) out of yellow, two-handled, one-and-a-half-pint pots, following each with a slug of clove-flavoured rum. This was our destination. And here it was plain that a chap like me could dream a whole summer away, considering it no less than his duty.

This diminutive Valhalla was haunted by a small, one-eyed sailor – a parson's son – who died more than 170 years ago. The walls of the small bar were covered with pictures of his gaudiest engagements. The landlord, Les Winter, was born just a few leafy lanes away, and so was Admiral Lord Nelson. It is a reasonable assumption that Les's great-great-grandfather, and the recent ancestors of many of his customers, dozed along with young Horatio through the sermons of Nelson senior.

In mid-career England's greatest hero spent five years at his father's rectory, waiting for a new command. When he left to join the *Agamemnon* he held a shindig for the local lads in the room above Les Winter's bar, and in the morning took a parcel of them off with him to serve as shipmates.

Anyway, this evening, after the martins had settled in the post office eaves, the men who bled at Cape St Vincent, four times removed, began to muster in Les Winter's tap room. They sat on the same high-backed settles that were there before Trafalgar. The nectar (Greene King Abbot) was drawn from the wood by spiggot without the aid of gas. And I swear that the talk that passed to and fro across the little room that summer night barely touched our century. They talked of shrimps and graveyards. They boasted about catching giant crabs . . . 'Half the size of this table, Frank, and still alive when the last customer went home' . . . Ancient friends belaboured one another with terrible insults in the accent of Nelson's Norfolk. The laughter was loud and frequent, the stories often ribald. But hardly a word was spoken, or sentiment expressed, that would have been surprising in the fo'c'sle of the *Agamemnon*.

Eventually, a small, elfish man began to play the mouth organ and the bones* both at once. Another virtuoso took up the beat with fingers drumming on the plywood seat of a chair he held like an instrument across his knees. And the songs they sang could be heard beyond the churchyard.

> 'Then up jumped a ma-a-ck'rel with stripes on 's ba-a-ack.
> Tis toim now ole Skippur to change the main tack,'

they sang.

> 'Then up jumped a lobster with only one claw.
> Come now ole Skippur, we'll pull for the shore.
> Oh, it's windy ole weathur,
> Stormy ole weathur,
> When the wind blows, we'll all pull togethur.'

---

* Pairs of shaped and polished strips of bone or ivory held between the fingers of one hand and rattled like castanets. Made popular by 'nigger-minstrel' bands but played by sailors and by small boys in working-class England until World War II.

The songs covered at least four continents, if you count Australia, at least three wars if you count 'Kroojer's', and a whole lot of sea. Which was all very right and proper for a village that was represented at the Nile and Copenhagen.

It was during this performance that John Temple, the farmer, arrived to pick up his weekly pin* of beer and drink a pint with Les. He was a tall, courteous man with a hundred-acre gaze, and having learned about my journey said – 'We're having a special service in the church at Wighton on Friday. Why don't you come? And we'll have a drink afterwards.' I said I would.

I walked out along the corridor. The yellow brick floor was channelled by the feet of three centuries of roisterers, Nelson among them. I passed a wall poster which read:

BRITONS!
Your NELSON is dead
GOD hath given us the VICTORY
BRITONS
Fear GOD, fear SIN, and then
Fear Nothing

The night air was soft on my face. There was a smell of hay. I decided to sleep near the Lord Nelson – which was probably called the Ship before Trafalgar, before the tide left and the river across the road became a stream, before the stickleback took over from the trout. A few hedges away I could hear someone still singing his way home.

'How's this for Paradise?' I thought. 'And how long will it be undisturbed?'

Until the coachloads from Düsseldorf and Denver find out, and begin to come up from Heathrow and Southampton.

'What route will they take? How will they find it?'

Ah! Now should I tell?

Well – you set out on a morning in early summer and take the little lane where the hedges are so heaped with blossom and the verges so deep with drifts and mists of fool's parsley, that it looks as though the world has been swept by an enchanted snowstorm. Then when you reach the crossroads where all ways look equally seductive, you ask two brown-faced men standing by a brick barn for the shortest way to the Admiral Lord Nelson.

You can't miss it.

* Pin – a cask with a capacity of four and a half gallons.

112

3

The village of Wighton stands on a rise about three miles inland. There is a horse pond at the top of the little hill and a few shops, a church just over the crest, and a pub called the Carpenter's Arms at the bottom.

One November night in 1965 at about half-past eight, a gale tearing in from the North Sea and across the marshes blew the church tower down. It was not, by all accounts, a spectacular fall. Weakened by 650 years of baking by the sun in summer and battering by all the winds of winter, shaken by bells every Sunday, holy day, wedding, christening and funeral, enough was enough. She just slid slowly down over the west front. And those people of Wighton who heard the sound of falling masonry above the windy rumble in their chimneys came out with electric torches and found the hilltop lane between Harrison's Farm and the churchyard blocked by a barrier of flint cobbles and Ancaster stone. And that, it seemed, was that. In other days a pious local magnate, anxious to ensure his place in heaven, might have fixed Wighton up with a new tower, but now bargaining with the Almighty on such a scale was out of fashion. After the first excitement Wighton settled down again to life without a tower.

It was seven years later that a Toronto engineer called Leeds Richardson became so curious about his unusual forename that he decided to take a holiday in England and perhaps solve the small mystery. He knew from entries in a family Bible that his father, grandfather and great-grandfather had all been christened Leeds. And he had heard of an ancestral connection with Wighton. Indeed, with that reverence for a European ancestry, however obscure, that is so engaging a characteristic of many North Americans, he had named his company Wighton Engineering.

So on a hot Sunday afternoon he turned up at the vicarage door. And after prospecting among his gravestones and parish registers during the next week or two, the vicar of Wighton was pleased to unite Leeds Richardson with his genealogical identity – with, one Robert Richardson, probably an itinerant ex-serviceman who, seeking work after the Peninsular War, had settled in the village and married Elizabeth Rogers, widow, in 1812. The first son of the union, baptised at Wighton's font, was named Leeds Richardson, perhaps in memory of his father's birthplace. It was Leeds Richardson the First who in 1837 – the year of Victoria's accession – took the Canadian trail with thousands of other English villagers, exchanging the grim uncertainties of the Industrial Revolution for the brave uncertainties of life in the new world.

Engineer Richardson was grateful for the vicar's help and he sent Wighton church a cheque for 250 dollars.

But the big, beautiful, transatlantic bombshell landed in 1974 when the vicar of Wighton – worried about the general dilapidation of his lovely church – received another letter from Toronto. Mr Richardson, it said, wanted to spend 100,000 dollars to rebuild the tower of Wighton. Or, as he himself put it rather more picturesquely – 'By golly, I'll put the tower back at Wighton!' and so he did.

On the day I walked down into Wighton I realised at once that something special was afoot. There was a feeling as if something really happy, something good, was about to happen. There were no flags or bands. But a retired army officer was marshalling a rabble of wild valerian in crimson platoons along the roadside verge. A sweet, shy, little woman on a bicycle flitted up and down the main street like a moth on some important errand. A couple of bobbies stood chatting importantly with villagers on a scrap of green halfway down the street.

And within the church – well, there had probably been no such occasion for decades. After Crécy, perhaps, when the old tower was dedicated? After Waterloo, Ladysmith, the Great War?

It is a large building and well-proportioned, with wide arcades between nave and aisles. It was packed with sunburned Norfolk villagers. Tall old men built like men-o'-war. Fair-haired little girls like the daughters of Vikings. Whole families of farmers and farmworkers. The piers were touched with sunlight from the windows. At least fifty people for whom seats could not be found stood at the west end around a font banked with Mrs Forster's dahlias. Methodists and Catholics had brought bouquets and the air was full of natural incense. The choir had obviously been schooled in heaven.

I was standing near the font when the bishop came down to the west for the dedication of the tower. He was an impressive man, in his mid-sixties maybe, with a lean, bronzed face. I was delighted to observe that the golden mitre on his head was adorned, not with the cross but with two sailing boats. His pastoral staff – I swear it – was a boathook. There were anchors and helm-wheels embroidered about his vestments which – lo! – were not the episcopal purple of convention, but shocking pink and turquoise in that summer evening light.

The text was 'The name of the Lord is a strong tower', and by heaven he gave it all he'd got. He towered in the pulpit above a sea of faces. And when it came to the ringing bits, the crescendos, he threw back his head and his right hand pointed – strained – towards the roof timbers. The names of ancient saints, the lighthouses and church towers of coastal Norfolk, landmarks for mariners since long ago, rumbled in the rafters and swept down the nave. This man, I learned later, had spent his early priesthood in the toughest quarter of North Shields. He knew his stuff about the sea.

And then he spoke of Leeds Richardson's gift to generations yet unborn, contrasting it with the selfish prodigality of the world. A classic horse race had been run some days before, and he'd read his newspapers.

'Twenty-five millions . . . *twenty-five million quid* on one race!' he cried in a voice like the thunder of the oceans.

Mrs Marion Richardson, wife of the philanthropist, wore a plain white frock hemmed with blue. She unveiled the commemorative plaque while her husband Leeds stood modestly nearby. It recorded that the new tower was to be called Trillium, after the flower of Leeds Richardson's native province, Ontario. The old tower had been the Crécy and bore the arms of Richard III.

After the service, coffee was served in the nave.

Then John Temple and I went off to broach his cask. That smaller ceremony took place in the kitchen of New Farm, Wells-next-the-Sea, during which he suggested I take possession of his carrot house for as long as I wished. I drove up the hill in the dark and was unable to take stock of my lodgings till next morning.

4

As carrot houses go, mine was clearly in the five-star class. It was a large building, two-thirds occupied by machinery for the sorting, grading, washing and packing of Norfolk carrots destined for the dinner tables of Europe. There were ladders and platforms and strange doors, the mysteries of which, I had been told, were perfectly understood by a band of women who took over the contraption at harvest time.

I liked the place. I like machinery even when I don't understand it. I certainly didn't mind sharing my dining hall with a carrot sorter. And by night the building creaked and groused in a most companionable manner.

There were practical advantages, too. The building occupied the flat crown of the rise where the dirt road broadened. If the day became intolerably hot I just ran the caravan backwards through the doors into the big cool hall where my cup, plates, pans, eating irons and boots were laid out on a convenient table. When I fancied a sea view – as I did each daybreak and evening – I drove out again. Steel bars became towel rails. I did not have to fold and stow my bed each morning. I hung my sleeping bag and blankets over a catwalk handrail for an airing, and at bed time just brushed off the carrot dust before turning in. There was a flush lavatory, a basin and electrically heated water in a roomy washroom of the *maison-concrète* style. Such trivialities become luxuries when you have been on the road a week or two.

There was solitude. Time for reading – or just listening to and watching this unusual countryside.

And company. Every morning between six and seven the rat-and-mole catcher crunched up the pebbly track on his way to remote barns and far-flung fields, and I made a point of stepping out and wishing him good day. The occasional rambler passed by, and if the kettle happened to be on we'd have fresh tea, and it was rare that I did not learn something from someone.

I learned, for instance, that the reason why so many Norfolk towers are round instead of square is that east of the carrstone district near Sandringham where the houses look as though they're made of gingerbread, there is little building-stone but flint pebble, which is not very good for corners. Stone for this purpose was sometimes imported from Barnack or even from as far away as Normandy, but of course that was expensive. It was therefore cheaper and more convenient to build round towers.

But to understand the north Norfolk coastline and see why it stole land from the sea in one place and relinquished cliffs and villages elsewhere, I had to carry a few books up the hill from Wells and sit with them above the shimmering saltings. Here is the explanation as I understood it.

Because there is nothing – nothing but three thousand miles of ice and sea – between Norfolk and the Pole, the wind that comes hammering down from the Arctic can pile up waves of great height and force. With this wild cavalry the sea attacks, and where the modest Norfolk hills touch shore it hurls pebbles and boulders against the map of England, claiming fields and footpaths, carving cliffs from soft ice-age deposits, then undermining and eroding them by a couple of yards a year.

The breakers, having taken their fill of chalk and flint and glacial detritus, then turn aside, still powerful, some racing west towards the Wash, some east then south round the bulge of Norfolk towards Great Yarmouth in what is understated as a longshore drift, eventually slowing and relinquishing their burden. Here the land advances. Two great salients of dune and shingle, like barrier reefs – Yarmouth Spit and Blakeney Point – have thus been formed, marking the routes of the spent sea force in opposite directions. Behind their shelter sea lagoons are formed where marine vegetation flourishes and dies in the calmer shallows, becoming an accretion of mud and weed which in time breaks surface, forming salt pans and marshes. Creeks drain the new marshland, becoming small bewildered rivers, twisting this way and that, seeking escape at the changing shoreline.

116

North Norfolk's travelling dunes are formed by the wind on dry days. It carries the sand up shallow beaches till it is halted by tufts of couch grass and piles up. After that the fresh winds whisk off the crests to form a new line of dune beyond, and so the sand advances. Such a process lost Eccles village its second church, built in the fourteenth century in what was thought to be a safe position. But creeping dunes buried it a hundred years ago. One way of halting the encroachment is by sowing marram grass, an ingenious plant whose broad blades direct rainfall into the tubular stalks so saving sustenance for dry days, and whose roots thrive in sand and bind it fast.

Another of my callers was John Temple who would lean against the carrot house and talk about marl pits, 1,200 gallon cows and other matters I did not understand. Close by stood a hut on wheels which I imagined was a Victorian bathing machine. I asked how it came to be rotting on a hill top two miles inland. Well, it wasn't a bathing machine. It was a shepherd's lambing hut. These days shepherds travel by Land Rover, and as often as not sleep in their beds at night. But not so long ago, John told me, the shepherds set out for their huts at the start of the lambing season, leaving razor and shaving brush at home, returning when all the lambs were safely delivered. Then honour and free booze went to the shepherd with the longest beard. And so began my elementary education in the history of farming.

5

The rolling fields of this Norfolk, with their hedges of green cumulus and their hidden lanes, look as though they have rolled thus from eternity and that they will, in their own good time, arrive back at the same place and start again. The farms and barns look as prosperous and full as their inhabitants. Here, it is pleasant to consider, young Nelson dreamed away his boyhood days. Pleasant, but in fact not so.

This corner of the county is also the territory of Coke of Norfolk whose great house Holkham Hall, with its terraces and pink marble pillars artfully arranged among avenues of trees and landscaped water, shimmers in the summer heat. It was a signpost pointing towards Holkham that sent me to the reference books. And there I read:

NELSON, 1st Viscount (Horatio). Born 1758.
COKE, Thomas William. 1st Earl of Leicester. Born 1754.

From which I deduced that Coke was but four years old when Nelson was born, and sixteen when Nelson went to sea at twelve.

And Thomas Coke it was who not only transformed this landscape, but with Viscount 'Turnip' Townshend of nearby Raynham and other eighteenth-century agriculturalists, helped to revolutionise the farming methods of the whole country, changing the lives of most countrymen and enriching the nation. He grew clover where previously fields lay fallow, brought in cattle for their life-giving dung, planted hedgerows and welcomed experts from abroad. He altered the old rhythm of the crops and the nature of the soil. In forty years he increased the annual rents of Holkham from £2,200 to £20,000. And he was a damned good landlord too.

Before Coke, this tract of Norfolk was a bleak, powdery, unproductive area bounded by a wilderness of salty marshes. It is said that here two rabbits fought for every blade of grass. That – not Coke's lovely garden – was the boyhood home of Nelson. And I wonder which one of them it was that in the end served England best.

Much nonsense has been written about the Englishman's love of the countryside. The cultivation of city window-boxes, the excellence of some urban parks, the trek to suburbia along the new commuter railways, the lingering regard for the garden city movement, and even the Dig for Victory campaign – all these have been produced as evidence that the English, having been town dwellers for a century, are still countrymen at heart. It is romantic poppycock.

A window-box, however admirable, is a piece of city furniture and not a racial memory. Public parks imitate the formal gardens of great houses and not farmland. When factory towns were building, farmworkers left the impoverished countryside in thousands. Rapid suburbanisation changed the conditions and the temper of the English once again, making of them neither city dwellers nor countrymen. Suburbanisation was not all bad, but it was propelled by an energetic building industry rather than an atavistic longing for field and heath. The Londoner who took the Metropolitan Line to Rickmansworth may have been drawn by the estate agents' Arcadian prose – but he had no urge to muck out byres, or even to stand close in the public bar to honest men who did. The plain truth is that most of us are strangers in our countryside, bored by its mechanics, unable to tell oats from barley or a field of cattle kale from cabbage. We are the most urbanised – well, *sub*-urbanised – society in Europe. By the 1930s the English people and their governments had so neglected their agricultural inheritance that farming was moribund and, by and large, farmers were a beaten lot who counted parsimony chief among all virtues.

But since the war, while we were transfixed by such urban entertainments as the decline of heavy industry, the farmers were astir, and a technological and economic miracle was being wrought in the fields – and we have barely noticed. It was a sensational performance we should not have missed, and all the more intriguing because it seems to argue with the most treasured prejudices of the ideologues.

It provides a lesson for those of the Right who believe that all state intervention is the death of enterprise and the harbinger of ruin. For Government – with grants, subsidies, education, advisory services and marketing boards – played both an initiating and perpetually supporting role. It is a poke in the blind eye of the Left which continues to believe that centralisation and the elimination of private enterprise are the tools of success. For without individual enterprise and a host of profit-making farmers it would not have happened.

Engineers and scientists, the universities, and the chemical industry, even the BBC and commercial television contributed to the new agriculture. It was as if all the ingenuity, energy, courage, good humour, patience, idealism and appetite for reform – all the virtues of Victorian England and few of the vices – had turned to the land. In 1939 British farming had the ability to provide only 30 per cent of the nation's food. When I record that it is now much nearer to producing all the essential food which can be grown in our climate, I understate the achievement for there are ten million more of us now, and we eat much better. Moreover, we have lost a million acres of agricultural land, and the labour force is smaller.* The annual increase in farming productivity is 5 per cent, a growth rate more than double that of general industry.

I do not exclude myself from the charge of ignorance about this renaissance without which we would all be poorer. Its extent dawned on me only during my stay in Norfolk. In a delightful book by Tristram Beresford† I was struck by a statement that if a farming Rip Van Winkle of the interwar years were to awaken now he would scarcely believe what he saw. There was a brief period in my youth when I found myself in the countryside, unaware that I had been transposed from one depressed area to another. There I learned such elementary skills as how to build and thatch a stack. And now I realised that such techniques would be irrelevant today. I was Mr Beresford's Rip Van Winkle.

* In Ireland 25 per cent of the population, in Italy and France 11 per cent, and in the UK less than 3 per cent are employed in agriculture.
† *We Plough the Fields – British Farming Today.*

6

Tristram Beresford says in his book that there are two philosophies current in agriculture. 'One,' he writes, 'is opportunistic and cynical . . . the application of a ruthless economic logic to the soil, to plants and animals, depriving them of all that is not strictly subservient to human ends . . . in order that we may have our way at the cheapest possible price . . . [It] may well be justifiable on the grounds of cost-effectiveness – at least in the short term.'

Well, we townies have been hearing for the last fifteen years about tycoon prairie farmers who have ripped out miles of hedgerow and produced milk from cows that have never stepped off their native concrete, men who have screwed every farthing from an acre regardless of tomorrow. We may have felt regret for the fading of an old romantic picture, but in the end we have accepted what we thought of as inevitable. People must eat, farming is a business, businessmen must make profits, you can't stop progress! We should, perhaps, be forgiven for assuming from stories in the popular press and unspecialised TV that farmers who do not comply with the logic of the biscuit factory are doomed to failure.

But it isn't so. There is another way. 'There has been evolved over two centuries a high farming system which is at one and the same time highly extractive and highly conservationist,' says Mr Beresford. 'It would be true to say that the more the land produces, the greater are its reserves for future production . . . In the opinion of "high farmers" . . . a grasping approach produces only a grudging response. To get the best out of nature, a man should use his heart as well as his head.'

Such a man is John Temple who is successful by anybody's standards. His prize Friesian herd is famous for its high milk yield. ('A farm is not a farm without livestock,' he says.) His fields – on Coke's old Holkham land – produce a wide and rich variety of crops that have made him what most of us would call a prosperous man. Once every three years they are spread with straw (80,000 bales) trodden and enriched by his cattle, which in turn have been hand-reared and fed on home-mixed concentrates and waste from New Farm's carrots, cabbages and sprouts and with beet pulp returned from the sugar factory. He fattens and sells 700 head of cattle a year. His grazing sheep – 340 ewes – help to fertilise the soil too, and produce 600 lambs which are also sold fat. John Temple does not stint and scrape and scheme like the factory farmers who specialise in one activity or two. He has a large permanent staff of twenty-four – including maintenance engineer, bricklayer, carpenter, lorry driver and vermin killer – which is considerably augmented during a harvest that lasts from August to February, from corn to carrots. He actually *plants* new hedges.

I had dinner with the Temples one evening at the bottom of the hill, and though John is a quiet, self-effacing man, I was able to piece together an honourable English family story which incidentally illustrates an interesting area of this century's agricultural history.

The first episode begins two years before the Great War with 34 rented acres and £84 saved by John's grandfather from his farm-labouring wages. The money buys two horses and two milking cows. Without meadowland, Mr Temple, then fifty, must rise at daylight to feed the livestock on the roadside verges around Wighton village, returning them at six for milking by his fourteen-year-old son James. Most of the milk is sold to villagers. With the rest Mrs Temple makes butter. Without capital, father and son must work on other farms to earn enough to carry on.

World War I takes James into the services. The father negotiates for another 30 acres.

During the Depression years the family work pitiless hours. At the end of a seven-day week there is rarely enough left over to buy an ounce of tobacco or a pint of beer. In 1933 John, now eleven, begins a milk round and before school each day delivers twenty gallons, refilling a 2½-gallon can slung from the handlebars of a lady's bicycle. At night when schoolmates fish or play football the boy starts work again, leading a horse and three-wheeled cart to the river for two loads of water for the stock.

In January 1940 there is crisis. Grandfather is dead. James has recovered after being run over by a horse and cart. John has been ill. Men and horses are working flat out. A promised colt has not been broken-in on time. The ploughing has not yet been done. Young John covets a £150 tractor but the family resources are £40 short. Eventually a relative gives John the money. He improvises horse implements for tractor work, and the Temple fortunes begin to change.

John, now in his late teens, finds he can not only work the 64 acres with the tractor, but carry out contract work on other farms. Wartime money is better. The Temples can now buy equipment they needed years before. Despite government encouragement for farmers to specialise and to economise with men and material, the young man has his own ideas. He believes in diversification and so dovetailing several operations that one activity aids another. Gradually the farm takes in more land.

In 1950, at the age of twenty-eight and now married, John makes his biggest gamble. 303 acres fall vacant. The land has been grossly mismanaged since the Depression. The previous tenant has been dispossessed by the Agricultural Committee. It seems such a hopeless proposition that when John takes it on, neighbours shake their heads and warn James that his son will ruin him. By ploughing in the poor soil and general tidying, John conceals the true extent of the land's poverty even from his parents, and begins to apply his 'high farming' ideas of generous rather than parsimonious cultivation.

Today, New Farm covers 1,040 fertile acres, including the original 34. Everything, marshland too, is under plough, James still lends a hand. John's sister is in charge of the profitable calf-rearing department, and son Stephen, with agricultural degrees from two universities, is the heir. As with Coke, specialists and students come from far afield to study New Farm methods, which Tristram Beresford calls 'a sophisticated exercise in fertility building'.

John Temple is a proud man in his quiet way, proud of his family, and also of his land and how he has cherished it. His success has been as much a product of his temperament – warm, generous, independent – as of hard and dogged work. The Beresford book says that John is an impresario rather than a tycoon. If so, he is the most kindly, unassuming and broad-minded impresario I have met. In short, he is the very best kind of Englishman. He also keeps good beer. And his wife Audrey makes the best Yorkshire pudding I have tasted south of the Tees.

14

Where the clock stopped in 1936, a meeting with 'Ron and Eth' by the seaside, a brief pilgrimage to Walsingham, and the memory of a naughty vicar.

1

I WAS RELUCTANT to leave north Norfolk. I had got my bearings in this odd but unspectacular hump of England. And I had become fond of Wells. People are often snobbish about it, I suppose, because of its candy shops and bucket-and-spade atmosphere. But Wells is a place for the connoisseur. The sweet Betjeman would love it. It is smaller than some villages I know, with a population of 2,450 not counting summer visitors. I dare say I could walk round its perimeter – pausing for an ice-cream tutti-frutti on the way – in less than an hour, yet it is solidly urban. At the back of town there is a tree-shaded village green where to judge by its name – the Buttlands – archery was practised. But now it is surrounded by substantial Victorian and Georgian houses with names like Casamaria, The Homestead, Glencoe House and Crown Hotel. Outside the Globe there are tables with red and white striped umbrellas. A nearby alley called Chancery Lane accommodates the Abbey National, a Commissioner for Oaths and other signs of urban importance. The town is full of shops where a wide variety of goods is sold with pleasant, unobtrusive salesmanship from behind well-stacked counters, and there is a big, old-fashioned draper's which is at least near-cousin to a department store.

Wells grew to something like its present size and character when the Great Eastern Railway, now alas departed, came along the coast from Lynn and turned inland for Fakenham in the 1860s. That, presumably, was when the narrow but prosperous Victorian streets were drawn in parallel and gradual descent between the Buttlands and the quayside, which is now a miniature esplanade and a berth for fishing boats and tiny coasters and has, besides the milk bars and gift shops, a grain elevator and warehouse.

There is an air of school holidays half-remembered about the place. It is as if some secret clock had stopped in the summer of 1936 and Wells was left suspended in a long, balmy day of Marcel perms, wooden spades and snowball teas when all that was expected of a week at the seaside was 'ozone' in the air, the mild excitement of unfamiliar streets and a trip in the *Skylark*. And if you were lucky enough to strike up an acquaintance with the assistant harbour master and his cronies you went back to school feeling that you had touched the edge of the world where plump men in blue jerseys smelling of Digger Flake knew about bum-boats and frangipani trees.

The first early morning I walked down into town I passed a window cleaner and said good day.

'And good morning to you, my good sir,' he replied with a smile.

I sat on an old anchor – the old, long, thin kind with curved flukes and a crow-bar stock. Across the narrow river a sea of marsh grass stretched to summer morning haze at the horizon. It was low water. The black stumps of an old breakwater stood on the silt bottom and the masts of holiday sailing boats leaned this way and that. A boy was fishing and there was a stir of twenty-two inedible crabs in his bucket.

'What do you do with them?'

'Chuck 'em back.'

An early fisherman had a big flatfish like a silver hot water bottle. He offered it to a pink man whom I took to be the harbour master.

'Oi don't moin', thankyew. Moi wife'll love tha'.' Then to me – 'Lovely morning isn't it! I enjoy it just for the getten-up you know.'

The low sun caught the first small sail of the day. Dad and Mum were sitting in the bottom of the dinghy with young Ron and Julie and Star the dog. They pushed off into the narrow channel but began to run astern opposite Don's Festival Amusements. The little boom swung over and swiped Dad. Small John, unperturbed, leaned over the gunwale and ran a hand through the passing water. They took almost twenty minutes to pass out of sight.

By now the haze had dissolved over the saltings. I could hear the town stirring. Vegetables had been delivered and someone was sluicing the roadway outside Country Garden Fruit and Flowers. Up three steps and beyond the genteel balustrades of the Mayshiel Restaurant (High Teas and Evening Meals) morning coffee was being infused. And a little later I swear I saw 'Ron and Eth', grown older and more sensible since BBC days – him in his blue, buttoned cardie and her in custard yellow – keeping abreast of world events with the *Mirror* and the *Sun*.

Beach balls, Gaz signs and binoculars in crowded plate-glass windows. Packets of home-made peppermint and aniseed rock. Treacle toffee, pear drops and fishing lines. Old couples in the snack bar taking tea with their hats on. 'Sizzerola – a game of skill for all ages . . . Flying Soucers [sic].' Sandcastle-shaped tin buckets complete with crenellations. G. B. and R. P. Walker – dafs and onions, tomatoes and pineapples, eggs nestling in straw, today's prices whitewashed on the window. Arcadia – specialists in beautiful gifts for the home. Milk-O Bar – Prop. C. H. Platten. Players No. 6 for Quality.

> In memory of eleven of the crew of
> the lifeboat Eliza Adams who lost
> their lives on duty in the disaster
> at Wells – October 29th 1880.

Clematis and wallflowers. Pale pink bungalow. Sea-pebble panels beneath each window. Shutters and a 'Tudor' door.

On my last Sunday morning I fell in step with the vicar. The church is almost surrounded by meadow. 'Do you mind if I come in jeans?' I asked. 'My dear boy,' he said, 'I don't mind if you come in bathing trunks.'

Through an open window in Green Dragon Lane a gramophone was playing.

> *Give me one minute more,*
> *Only one minute more.*
> *Give me one minute more in your arms . . .*

I left the carrot house on Monday morning. The sun had just come up again like clockwork.

Of course I should have turned west straight away, then on to Yorkshire, but I didn't. I took a curve inland to Little Walsingham, reasoning that if Henry III thought it worth twenty visits and if Henry VIII walked there barefoot, I should at least take a look. It was – and by some people still is – believed that in 1061 the lady of the manor there had a vision of the Virgin Mary, and in the Middle Ages it was second only to Canterbury as a place of pilgrimage. Some friends advised me not to go, saying it was in some way sinister. Morton and Priestley had passed it by on their English journeys. Therefore I was pleased to find it congenial and full of small architectural surprises – timbered buildings, splendid inn and a town pump like a gigantic beehive. Although it stood on a rise a few miles from the sea it was a warm, inland sort of place, unlike anything on the coast. A fifteenth-century gateway led to the Abbey ruins. But was this the site of the famous miracle? Or was the building put up by the Anglo-Catholics in the 1930s the place of the true shrine? I gathered there was disagreement, so before I got hooked myself I drifted on and struck the coast again at Blakeney, all brick and flint and holiday-craft sails.

Rounding a bend I found myself in Stiffkey (pronounced Stewkey) a name that riffs back from the thirties like a blast of saxophones. There was a time when the delightful little church, now tree-screened on my left, was packed with 500 people of a Sunday and hundreds standing in the churchyard. The pilgrims poured in by train, by bicycle and special buses for a glimpse of a little rector called Harold Davidson whose weakness for young girls – actresses, fallen women, Lyons' Tea Shop nippies – made him the stuff of headlines for almost a decade. This small village, which had hitherto been known only for a succulent variety of oyster, became, in the words of one writer,* 'as notorious as Babylon, and its incumbent as celebrated as Al Capone'. I find this story oddly haunting. It reeks of the 1930s, a period already losing its real presence in the public memory.

As I neared King's Lynn again I remembered that Captain John Smith, the 'Father of Virginia' whose life had been saved by the Red-Indian princess Pocahontas, had begun his working life as an apprentice there. In fact one could fill a chapter with Norfolk's North American connections. Captain John Mason, Governor of Virginia, came from Lynn. So did Captain Vancouver who went to the west coast, and left his name upon the map. Lincoln's ancestors came from Wymondham. Tom Paine

* Ronald Blythe, in *The Age of Illusion*.

was born in Thetford. Ben Franklin's grandfather was from Norwich. Three Yarmouth girls were hanged as witches in Salem, Mass. During the great emigration of the 1830s Norfolk families flocked to the quaysides to embark for America. In the first half of 1836 alone 3,200 sailed from Lynn and Yarmouth for a steerage fare of £6 10s apiece. Another, but this time entirely female emigration followed the returning GIs in the forties, though some American servicemen liked both girl and place enough to stay. But the first truly American *immigrant* was Princess Pocahontas herself. She married John Rolfe of Heacham near King's Lynn, one of the first tobacco planters. He brought her to London where she met Charles I and she lived on the Rolfe family estate where there is a memorial to her. I thought of making a detour to that seaside village but instead turned into the gates of Sculthorpe air base where a small staff remains.

There are few more melancholy places than a disused wartime airfield – especially an American airfield with just enough men still about to remind us of that noisy, swashbuckling tribe of foreigners who were never quite foreigners, and soldiers who never quite accorded with our stiff-necked notions of military behaviour. They brought a special spice to those taut but exhilarating days. How relaxed they seemed! How confident! Yet in a way how vulnerable and innocent. Historians will no doubt record their arrival as a logistical and strategic exercise, but that gay invasion was also part of our social and emotional history and is remembered with affection by many people in this part of England and elsewhere.

I knew the place well when it was still jumping in the fifties, when airmen lounged in canvas chairs around the hutments, the PX was still going strong and dozens of radios were tuned in to AFN. This day, though, I followed a pick-up truck along cracked, deserted roadways. I was conducted down glum, hospital-like corridors and past offices in which a few men sat in tilted chairs and legs were disarrayed on tidy desks. In one room a belching contest was in progress, but it lacked zest. The few chaps I spoke to were correct, polite, withdrawn. I sat in a large room – the CO's office. Rabbits gambolled fearlessly in the heat outside. The CO was a mild, genial man. He talked for a while about darts, skiffleboard, and dominoes and then ordered in some recent station records for me to study. There I read:

> August gave us the opportunity to host the largest and most fascinating social event of the year. This was an authentic [sic] Hawaiian Luau. Prepared by members of the USAF Wives Club our English guests dined on Hawaiian foods, tasted punch from a coconut shell and wore leis about their necks. Some even attended in Hawaiian attire.

Still, there are even worse things than American punch, and when I paused at Lynn again (for a pork pie to keep me going) I found some. I wouldn't put anything past local planners, of course, but it is hard to understand why the people of Lynn permitted the desecration that has happened since the 1950s. There they lived in a fine little North Sea port that proclaimed the good sense, enterprise and sensitivity of their fore-bears. It perfectly expressed their place in the world and I would have thought that some of its serenity would have entered their souls. So what came over them? Had there been no rioting in the streets? Had the chief planner not been burned in effigy or the town clerk not chased trouserless across the Tuesday Market? Alas, no!

Streets were renamed. Others had disappeared. And there was a new-pink complex of shopping parades called the Vancouver Centre where every variation of plastic, ranch-house architecture, pseud-art-nouveau and side-show oriental were on display. Among the She-Girls, Easiphits and Stone-Dris, a few of the old shops remained to emphasise the collapse of taste – a saddler's with windows full of dandy-brushes, embrocations and neatsfoot compound. Taylors the seedsmen (est. 1770) with an array of seed packets as gay as a garden (Pyrethrum hybridium, Bellis pirennis, Stock Brompton, Canterbury Bells), and W. H. Smith in a fine, white building with a cast-iron gallery. But I would not have bought pies in the Vancouver Centre if they had been stuffed with venison.

Outside the 'development' area, however, the real Lynn still exists. In a narrow street I found a shop called Scupham's with a glory of whole-some eatables in the window. Now if they had put Scupham's pies in the Tate, instead of Carl André's bricks I would have understood. Noble caskets they were, and in such a variety of sizes that you felt each should have a name to suit its character – from Monarch and Dauphine down through full-blown Duke and Duchess to Knight, Baronet and Esquire. I bought a fine specimen of medium girth and ate it somewhere in Lincoln-shire with half a Guinness.

There were many temptations on the way north. The grand old port of Boston whispered to me from the east about its timberboats, a summer view from the top of the old Stump and soft, bright light reflected in Georgian windows above the river Witham. But I drove on. I nearly paused in the market town of Sleaford. There the legend 'Higgs for Cigs' used to be scattered through the local paper apparently at random, and surely there must be fun in such a poker-faced town. Lincoln's lovely crown was the greatest temptation of all. I even considered a short trip west to Nottingham for an evening in the Trip to Jerusalem and a night-cap in the Salutation Inn as other Crusaders had done before me. I almost took the road to Scunthorpe.

But at last I arrived at Bawtry, which used to be on the old A 1. If I had arrived a few hours earlier I might have overheard the sober executive of a famous banking house complaining that he was being visited by a lady in his room at night. Why in heaven he objected, and how for the first time on this trip I almost lost my way, I will relate in the next chapter.

15

About ghosts in Bawtry, about Mallard, Windsor Lad
and Papyrus *in Doncaster – but chiefly a consideration on
whether Yorkshiremen are myth.*

1

FOR ME, and maybe for many others who drove down the old A 1 out
of the industrial towns and villages of Northumberland and Durham,
Bawtry used to be rather a special place, with its broad main street,
coaching inn and brick-built Georgian air. Although it stood on the edge
of the Yorkshire coalfield – its inhabitants but a mite more affluent than
those of Tyneside – it seemed to reflect the comparative security and
certainty-of-mind of lower England. It looked warm and easy-going – as if
it were the threshold of the South. I had not passed this way since this
section of the A 1 had become the A 638 and the Doncaster by-pass had
replaced it to the west. It would be interesting, I thought, to see how
Bawtry had survived separation from what had been its lifestream for
perhaps 2,000 years, so I disembarked outside the inn – a long, stuccoed

building of two storeys that still called itself 'The Crown Hotel and Posting House' – and entered the front bar.

The walls were covered with those coaching prints whose eighteenth-century humour means little to the motorist but whose presence suggests a traditional hostelry, the prospect of wholesome food and, perhaps, amusing conversation. This impression was at once confirmed by the amiable creature behind the counter. Of middling age and volume, she wore a crisp, striped summer blouse, she had a welcoming smile, and her name was Mary Partridge. I took a windsor armchair, ordered best bitter, cheese and salad with brown bread, and – after a brief exchange about the weather – I was soon being told of the businessman who had changed his room that very morning. Oh yes, a nice quiet chap he was . . . not the sort to make a fuss . . . yet he had approached the reception desk and asked for fresh accommodation. No, there was nothing wrong with the amenities. It was just that – well – he was being visited at night by a strange woman. *By strange he meant she wore a crinoline!*

Now this incident might have been passed off as one man's eccentricity had it been the first (here we are joined by Freda Mugglestone, thinner than Mary and with an impressive repertoire of corroboratory nods and glances), but there had been previous appearances. One guest claimed to have met the same apparition on the stairs, for instance. And Pauline, a former receptionist . . . sensible sort of girl . . . not one for exaggerating, Freda testified . . . had been awakened by an intruder in her room. She had kicked out, striking her big toe on the radiator as the figure vanished. Mary had a theory – she said she had heard about a woman guest who had arrived . . . oh, a long, long time ago . . . to meet her lover. Some said he had been killed on his way to the tryst and that she, poor thing, had been waiting ever since. But that, of course, did not account for the appearance of the mysterious parlourmaid.

'Parlourmaid?' I asked. 'Another ghost? . . . May I have just a little more of that excellent chutney? Perhaps you would refill my glass. But please go on.'

Mary Partridge, Freda Mugglestone and a pretty receptionist who had now joined us, all said it was a pity that I could not meet the head porter now off duty, for it was he who, at about five o'clock one morning, had seen a figure entering at a side door and thinking it was a member of the staff, called a greeting. A moment later the stranger was standing at his side, a young girl dressed in black and white, with her hair done in a bun. And in another moment she had disappeared. 'When I came past a little later, he was standing there,' said Freda. 'White as a sheet, he was. And there was this cold feeling in the air.' Someone remembered that soon after World War II a chef had strangled a young waitress, then hanged himself.

I had now dealt with the cheese and salad. Through the window I could see that the sun had moved behind the Crown and I had not yet made up my mind where to pull up for the night. 'Did you ever hear of the saddler who was hanged for not drinking up his liquor?' I enquired. No, they hadn't. I looked at my watch and noted the level in my glass.

'Well – I am not sure when it happened,' I began. 'Probably late in the eighteenth century when the Great North Road, particularly round here, had a reputation for highwaymen. The Earl of Dumfries had been robbed barely a mile down the road. Or at least he *claimed* he had. There was some doubt about it, but him being an earl and all that, two local chaps were hanged. But to the saddler . . .' I paid my bill. There was still beer in my glass.

And I told them the story about the traveller on his way to Doncaster with his saddlebags full of money. He paused at Bawtry for refreshment and to have a broken harness fixed. Before leaving he bought the saddler a drink. At King's Wood – a dark stretch along the nine-mile road – he was robbed by a masked man, and hurrying back to Bawtry to report his misfortune he found the tankard with the contents still untouched. A hue and cry was called for the saddler who was caught, tried and hanged at York. 'And the moral of the story is "Allus sup up",' I said. Which is excellent advice to this very day for anyone who wishes to avoid suspicion north of the Trent.

'And quite right too,' said someone as I disposed of a last crumb of cheddar and drained my tankard. At which point the firm of Partridge, Mugglestone and Entwisle was dissolved with mutual expressions of regret. Outside, a saddler's shop was still in business across the street.

Since my last visit Bawtry had been incorporated in the Metropolitan Borough of Doncaster. The demotion of the main road seemed to have made little difference to the volume of traffic. I dare say there are plans for the eventual submergence of Bawtry. The lads down at the planning office will call it Progress. A future mayor will no doubt make a speech about 'courage, faith and the crowning of a great scheme', and some developer will install a new swimming-pool in his Surrey back garden. Doubtless by that time the Crown Hotel and Posting House will be a suburban pub.

2

People who know about that soporific ritual called cricket tell me that to play for Yorkshire one must have been born within its boundaries. It seems a sensible requirement which, if adopted by professional football, would inject some mortar of common sense into that irrational edifice. Imagine it – every man jack in a canary strip would be a true Norwich man. Arsenal would have to scour Highbury for players and suffer penalty for fielding a man from, say, Kentish Town, and a candidate for Newcastle United would have to prove by birth certificate that he was a North Tynesider. Football hysteria would still have no rational basis, but at least the supporters of a successful Sunderland or Middlesbrough would know the winning goals had been scored by a fellow townsman and not by a hired Londoner or Liverpudlian. The nonsense of transfer fees would be ended, and footballers might once more play for fun.

The rule applied to Yorkshire cricket, though, is a different matter. It has been calculated that there are more acres in the county than letters in the Bible. Before the boundary-changers mucked about with it Yorkshire was the largest piece of England under one High Sheriff, though it had three Lords Lieutenant and now has three of each. Upon these acres and beneath that one High Sheriff lived well over five million people. Quite simply, Yorkshire had more cricketers to pick from.

Which brings me to the 3,897,940-acre question – what is Yorkshire? And what is this Yorkshireman that people – especially Yorkshiremen – talk about? I have some Yorkshire ancestors. I was born in one adjacent county and brought up in another. I have shared barrack rooms with men who called themselves Yorkshiremen, and I have worked with them. Yet still I can discover no common characteristic that distinguishes the people of that large area which, even from sparsely populated Saxon times, has had to be divided into three separate counties known as Ridings (Saxon third-ings). Of course the stereotype of a bleak, unimaginative race, taciturn and tight-fisted, could only be believed by those who never take their brains for exercise outside London. What is mistaken for insensitivity is often a wicked sense of humour depending on a poker face. Yes, I have met careful men in Yorkshire who do not blab their business or your own, but these are mostly farmers from the west. Wordiness is not for those who can read a face, a handshake or the way a man walks up the road as surely as they con the weather on the fell tops. They are an admirable kind of Englishman.

But they are comparatively few. In York itself – a generous city and a lovely one – people tend to be chatterboxes, ever willing to discuss their private affairs. And can there be much in common between the fishermen climbing the steep streets of Whitby and the manufacturing inhabitants of Todmorden who shelter in the Calder defile between Heptonstall Moor and Turley Holes Edge? Is it not probable that the city of Leeds has moulded a very different people from those whose homes cluster about Richmond Castle or Ripon Abbey? There are parts of Yorkshire that are psychologically in the Midlands, and places – oh, Middlesbrough! – that now occupy a special limbo known as Cleveland, and which even in the old days I could never think of as a part of Yorkshire.

Have I overlooked something? Is there some subtlety of character shared by all Yorkshire men and women that I have been unable to discern? I am yet to be convinced.

As I drove into the many lands of Yorkshire the question was which one to choose. After the tranquil southern scenery shimmering in the heat behind me I would have liked to see the Dales again, where villages lie like low outcrops of fieldstone that have been there since the ice retreated. I wanted to smell sphagnum moss, to climb into Gordale Scar where the white beck drops three hundred feet from rock to rock with no one there to hear the echoes but myself. For such solitary pleasure I would have to veer north-west.

On the other hand, I knew a valley beyond the Wolds where men grow gooseberries as big as prize tomatoes and do so with the pride and reverence that others give to roses. Once a year each grower parts the heaviest fruit from the parent stem and walks down to the village hall at Egton where it is weighed to the dram, measured round the middle and circumnavigated by grave judges who, after solemn conference – and perhaps a little lubrication from the pub next door – announce the winner. To the champion of the Egton gooseberry fair belongs such honour as would satisfy any modest man. For sanity like this I would have to drive north-east.

And of course there were the mill towns. I like the Yorkshire mill towns. I like the mills themselves – great eighteenth-century vessels landlocked in the wayward steepness of the Pennine streets. How men who can abide the flat roads and lives of Beckenham and Penge and sing songs of praise to Sidcup can arch their brows at Hebden Bridge and Halifax is quite beyond my reckoning. It was a London visionary who wrote that line about dark Satanic mills. But had he actually seen the great chimneys, their wondrous brickwork clustering above purple ter-race roofs? Had he seen houses, not sitting smugly in suburbia, but engineered into the pitch of the terrain with steep, worn steps and iron handrails turning up to stout front doors . . . rough surfaces of squared stone blocks stained black and gold with sooty rain . . . short emerald grass between the granite setts and brown bracken cantilevering from walls? Had he ever looked down through iron railings into mossy yards . . . observed the grain and colouring brought out from pavement stones by frost, rain and the emery of not-quite-forgotten clogs? And felt the sweet, soft dampness of the air? House, street, chapel, mill – and then the great, green, quiet hills around. There have been worse Jerusalems.

While I was dreaming about mills and becks and giant goosegogs I came to the outskirts of Doncaster, and nobody can say that Doncaster is fair of face. Yet there was a time when it seemed to me a place of high romance. It was in the 1930s. I was a small boy from Sunderland, County Durham, a raw, uncomely town for which I still have some tenderness. Sunderland was ailing. The Slump had stilled the shipyards and engineering shops. Even the mining and shipment of coal had fallen on thin times. Young as I was, and knowing no other condition, for me the Great Depression – the poverty of friends, tuberculosis, the despair of men who sat at our table and wept for want of work – was no abstraction.

Anyway, once or twice in that period I was put into a third-class carriage and sent to spend two weeks of my school holidays with a Non-conformist minister of fundamentalist persuasion. *He* it seemed to me, was rarely off his knees. And *she* talked of the royal family in terms her husband would have reserved for the Holy Ghost. However, from this atmosphere of piety I escaped each day to sit on a fence overlooking the mouth of a railway tunnel, returning only for meals, bed or to be currycombed and declared fit for church. That tunnel, I thought, was what Doncaster was all about. From its dark mouth there leapt, in clouds of steam, all the great shining monsters of the modern world, hurling themselves at London, thin white streamers flying from piston valves, gathering up their roar and rattle in their wake. *Mallard* . . . *Papyrus* . . . *Windsor Lad* . . . *Dick Turpin* . . . *Spion Kop.*

Then in the distance, down beyond the sidings, coal towers and loading gauges to the south, there would come the distant warning of an A 4 Pacific, part growl, part wail, part chime. And up she strode in gleaming green, piling up her noise in a great Doppler wave before her, till – POW! – she plunged into the black arc and there was only the ring of receding wheels on metal. *Falcon* . . . *Merlin* . . . *Osprey* . . . *Kestrel* . . . Twice a day down came the *Coronation*, a flying serpent all in blue. *Dominion of Canada* . . . *Empire of India* . . . *Union of South Africa* . . . Twice a day the *Silver Jubilee. Quicksilver* . . . *Silver Fox* . . . *Silver King* . . . *Silver Link* . . .

For that fortnight Doncaster was alternately my Purgatory and my Paradise complete with saints. Had not the great Henry Alfred Ivatt worked here in his beard and bowler designing the Atlantics with their four big driving wheels and tall stacks? And was not his successor, Sir Herbert Nigel Gresley, at work half a mile away, and were not those great chiming A 4 Pacifics his own and Doncaster's creations? *Golden Eagle* . . . *Blink Bonny* . . . *Captain Cuttle* . . . *Kingfisher. Cock o' the North* . . . *Green Arrow* . . . *Roedeer* . . . *Alnwick Castle* . . . I eased my bottom on the railings and took down the sacred names as they flashed before me.

But one day, just before I left, I was taught a lesson by the pious parson and his wife. There was some mention of Sunderland and unemployment. Their faces stiffened.

'Un-em-*ployed!*' boomed Mrs Reverend.

'*Loafers!*' echoed the wee man.

'Those people just don't *want* to work,' declared the matriarch.

'Just lazy, idle, good-for-nothings!' put in her husband.

There was nothing I could say.

A few minutes after leaving Bawtry I came to a road junction surrounded by subtopian mess. Doncaster. But no, I did not fancy it tonight. Besides, the old steamers had faded away with the *Evening Star,** and I knew my wooden fence had been replaced by a concrete barrier. I would join the A1(M) and make for York and sleep in a hotel bed for a change.

3

I have mentioned Ferrybridge power station before. It stands alongside the canal-like river Aire near the crossing of the A1 and M62 and it is the most impressive sight for many a flat mile of road.

The Normans, who were pretty good themselves at building big and round and high, would have been amazed by the eleven cooling towers guarding the entrance to the North. There was never such a castle. Eight of them are 375 feet high – 141 feet taller than the great lantern tower of York Minster. Two chimneys stand 650 feet – more than half as high again as England's loftiest spire at Salisbury. Ferrybridge is actually three power stations (A, B and C), the first of which was opened the year Morton set out. The last is a 2,000 megawatt job, which means it could run two million one-bar electric fires all at once. Until a few years ago it was necessary to slow down as one approached, then make a double right-angled turn to cross an eighteenth-century bridge with graceful arches reflected in the water. Now a dual carriageway runs straight past and perhaps the narrow bridge is down below there somewhere out of sight. But you can still see coal barges lined up like toys below the three towers of Ferrybridge B, and coal trucks still trundle along Hornby rails to deliver their morsel loads to my lords turbine, Olympus, Bristol Siddeley and Brush.

Ferrybridge stands on coal. It devours coal at the rate of five million tons a year. And this is power station country. Almost within sight,

* The last steam locomotive (1960–5) built for British Railways. Now in the National Railway Museum, York.

Eggborough and the mighty Drax are deployed like sister fortresses, their steamy pennants flying above the green plain, consuming ten million more tons of the black, primeval swamp in which they are rooted.

People have their own ideas about where the North begins. Many a Londoner feels he is in *terra incognita* beyond High Barnet and the old joke about the North starting at Watford merely puts a laugh to his real unease. On the other hand, there are Northumbrians who feel so remote from Manchester and its ways that the cotton country might as well be in the South. Political bounds drawn by administrators do not always correspond to the instincts of the administered. Graham Turner in his study of the north country* discusses boundaries for five pages then ends up including Cheshire and parts of Derbyshire and Lincolnshire. Well, I suppose it all depends on one's associations. The North in which I can believe, however, begins at Ferrybridge and no sooner. The frontier marches from the south bank of the Mersey to the north shore of the Humber and there might as well be moorland watchtowers along the southern side of the M62.

As I drove on, the sun was losing height. There was a moisture in the air that was almost visible. The cars ahead – brake lights and indicators twinkling – seemed to shrink as they ran down the long decline towards the chalk-grey towers. And above the softly-breathing rims of concrete great columns of vapour rose to Himalayan height and filling the whole northern firmament joined and mingled, turned pink, crimson and lowering purple. Perhaps thus the sky was once transformed above tumbling Jericho, burning Persepolis, dying Pompeii, London in 1666 or Hiroshima. But surely it was not until the nineteenth century, and then perhaps only in the humid air of northern England, that such vast, apocalyptic, man-made skies regularly outgrew nature, inspiring artists like John Martin† of Tyneside to fill canvases with Pandemonium, and his arsonist brother Jonathan to set fire to York Minster.

It was a fine, fierce, barbaric spectacle I drove towards. I do not say that such industrial drama typifies the upper part of England, though there is almost as much of that as there is exquisite parkland, quiet forest and lonely stream. I *do* say that the North is a land of contrast, visual, social and temperamental, and that all this produces a kind of tension, a vital restlessness that is absent further south. A northerner – at least a north-erner like me – may sometimes wish for what he thinks of as the serenity

* *The North Country.*
† John Martin (1789–1854) painter of prodigious scenes and townscapes. His brother tried to burn York Minster in 1821, damaging the choir and destroying medieval woodwork. He was tried, and held in an asylum till his death in 1838.

and emotional security of the sweet, soft South. He may lightly fall in love with smooth downland or the bright, timbered towns of the southern counties (as indeed I had so recently been seduced by Kent) and persuade himself he could rest there for ever. But eventually there comes a vague impatience, a hunger for abrasion, a time for trumpets. The condition has a name. It is homesickness.

4

Beyond Ferrybridge a great plain spreads out between the Pennines and the Wolds. There the Yorkshire Ouse winds down from the Vale of York bringing the waters of the Swale, the Ure, Nidd, Wharfe and a dozen lesser streams born in the northern hills. From the western moors the Aire and Calder join the flood. The perverse Derwent, rising near the coast behind Scarborough, flows inland, dividing North Yorkshire Moors from Yorkshire Wolds and eventually emerging from the Vale of Pickering. The Hull makes its short, southbound sprint, and up from the south come Don and Trent. All mingle in the broad Humber, enhancing the ancient and future fame of that strange state of mind known as Kingston upon Hull to its inhabitants and plain Hull to the rest of us. It is what Daniel Defoe in A Tour Through the Whole Island of Great Britain called 'a wonderful conflux of great rivers', recognising their importance as channels of trade, the way by which much English wool and cloth reached the quays for export.

He noted that 'all this part of the country is so considerable for its trade that the Postmaster-General has though fit to establish a cross post through all the western part of England into it, to maintain the correspondence of merchants and men of business'. This 'throughway' began at Plymouth and went by way of 'Excester', Taunton, Bridgwater, Bristol, Gloucester, Worcester, Shrewsbury, Liverpool, Manchester, Bury, Rochdale, Halifax, Leeds and York, to Hull, whence English goods were shipped to Holland, Bremen, Hamburg and the Baltic. Defoe's Tour was published early in the eighteenth century, but four hundred years earlier cloth manufacture was moving from East Anglia to the running Yorkshire streams more suitable for cottage fulling mills. Gradually the processes had become more specialised. The organisation of collection, storage, transport, marketing and investment had evolved in a great, slow industrial revolution preceding that of Defoe's 1700s, not only to put red gold into England's arteries and place the Lord Chancellor on his Westminster Woolsack, but to lay the foundations of two English empires.

It is a rich and gentle plain studded with great abbeys, handsome houses and fine towns. There are castles too, of course. Romans, Danes, Yorkists and Lancastrians, Roundheads and Royalists swept over it, fighting some of England's bloodiest battles. But unlike Durham and Northumberland with which it once made up the kingdom of Northumbria, it has long put off its warlike mien.

In those more northern counties close to the Scotch* border, where farmsteads are fortified and vicarages built like keeps are still inhabited, the marauding days are still part of local consciousness. There children still learn the old warlike ballads, and Northumbrians called Charlton, Milburn, Dodds and Robson are aware that they bear the names of great border bandit families. In north Yorkshire such stories have the unreality of legend. Castles are fewer. The walls of York still embrace the inner city. One thinks of them no longer as a military cordon, however, nor of the gateways as sallyports from which armies marched out, but rather as a sensible insurance within which the gentler arts of commerce were practised, where men grew prosperous, built fine houses and cultivated gardens by the riverside, wrote and published books, sent their children to good schools and went to church. The northern gateway, Bootham Bar, endured the great siege of York as recently as 1644 but the modern notice on the postern refers chiefly to the guards stationed there to conduct travellers safely through the forest and protect them from the wolves.

I arrived in York at nightfall and put up at a large Victorian hotel with three iron-railed galleries encircling a lounge from which ascended a grand stairway broad enough to accommodate half the board of the Great Northern Railway line abreast. And at the rear there was a heavy revolving door to catapult hotel guests directly into an echoing world of platforms, porters' trucks and girders decked out in heraldic colours. In the basement there was a splendid bar-room with plenty of cast iron, mahogany, plush and terracotta. The walls were decorated with the nameboards of long-abandoned but affectionately remembered stations. The staff were cheerful. The drinkers seemed mostly to be railwaymen and regulars. And there was a fireplace of wonderful vulgarity that must have scorched the coat-tails of many a fog-bound businessman on his way north to open a branch line.

Sleep did not come easily in York, but I did not mind. It was my first

---

* Schoolmasters and news-subs insist on Scottish but I agree with A. J. P. Taylor who, in *English History 1914–1945*, writes: 'The inhabitants of Scotland now call themselves 'Scots' and their affairs 'Scottish'. They are entitled to do so. The English word for both is 'Scotch', just as we call les français French, and Deutschland Germany . . .'

bedroom in a city since leaving Calais and the nights were full of unseen movement. I spent hours reading at my first-floor window overlooking public gardens just outside the medieval walls. Gleaming white among the lawns, they dipped gently down towards the river, entering darkness somewhere near Lendal Bridge. Cars whispered by, disappearing through an arch into the labyrinth. Church clocks in the dark mass of the city marked off the hours. Even the birds below me stayed awake, chink-chinking their alarms among ornamental bushes. And all night long there was the low, interminable roar of railway business . . . the tethered throbbing of a stationary Deltic . . . the whine of a two-engined '125' snaking past deserted platforms in the wide nave of York's second cathedral of 1877.

I dare say York itself had never slept since Governor Quintus Petillius Cerialis marched up the Vale in AD 71 to parley with the natives and set up a camp that became Eboracum, Altera Roma, the other Rome. Or since Constantine the Great walked the pavements that still exist beneath the Minster, was proclaimed Emperor by his troops, then set out to found Constantinople and legitimise the religion which men still observe down there in Holy Trinity Goodramgate, St Cuthbert Pease-holme Green and St Martin-cum-Gregory Micklegate.

16

A confrontation with 'Supermac' and 'Bombardier Gloria'
among the kings of England, and a discussion of the art of
window-peeping on the ramparts of the city of the Caesars.

1

I DOZED before the dawn and when I awoke the sun had set fire to the
Minster. That great, fat crossing tower always looks truncated to me,
as if it wants a spire, but that morning it was made of molten gold.
Downstairs I was served an indifferent meal, charged exorbitantly for
withered toast by the lordlings of the breakfast room and bade them bear
it thence, which they did with an *hauteur* as if I had turned up my nose at
some rare antique, which probably I had.

I looked up what John Boynton Priestley, a Yorkshireman of note, had
said about these parts when he arrived in 1933 on a journey like my own.
The book he wrote* is full of sound observation and gentle wisdom and

* *English Journey.*

will deservedly be read for yet another fifty years by armchair travellers. About York, however, he recorded grumpily that 'for all its Eboracum airs, its walls, its Minster, York has never enchanted me'. After which he fell out with a publican, went to the pictures, saw a rotten film and left next morning. Ah well, he was suffering from a cold and came from Bradford. May the great man be forgiven.

Morton, who arrived by car, wrote that York was the only city left which a man should enter on horseback or on foot. I disagree with him as well. York is one of the last places – Durham and Newcastle are others – which for maximum enjoyment demand disembarkation from a train. I had squandered my arrival on this occasion. But I attempted to repair the damage by negotiating the revolving doors, emerging on to the station and crossing the footbridge that takes you up among the ornate capitals and the crests of former railway companies to the Mall platform in the middle. What an arcade! What a lightness of vaulting! What a place!

The 'nave' itself runs 800 feet. That is 240 feet longer than the overall plan of Liverpool Cathedral, the biggest church in Europe outside Rome, and 200 longer than St Peter's Rome itself. In parallel are the three side aisles of lesser height. All four span 234 feet together. But what gives York station its sense of architectural mystery is the way it curves, so that one cannot look along a main platform from one end to the other. Every fourth span – and all are ornately pierced for lightness – leaps over track and platform from a freestanding Corinthian column of cast iron, the intervening spans appearing, deceptively, to be unsupported. Each one thus steps out ahead of its nearer neighbour. The biased pattern of semi-circular ribs so created – and repeated in each aisle – combined with the optical illusion of perspective, replaces in the receding horizontal the mathematical excitement that all great Gothic cathedrals possess in the vertical. This, along with the comparative lowness of the roof vaulting (York's main train shed rises 81 feet above the tracks while the nave of Liverpool soars to 173), provides an appropriate sense of motion. Trains do not pull up at York. They swing alongside. And the arrival of the High Speed Train with its smooth, continuous lines, is particularly stylish. The cost of this elegant building nudged £400,000 in the 1870s, causing one shareholder to protest that it was a 'very splendid monument of extravagance'.

Splendid indeed! I stood on the footbridge close to the girders. Shafts of yellow sunlight lanced the curved roof, striking paintwork and gilding untidy platforms exactly as the engineer-designer Thomas Prosser had intended. But now there were no shifting pillars of steam to dramatise the play of light and make the caves and forests in the air which must also have been part of his sumptuous vision.

Walk out into York quietly. Having arrived by train, now follow the advice of H. V. Morton and proceed on foot. Don't take a taxi. Don't clatter round the sights behind a guide. It's a town you're in, not a museum. Don't dash up to the Minster straight away and polish it off in an hour or two. Save it till last. Or, better still, slip in there on your second day and stand at the crossing of nave and transepts and take in one of the loveliest interiors in England. Leave within half an hour and doddle down Stonegate. Look at the handsome little shops. Buy a *Yorkshire Post*. Or just stand at a timber-posted corner watching the citizens of York. Forget that George V said that the history of this pocket city was the history of England, or that Roman emperors walked this way in purple. Better to recall that Laurence Sterne, the irreverent and penniless cathedral Reverend, lodged here a few doors from his French inamorata Catherine Fourmantelle, and that when his *Life and Opinions of Tristram Shandy* was published just across the pavement – under that sign of the swinging Bible – some of his neighbours were affronted, believing they had been portrayed, and the rest were probably delighted. On one corner a ship's figurehead of Minerva, patroness of arts and trades, surveys one of the happiest little streets in England. And under the eaves of No. 33 a delightful devil, red and naked, presides in derisive lavatorial pose over the traffic of his fellow townsmen. No motor traffic here, though. Just idlers, shoppers, tradesmen. First-floor geraniums dripping in their window boxes. Smell of coffee.

Walk through the streets from Whip-Ma-Whop-Ma-Gate to Piccadilly across the working river Fosse (remembering that a 'Gate' is a street in York, and a 'Bar' is a gate), from Lord Mayor's Walk to Nunnery Lane across the working river Ouse. Call in at the Black Swan, Peaseholme Green, as much for the smell of hot lunches on the hob as for the notion that General Wolfe, the hero of Quebec, was dandled here by his Ma among the domestic oak and plaster. Or drink your ale at a bar counter in Sampson's Square with your bottom on the parapet of a Roman bath. I suggest no itinerary, no route. The accidence of streets is too complicated. Saxon upon Roman. Viking overlaying Saxon. Medieval upon Danish. And a few alterations by Nazis and developers. Talk to people when they talk to you (as they surely will), and when they mention money (as is likely) talk money back. For money is to the citizens of York what the weather is to other Englishmen, a civilised topic of conversation, a social lubricant. It has probably always been so in York.

Then . . . refreshed by the profane, return to the cathedral a second time, a third time . . .

The air was charged with the scent of flowers as I passed through the city walls, walked down to Lendal and bought tobacco from the corner shop in Tanner's Moat. The penny-coloured Ouse was tarnished at the edge with images of trees and buildings. A barge unloaded reels of newsprint into the *Yorkshire Herald* office at about the spot where York Minster had been landed stone by stone and carted up Stonegate – hence, the name. Waiters were astir on the balconies of riverside restaurants and pubs. Pedestrians thronged the sidewalks of the cast-iron Lendal Bridge at each end of which former toll gates, like little castellated forts, had been converted into shops and were already doing brisk morning business. A man in a blazer and straw boater – he could have been Jerome K. Jerome thinking his idle Edwardian thoughts – leaned on the parapet apparently engrossed in the rooftiles of a medieval tower, and a boy vainly tried to spit on the roof of the waterworks below (1682) before proceeding to his office desk or grocer's counter. An explosion of midsummer foliage hid what was left of the old Roman walls. There is no other city in the land in which the centuries live so harmoniously together.

A delightful creature at the city tourist office, hearing I was a passing journalist, had proposed to guide me round the ancient walls, to send me on a guided tour of haunted houses and to provide me with entrance tickets to this museum and that. I was even offered an audience with the Lord Mayor. I declined – I hope with grace – and I am glad. For if I had got myself involved with itineraries and aldermen I would not, for instance, have found myself among the tarry smells and piled up shelves and hanging cards and cables, straps, buckles, harnesses and snares of Ralph Ellerker Limited . . . 'Rope Twine and Canvas Merchants Estb. 1795 . . . Practical Men Sent Out to do All Kinds of Repairs . . . Wagon Sheets and Tarpaulins made repaired and hired quickly . . . Stack Sheets . . . Small Covers . . . Ducting Shutes and liners . . . Advertising Banners . . . Diving Air Bags . . . Saddlery and Harness made on the premises . . . Quality Ferret Collars and Lines . . . Purse Nets . . . etc.' Which would have been a pity. What a shop!

Nor would I have met the large, friendly fish trader who spent much of an evening telling me where he bought his merchandise, how he made it pay, where he kept his van, what time in the small hours he set out for Grimsby and when he would be back – before emptying his pint pot and setting sail for breakfast at 11 p.m.

Had I been sealed in a sightseeing coach I could not have been stopped by the man unloading cartons from his car boot in an ancient street. 'Bit cool,' he said (it wasn't) in that clear, well-articulated accent of straight-forward vowels which is the way they clean up English in these parts – then kept me half an hour telling how he began his business, how he had prospered, how his family had grown, how much they earned and what ambitions he had for them.

If I had followed the tourist track I would not have met the shopkeeper who took me upstairs to see the great Jacobean ceiling beneath which he ate his breakfast every morning and watched television at night, instruct-ing me on the niceties of stained glass window colouring said to have died with the old craftsmen. Nonsense! he said. Why . . . the Victorians had made medicine bottles with tints of equal subtlety!

And if I had been padding round the Minster behind a guide I would not have met Harold Macmillan almost as large as life among the kings of England in the fifteenth century stone screen. They stand in niches across the choir's breadth, William the Conqueror on the left, Henry VI on the right and thirteen others in between. They are a lively crew, almost ready to burst into conversation with anyone advancing up the nave. There is something impish in this parade that took one Norwich man a quarter of a century to carve. Why does King Stephen (1135–54) wear a little skirt and fluffed out hair instead of scholarly regalia or armour like his fellows? Is he the Bombardier 'Gloria' Beaumont of this royal concert party? And then . . . yes, I swear it . . . installed in a Gothic sentry box second from the left, there stands Supermac as bold as brass in kingly robes. There are the familiar drooping eyes, the face composed in comic sleepiness. I looked them over, right and left. Is that the joke they have been sharing for five hundred years?

I read somewhere that an American authority had listed York among the ten most 'glamorous' cities in the world. That word smells of show-biz. I resent its application to England's finest city. Anyway, I bet that when they drew up that list, St Helen's Square was not even in their minds.

St Helen's Square opens at the foot of Stonegate – but not much. There is hardly room to swing a taxi there. At one end stands a church with an octagonal tower of open tracery, formerly the glass-painter's guild church and now the official place of civic worship. Directly oppo-site, and filling the whole end with its back towards the hidden river Ouse, sits the Mansion House, all pink brick and cream stone pilasters, as Georgian as a beadle. It is not particularly grand. That is its virtue. Resting foursquare and mildly prosperous, it could have been the resi-dence of a minor eighteenth-century peer and would have looked well in parkland. Beyond its four front steps and double doors lives the Lord Mayor of York with his Sword of State, his Great Mace of Office and his seventeenth-century chamber pot.

Church and mansion keep company with only half a dozen or so other buildings. One is Betty's the confectioner's and caterer's. When I found St Helen's Square that morning cakes were being delivered fragrantly from the bakery in Harrogate and an enormous marzipan-coated frog tenanted a corner window. I am not a creamcake man, but Betty's smells of quality.

There is a corner savings bank of 1829, a Barclays, the Yorkshire Insurance Company building raised in 1840 when such engines of finance were disguised as Italian palaces, and a neo-Georgian office block of 1929. There is also Terry's. 'Terry's of York', that is, with its four Corinthian columns, a hat-trick of pediments and three little balconies beneath. I thank the sudden shower that drove me in there for one of those small surprises that almost every English town hides from the urgent visitor and – thank God! – leaves out of all the guidebooks. Head down and blinded by the rain I took shelter in the doorway and, retreating further, found myself in a sumptuous restaurant lined from floor to moulded ceiling with magnificent mahogany panelling, every square and oblong cared for, highly polished, grain alive. On my right was a splendid timber staircase and overhead a delightful little dome. It was like walking from an inland city street and finding myself in the public rooms of one of those pre-1939 Cunard White Star transatlantic palaces. I climbed the companionway to another deck and found myself in a stateroom of equal splendour . . . 'this room has a special sprung floor, and lovers of the terpsichorean art will delight in its resiliency', said a deckle-edged brochure. It also told how Terry's began with a man rolling pills in a back room in 1767, then on through throat lozenges for chilled coach travellers to almond dragees, 'All Gold' chocolates and royal christening cakes and wedding breakfasts, with members of the Terry family still on the board.

From some crow's nest at the head of yet another stairway came the sound of masculine cheers. The York Round Table was at lunch. Ah, provincial England! Oh, happy York!

Now why take space to recommend St Helen's Square when I could be praising the ingenuity and charm of Castle Museum which houses one of the most entertaining social history collections in the country? There, in what used to be the women's gaol, they have made a Victorian street, complete with cobbles, shops, pub and hansom cab – Joe Hansom having been a York architect who must have made a pretty penny from his coach design. Maybe I should have been standing over the grave of Dick Turpin – a loutish blackguard who never actually made that famous ride to York. Or drooling over the Shambles, in which quaint timbered street it is said that neighbour could shake hands with neighbour through outward-leaning bedroom windows – though I cannot conceive of sober Yorkies doing anything so unprofitably daft. Or pausing piously at No. 35 where lived St Margaret of York who was pressed into sainthood in 1586 – she was a butcher's wife called Mrs Clitherow, judicially crushed to death for harbouring Jesuits. Or tracing the real birthplace of Guy Fawkes. Or the fictitious birthplace of Robinson Crusoe. Or speculating on which house in Castlegate Sir Walter Scott's Rebecca and her father Isaac might have succoured the hero of *Ivanhoe* in. Or rhapsodising over the city's eighteen medieval churches. I could have filled a chapter with such entertainments. The answer is that St Helen's is one of those vantage points where one may sit and watch the real live York.

From a window behind one of the first-floor balconies in Terry's, with a cup of best Ceylon steaming at my elbow, I looked out on a prosperous European city with the air of a provincial capital but no self-conscious flourishing of ancient lineage. Here were no signs that St Helen's Square was once the Praetorian Gate of Eboracum, the ceremonial portal of a Caesarian Simla. No noticeboard announced that York was once the royal capital of Northumbria. It was just a working city, civilised and confident, respectfully keeping the past in its proper place where canny Yorkshire pennies have successfully been turned into fat Yorkshire pounds. Substantial! Yes, that's the word for York. Thoroughly substantial.

By and by I made my own way to the walls, by way of Exhibition Square which, unlike St Helen's, is not a square at all. One side is ruled fairly straight by the ramparts, themselves interrupted by the portcullised Bootham Bar. It then forsakes geometry and does not even make a decent triangle. But who cares! Many a metropolis would boast about such a cockeyed square as this. Wrought-iron balconies and trees. Rectangular tower with red pantiled roof. What was once the mess of a stylish regiment now on duty as a pub and tourist office. Signboard advertising the 'York Pullman Bus Company' offices. Monument to a painter I have never heard of. City art gallery, Italianate with its five-arched portico. And the Theatre Royal – yes, now there's a place! Built against the wall of a twelfth-century hospital, it has been drawing audiences since 1740, has an art-nouveau auditorium and with its open arcade of 1877 looks like a seaside town hall in North Wales. Or at least it would do so had not some architect had a vision of a glass pavilion just ten years ago – a many-sided little dream of tall, narrow panes and sweeping concrete canopies clasping the theatre about one corner to serve as restaurant and foyer. A little beaut, a fragment of the mirage of postwar architecture which we so briefly glimpsed before the dull reality of curtain wall and tower block engulfed us. From this congenial plaza I mounted the stone stairway inside Bootham Bar and took to the ramparts.

Much has been written about the walls of York. Writers full of English breakfast, circumnavigating battlements and barbicans, have seen archers at the loopholes and heard sounds of battle – as comfortable a way of going to war as any, but not my picture show. You stand on earthworks piled up by Danes and Normans, and as you walk north-west from Bootham you look down into the bubbling pot of the old city. But on the left, from constellated ramparts and raised platforms, you can see the streets, roofs and yards of a richly mouldering Victorian suburb. No other city has such a convenient 'gods' for the observation of other people's business. The ramparts do not rush you on like those elevated railway tracks that tantalise with flashes of room life in once-Georgian Lambeth or Victorian Herne Hill south-bound from Charing Cross. Here, at walking pace and from your superior height and unconventional angle, you may peer down at leisure at the horticultural arrangements of deans and prelates and the kitchen parts of fine Jacobean houses.

Here, in an apparently unharried world of walled gardens, terraces and balustrades, tall windows and substantial bays, a french window stands ajar, revealing books, rugs and the faint hints of India that still haunt pukka English drawing-rooms. A girl in jeans – god-daughter of Mrs Miniver? – walks down a path with pruning shears. Silk lawns run to the buttresses of the rain-rusted Minster. On the other side, below the battlements, monstrous lorries from the north rumble down Gillygate seeking a way into the city. The great, grey-purple tide of Victorian domesticity that swelled into this century subsides at the foot of the green dike, depositing a flotsam of outhouses, pub yards, washing, small businesses and expired gardens.

The walls lead on, undulating slightly, curving through treetops, between chimneypots, past workshops and sculleries. Here you could lean through an open window and steal some tarts cooling on a kitchen sill. There you could snip cuttings from a collection of potplants. Did the publican have a full set of the *Decline and Fall* and had the Reverend actually read the *Kama Sutra*? Now a break in the masonry near an engineering works in sight of the river Foss, which is industrial and mucky, more like a Lancashire canal than a Yorkshire stream. Again more leafage, red pantiles, bandy medieval streets.

I will not detail that perambulation. Each man to his own window-peeping. But occasionally something beckoned me down into the streets. I descended into Goodramgate to look at the window of a model shop full of Junkers 87s and Liberators. I found two brews in two pubs in a single house and tasted both. Through the archway of a timbered fifteenth-century house where Charles I had set up a Civil War-time mint I walked into a delightful Georgian courtyard. I watched prosperous mothers delivering their offspring to morning school. I argued with a shop manageress who refused to sell me wine glasses.

And so, by way of such commonplace adventures, I came round to Lendal Bridge again. Descending to survey a luxurious motor yacht moored plumb in the city centre at Queen Staithe, I entered the King's Arms among whose flood-marked posts and beams I ate a fine pub lunch and found that my hosts were called the Wombles. Roy and Mary Womble. A happy and hospitable pair – and that's as true as there's a common down in Wimbledon!

4

The beautiful young woman at the city tourist office said: 'You simply cannot visit York, Mr Entwisle, without seeing the Cathedral undercroft. Haven't you heard what . . .'

Yes, I had heard. I knew what they had been up to beneath the Minster these last few years having seen them at it on a previous visit. Where there might have been a dim religious light and a touch of the peace that passeth understanding there were noisy compressors, scaffolding and tarpaulin screens. Wooden footbridges spanned floodlit caverns beneath the floor where you could see men at work like miners, strengthening the foundations of the central tower. I also knew that while they were at work down there they had found some remarkable Roman relics. It had all cost two million pounds and now that the schemozzle was over the Minster was safe from collapse for at least another thousand years and they had turned the big hole into a subterranean museum with an entrance fee and pay desk.

None of this appealed to me. I can feel kinship with Dane and Saxon, distant cousinship with Celt and Norman, and as for the medieval English, it is as if they have just left the room, the air full of their unfinished sentences. But I had been bored to truancy by school teachers droning in unheated classrooms about the ingenuity of hypocausts and the use of javelins in campaigns that got no one anywhere in the end. But she was a beautiful young woman. So I went.

I'm glad I did. There is sorcery down there beneath the clay of York, something so disorderly that it could have been arranged by no curator. We have been taught to think of the 'ascent' of man as a linear process an accumulation of technology, but down there the convention of time has been jarred out of sequence in a way that seems to express a poetic truth about the blink we call two thousand years. Eleventh and fifth centuries lie side by side. Nineteenth-century vault stands over the 900-year-old battle horn of Ulf, twelfth century precedes first, and Roman engineer shares time and space with Norman and Victorian. There Rome breathes! I met the great Constantine among the roots of York. His sandstone ears had gone missing since the troops proclaimed him Emperor at the end of Stonegate. I saw he was short-haired and had fat chins.

A notice said that Roman sappers had constructed a system of drains and culverts 1,800 years ago to carry rain and waste from streets and roofs. It was found in working order, so twentieth-century engineers re-conscripted it to control the destabilising rise and fall of water beneath the medieval tower.

'You now stand in the headquarters building . . . the 5,600 men of the Heavy Infantry Legion, drawn from Europe, were replaced by Britons . . . here was the street separating it from the barrack blocks of the 1st Cohort . . .' Now there was something I could understand – stores, workshops, orders . . . morning muster on a keen northern morning!

This central hall was longer than the nave of the Norman Minster . . . 225 ft wide . . .' How the dickens did they keep the roof up?

A likeness of Septimius Severus. A head of Hadrian. Sepia tesselations. Browns, reds, blues, greens. Here a boulder I would not care to lift. *'This stone fell on the head of Roger of Ripon during a service'* to commemorate St William of York, an archbishop. *'By the Saint's interception the man was unharmed.'*

Stainless steel bolts in cliffs of concrete binding the foundations of the tower above. The 'York Virgin' carved in magnesian limestone. Celtic gravestones. Medieval grotesques.

'Emperor Septimius Severus ruled the Roman world from his palace in York for two years before his death here in A.D. 211 . . . The British population became Roman citizens, erected massive public buildings and worshipped at the temples of Mars, Hercules and Mithras . . .' Fall out Methodists, Presbyterians and Baptists!

A deep booming sound smote the subterranean air. It swelled, vibrating out of concrete floor and roof and ancient masonry like the throb of a great gong struck in the earth's heart. Before it died it was overtaken by another, then another, three seconds between each stroke, and when I climbed back up to the Cathedral nave it seemed to possess every molecule of pier and vault, filling the huge chamber. It was noon and Great Peter, the deepest-toned bell in Europe, was speaking to the citizens of York.

I met a nun in the choir stalls and she told me that the sexton pulls the bell rope once then cycles off for lunch, racing to get home before the tolling stops. 'One pull, and it rings a hundred times – about five minutes.' Her figures were correct . . . one hundred chimes . . . one each three seconds . . . five minutes on the button!

As I passed the transepts I looked up again at the five slim, austere and lovely sisters that Dickens loved . . . five lancets, each five-and-fifty feet in height, filled with thirteenth-century glass in small, grey-green geometric patterns . . . five membranes of translucent gossamer washing the whole northern limb of the Cathedral in pale green light.*

Outside, the last note of the holy cannonade had rolled off down Museum Street and across the railway sheds. The sun had now moved around, catching the great west front aslant. It looked as though someone had unrolled a cascade of glowing lace down from the sky. Cream, brown, coffee, gold, it tumbled into High Petergate. I wondered whether awe was a healthy state of mind for a twentieth-century man and walked off down Duncombe Place relishing the idea of a cathedral sexton, spectacles gleaming, cycle clips in place, hurtling through the streets of York to beat Great Peter to his fried fish fingers.

5

In the Railway King that evening I met a Scotch fellow who said he had come to York for a six-month business stint, had stayed twenty years and had no intention of ever leaving. At first he called it just a *village* – 'a big one, but just a village'. Then he was extolling it as the university *town* it is. At night the new, white, floodlit, academic buildings seem to float on the lake of a 190-acre park. Then he was calling it a working-class and beer-drinking *city*. 'There used to be a hundred pubs within the city walls alone – tremendous! – and twenty-seven in one short street.' Insurance . . . engineering . . . a quarter of the working population feeding the sweet tooth of the world from three chocolate factories . . . *and 7,000 railwaymen.* Ah yes, the railway!

The house in which we supped was named after George Hudson, the railway tycoon and swindler who was thrice Lord Mayor of York. So was the street. With an eye on the tourist trade the city fathers had rehabilitated him, rehanging his portrait in the Mansion House and giving back the name Hudson to the thoroughfare that had been called Railway Street since his disgrace. Yes, York, for all its 'Eboracum airs', its Roman ghosts and its eclairs, was still a great railway town and I must therefore visit one more museum before I left.

* The likeness of the Five Sisters windows to some wondrous textile struck Dickens too. He wrote a tale about five young women, sisters and citizens of York, who wove five tapestries. When they died their needlework was miraculously changed to glass.

In north-west London, on the edge of one of the biggest concentrations of humanity in Europe and one of the world's greatest tourist centres, a Royal Air Force museum preserves the aircraft that saved the West just four decades ago. Beautiful machines they are and it is not surprising that in the year it opened (1972) 600,000 children of the airborne age went to feast their eyes and their imaginations on the Spitfire, the Hurricane, the Halifax and their less famous sisters. Next year the figure dropped to 400,000, but that was still a tidy multitude.

York is two hundred miles from the capital, far from Channel ports and international airfields. Its National Railway Museum opened in 1975 and in the first twelve months 2.1 million went to see it. When the novelty wore off the small staff still had to cope with 1½ million visitors in a year. That so many people appear to prefer puffer trains to warplanes might say something for the excellence of the York museum. I think it says a great deal more about the English.

What do they get for their money? Well, there is no entrance charge. They just walk in. Then if they turn right they may climb to a balcony and look down on the two acres of the main exhibition hall. It was one of the Main Motive Power depots of the old North Eastern, and I like to think it is the place that H. V. Morton visited one night in the year that I was born and listened to the green giants, 'The Olympians', basking on the turntables as they waited for the night runs.

> There is no sound . . . but the drawing of furnaces as the clock moves on. Then far down the main-line track . . . is a far scream and a gathering thunder . . . A big green Pacific crouching over the track, a sudden meteor flash . . . and a short pinkness of dining car windows. Then deeper darkness . . .
>
> 'King's Cross,' says one of the Olympians, 'and dash my connecting rods, six minutes late!'
>
> 'You've never brought in the King's Cross,' comes an oily rebuke from the shadows; and no-one replies. A Pacific has spoken. (No-one back chats a Pacific except a very shabby tank.)
>
> 'Haddock – haddock – haddock . . . haddockandplaice – haddockandplaice – haddockandplaice – haddockandplaice . . .' pants a deep asthmatic voice as a high, dark shape passes No. 4 shed. The fish has come from Hull.

And there they are, noses in towards the centre on the forty-four radiating tracks of the two vast turntables. And there are some of their ancestors. Old gaffers like *Gladstone* that ran on the Brighton & South Coast Railway, painted in 'Stroudley's Improved Engine Green' which is actually a toffee brown. Old Coppernob (Furness Railways 0-4-0 1846) with his huge, gleaming dome, shrapnel scarred in World War II. One of Stirling's magnificent 'Eight-footers' (Great Northern 4-2-2 1870) with its huge driving wheels. Old *Agenoria* himself (1824) with his towering black lum, a contemporary of the *Rocket* and a sister of the *Stourbridge Lion* which – exported to America – became the first locomotive on that continent. A Bo-Bo Electric of 1904 that worked trains down the steep tunnel to Newcastle quayside for sixty years.

And some of their descendants. *Green Arrow* (LNER 2-6-2 1936) – ah, how she pranced through Doncaster! *The Duchess of Hamilton*, LMS Red, most powerful steam loco built in Britain, rescued from ignominy at a Butlin's holiday camp. *Ellerman Lines* of the wartime Merchant Navy Class with her side cut away to show her innards. *Evening Star*, last of the steamers, Swindon 1960. And standing alongside in all her streamlined glory, *Mallard*, kingfisher blue and black, whose 126 miles an hour between Grantham and Peterborough has never been beaten by another steam train.

Here is the clock from the station on Gravesend Pier, stopped for ever at ten o'clock one summer day in 1945, still secure in its wooden tower of cream and green. On which of its surrounding seats did I rest my leave pack?

And occupying the end wall like a colossal reredos celebrating the nineteenth-century gods, the cogs and giant flywheel of the stationary Weatherhill Winding Engine that used to haul wagons into the hills of upper Weardale. I remember how, disused, it still reigned in the empty landscape where there were no trees, no other works of man in sight. And now it works with an electric button.

Perhaps one day there will arrive a generation for whom those boilers and fireboxes, the gleaming con rods, valves and pistons, the dashing company liveries and lettering, the peculiar incense of hot oil and coalsmoke, will mean nothing. They will not believe then that drivers and firemen once so loved their cabs that they grained the metal parts with paint and polished up the copper tubes before each windy journey on the open footplate – that there were grown men whose hearts would leap at the sound of a tank engine heaving dirty coal trucks up an incline a mile away. But that bleak day has not yet dawned, nor is it close at hand.

That last afternoon in York I entered a side gallery. On the walls were railway pictures – carriage scenes of haunting intimacy, and those great tumultuous platform panoramas in which all the vitality of Victorian England are crammed in a turmoil which no camera, and I think no modern artist, could ever reproduce. Life-size figures of former railway workers were displayed in glass cases – the ticket collectors, waiters, signalmen and clerks who stood so importantly in the smoky shadows of my childhood. It was as if they had been frozen in mid-gesture, the glances fixed for ever.

I was looking at a Stockton & Darlington Railway guard of 1860 – frock-coat, peaked cap, muffler and lantern – when, for some reason, I was seeing instead a poisoner of rich old ladies. An LS&WR porter of the 1890s in Dundreary whiskers looking at his pocket watch seemed to be the perpetrator of some obscure sexual crime. A stationmaster, very smart, black-braided coat, wing collar, rimless glasses – a mother poisoner. And, most sinister of all, a smart young hotel page of the 1950s with chocolate-coloured suit, three upright rows of buttons on his double-breasted waistcoat and carrying a hat box which – I had a nasty feeling – contained something more grisly than a hat . . .

I went back to the paintings, marvelling at their detail. A little later I met Peter Semmens, Assistant Keeper and one of the creators of this magnificent museum. We realised we had met years before on a disused station – the former private halt of the Londonderry family. I told him what I'd felt in his gallery. He gave me a swift, old-fashioned look and said: 'Do you know where we got the wax figures for those exhibits?'

'No – how could I?'

'They came from . . .'

'Madame Tussauds?' it suddenly occurred to me.

'Right!'

'Perhaps discarded from the Chamber of Horrors?' I ventured.

'Very probably.'

In the main hall the air was full of ghosts. There were loudspeakers in the girders. The sound of an express goods rattled from nowhere into history. An Atlantic whistled from oblivion. An A4 started up, driving wheels spinning on the lines, exhaust roaring.

On the white brick walls a cast-iron notice read:

> These closets are intended for
> the convenience of passengers.
> Workmen, cabmen, fishporters
> and idlers are not permitted
> to use them. BY ORDER

The yearning cry of a Super Pacific filled the hall and dissolved into the distance.

17

Illustrative – among the clouds at Blubberhouses and the cascades of Kettlewell – of the old proverb that 'there's nowt as queer as folks'.

1

THE DAY was as bright as a blackbird's eye when I trundled up Petergate, through Bootham Bar and out into the Ridings. I could, of course, have been across the Tyne Bridge by midday, under and over Newcastle by the new urban motorway and in my own Northumberland bed that night with my rowan tree whispering outside the window and my little river talking the dark hours away. But there's a whole kingdom between York and the Border and plenty of temptations. I saw a sign to Harrogate and decided to look up a friend.

Harrogate is one of the oddest towns in England. Halfway between the west coast and the east, halfway between London and Edinburgh, with stylish shops and great Victorian hotels that would not shame St Petersburg, and miles and miles of public gardens full of flowers, it is a wonderful incongruity out there in northern Yorkshire. I must have crossed its boundaries half a dozen times on my way to somewhere else and never got the hang of it.

Oh, I knew the essential facts. Discovered in 1571 by a Mr Slingsby who thought the water foul enough to be medicinal, it became one of the great health resorts of Victorian Europe, dispensing hot mud poultices and a thousand glasses of sulphurous water in a single morning. It had a Kursaal (German for cure-room) and a Royal Pump Room and you could get the treatment on the National Health not so long ago. What I did not, and still do not know, is what brought all the wallowing and swallowing to an end. And now that it's all over and the place hires itself out to conferences and exhibitions, what do Harrogatians do when the gabbing season's over and snow lies on the glass dome of the Sun Pavilion and the Assembly Rooms are silent?

My friend worked for the Regional Hospital Board so I met him in what looked like an airport concourse but was in fact the bright reception area of a modern hospital. The patients sat on comfortable sofas sipping coffee and soft drinks, as healthy and relaxed a crowd as I've ever seen. It must be something in the water.

We lunched in a pub in a small isle of houses surrounded by a green sea of municipal parkland and when we parted and I was back on the A1 I still knew no more of Harrogate.

Knaresborough called me next – the Mecca of a million Mothers' Union coach trips. Here there is a castle on a cliff, and a well that turns small objects into stone, and a cave where Mother Shipton, the fifteenth-century witch, forecast cars, aeroplanes and air raids and said the world would end in 1981. Not much time left! I motored on.

Ripon beckoned. And it would have been pleasant to pay my deep respects to the first and best of the world's seventy Richmonds, a glorious, humpetty old stone town, far superior to the London suburb of that name, and birthplace of the 'sweet lass' of song. There people still see plays in the delightful little Georgian theatre, and climb the eleventh-century castle keep to see the woods towering above the hurtling Swale and to contemplate the undulation of green dales swinging down towards the Vale of York.

My patience with the A1 lasted till I saw a sign to Bedale and there I took to another world – a world of stone villages where you can wander through five hundred dales and still have four-score to see.* A world of great horizons where clocks and men run slow.

On an unfenced moorland road a man and two dogs were sauntering

* The number of dales in Yorkshire causes unending debate. One school says 565, the other 581.

several million sheep through thin, yellow sunlight to a destination a decade or two ahead. The shepherd knew I could not pass, but it did not cross his Yorkshire hillman's mind to make way. So I parked, sat on a tussock and watched the moorbirds in the empty valley at my feet.

I caught up. He could have let me go by twice when we came to road gates, but he didn't. When his flock ran off and scuttled down into the wilderness I helped round up his strays. He did not say a word. So I had to doddle on another year or two until I saw my chance at yet another gate and nipped through his protesting herd. I bore him no resentment. I've no doubt he had his priorities the right way round.

Now I descended into a deep, green well full of houses, trees, the smell of woodsmoke, and everywhere the sound of running water. A barrier of white cliffs stood behind the village. Was it Kettlewell? If so the kettle leaked and the well overflowed. I found a pub where there was fire and food and there I met a gypsy lad in a hat of imitation leopardskin who said he was part of an official team seeking new water sources. Water? Water here? Well, yes – but there was time left over to pursue local girls, and with some success, for he regaled me the whole lunchtime with his harum-scarum tales of conquest and of how, in between times, he found water in high places.

In a cloud on the road to a place called Blubberhouses I paid some small coin to a woman at a hut beside a wayside hole and she took me down inside the fells to caves where stalactites hung like Christmas streamers. And I spent the night in a big stone house in a clump of trees over Coverdale where I found two dear old friends, Ciss and Robert, who I had last seen in Northumberland. They were getting on a bit and it was a lonely place but they told me that if by accident they left a door open late or early, or if no smoke rose from their chimney, neighbours would telephone from miles across the fells, or drive over to ensure that all was well.

That night it was pitch black. Robert and I walked down into the village and felt our way along the crooked street where the humps of houses looked like outcrops of the valley rock. We entered one such mound of boulders and were in a long bar-room with an open hearth. The other customers, weather-creased and lean, sat round the walls on benchseats and most of the time the loudest sound was the shifting of an ashen log, the flaring of a pipe-match or the gush of a fresh pint being poured. There *was* conversation, but it was not the superficial crackle of our lowland world. Sentences were short and practical and each was followed by a digestive silence. The subject was a mysterious process known as 'tupping', about Leicestershire and Suffolks. Jim would not part with his hardy Suffolk-Swaledale crosses. 'They could stand the draught,' he said.

Robert, an ex-coalminer and pigeon fancier, contributes his sage portion to these deliberations as if he had lived there all his life. We two sat at a great oak table – 'older than the pub . . . old when it was brought here from a dissolved monastery'. His deep, rich r's rolled out from some recess with which only true Northumbrians are endowed. But he made no discord with the Yorkshire speech of his companions; he had their rhythm to perfection and I began to wonder whether the talk was all some lumbering Nordic joke, but no one smiled. Then once he said quietly in aside – 'They knaa Aa knaa buggor-aall aboot sheep, man Frank, but they knaa Aam lornen.'

Next morning I turned down the offer of a day's beating with a shooting party and set off again. I had completed a great loop into north-west Yorkshire. Emerging on to the A 1 again, I headed for Scotch Corner and was there within the hour. A car in the forecourt of the Scotch Corner Hotel displayed a rear window sticker which read:

'Divvent dunshus wah Geordies!'*

I was almost home.

2

Some may dispute that Ferrybridge is the gatehouse of the North. I grant them latitude. There can be no argument, however, about where the North-east starts. For Great North Road travellers it begins where the A 66 takes western flight for the Bowes Moors and the high, heathered wastes of County Durham, where a B-road trickles east towards the industrial Tees and where the A 1 itself becomes a motorway and surges off to Tyneside. The place is called Scotch Corner.

It is not a political boundary. It falls a few miles short of the river Tees which used to mark Durham off from Yorkshire before Local Government Disorientation. Nor is it visually dramatic. There is just a roundabout and the big redbrick hotel. It is the point, though, where the wayfarer must choose his path into this strangely unknown region. And more important than lines drawn on maps by clerks in Whitehall, it is an emotional frontier post. Beyond Scotch Corner the inhabitants know they are a different sort of people. It is not that they are Geordies. Geordies live on Tyneside only and have their own variation of the north-east way of speaking. Yet the *difference* they feel is deeper than the divisions between Devonians and Cornishmen, between Lancastrians and Tykes, Southerners and Northerners. It is one of attitudes towards

* Don't bump into us. We're from Tyneside.

the world of other Englishmen. It is one of tribe. A north-easterner meeting other Englishmen abroad will single out those of his tribe immediately. At once a flame of kinship will be lit, and humour is the tinder. North-easterners are given to self-mockery. They are vastly amused about themselves, about their weaknesses, their insularity and the myth of their superiority, knowing it all the time to be a myth.

An exhausted Northumberland Fusilier lost from his unit in the Libyan desert stumbles on a Durham Light Infantryman lying face down in the sand in the last stages of dehydration. The two exchange information about birthplaces, home gossip and the small chance of their survival for another day.

'Bloody m-a-a-a-rvellous, isn't it,' says the Durham lad. 'You come here all the way from Spennymoor, get lost in Africa, and the last man in your life you come across is a chap from yem [home].'

'Aye,' says Geordie, 'an' d'ye knaa what day it is?'

'Aa've telt ye man – Aa've lost coont. Is it Sunder?'

'No man! Aa mean what *day* is it. It's the day o' the Big Meet'n [Durham Miners' Gala].'

The Light Infantryman raises his head, scans the horizon and the burning sky. 'Aa'll tell thoo what – mind, though, but . . .'

'What's that, bonny lad?'

'They've got a bloody m-a-a-a-rvellous day for it, heven't the'!'

The joke is not about courage in adversity, like a Bairnsfather cartoon. It mocks north-east insularity and it is in praise of tribe.

Graham Turner, in his survey of the North, said that when he crossed the Tees the change was hard to define and yet more marked than the sensation of entering Wales or Scotland. And so it is! It resided in the attitudes of those he met, their unspoken indication that they were a race apart. And that they are! He put it down to centuries of isolation, the poor communications with Scotland and the rest of England, and to a separate Palatinate administration ruled from Durham by Prince Bishops with Church courts and their own exchequer. That is what he must have been told. But it cannot be so. The broadest of all highways – the North Sea from Tynemouth to London River – had been used for centuries to carry coal, fish and men. Ecclesiastic sovereignty was broken by Henry VIII. And anyway, the north east culture is more proletarian than peasant. It took warmth from the smoky streets and garths of the eighteenth and nineteenth centuries along lower Tyne and Wear and the mining townships that flourished in the age of steam, from the astonishing new movement of coal, iron and manufactured goods on north-east invented railways. Communications – not isolation – mothered it.

The best-loved folk-songs of the region – sometimes wistful, nearly always comical, often both – are industrial and urban. They are about streets and pubs and pitmen. Many, indeed, are about communications. 'My Bonny' lay 'Over the Ocean' because he was a sailorman, and when Kathleen Ferrier crooned for 'The Wind' to 'Blow Southerly' she echoed a lament that had long been sung by sea-widows along the Tyne. The famous keel song – 'Weel May the Keel Row' – concerned the midstream loading and unloading of cargoes.* 'Keep Yor Feet Still Geordie Hinney' – one of the comic-wistful songs – is about the disturbed dreams of two Tyneside lads obliged to share a bed in a Tyneside lodging house. And 'Blaydon Races' – what north-easterners call their *national* anthem – begins at Balmbra's Music Hall in central Newcastle one wet summer afternoon in 1862 and documents such urban furniture as factories (Armstrongs – now Vickers), railway bridges, dispensaries, infirmaries, omnibuses and a mechanics' hall. It immortalises real Victorian eccentrics – like Coffee Johnny in his white top hat – such as only cities breed. Despite the rain . . .

> There wes spice stalls an' munkey shows, an' aad wives
> sellin' ciders,
> An' a chep wiv a happeny roondaboot shootin' 'Noo me
> lads for riders!'

These songs, and many more, are not museum pieces disinterred by trendy folk groups. Nor are they sung with the chauvinistic maudlin of po-faced Scots. They are still real. And they are roared for joy by housewives on factory coach trips, in pubs and clubs and parties, and best of all in lovely, beery, unsophisticated Balmbra's Music Hall, still alive and kicking.

I used the word *tribe* for the want of a better noun. It is no tribe of *blood* relationship. Cornish and Welsh miners, Scotch fishermen and Irish peasants, itinerant workmen from all parts of the islands, poured into the North-east in the days of new-sunk pitshafts, iron steamships and gun factories that outclattered Krupps, thickening the Tyne and Wearside broth. And there has been an Arab community in Shields for as long as anyone remembers. The marvel is that the north-east dialect survived this human deluge, becoming a binding agent in the end.

It has been said that language is the mirror of a people's soul. North-easterners use some different words from other Englishmen, though I don't suppose their vocabulary is much bigger than elsewhere. A horse or

* A keel was a Tyne lighter propelled by oars.

pit pony is a *cuddy* or a *gallowa*. A butterfly is a *lowie*, a moth is a *logger* and a toffee is a *bullet*. Mud is *clarts*, a lavatory is a *netty*, a knife is a *gully*, a lane is a *lonnen*, a pitman may be a *yacker*, coal being *yak*. Frail is *femmer*, dirty is *hackey*, a sparrow is a *spug*, a pig is a *gissie* and to throw is to *hoy*. But much north-east eloquence is achieved by sweeping modulations of the voice. The word *canny* has an entirely different meaning than in the rest of Britain. Put it on a Geordie tongue and project it with a Geordie voice and the word takes shades of meaning from execrable to excellent according to the intonation. The word bugger, too, can be a word of comradely affection as in the American mid-west. In this mildly comic usage it appears to have a different source from bugger (derivation Bulgar) as used elsewhere. In the north-east it may be kin of boggle or bogie, a legendary monster. In Northumberland and Durham a 'canny aad bugger' is not a mean old homosexual but a good-natured friend.

But it is not just words themselves that are referred to in the proposition that language reflects a people's nature. There is vividness, vitality and a dash of poetry about the way north-easterners use their kind of English. A nosey-parker will be described as *nebby*. An unmarried, pregnant woman has *fallen wrang*. A woman's footfalls are described as *tappy-lappy* – 'doon the street she gans, tappy-lappy'. A sharp-tongued wife remonstrating with her husband is giving him tubs to mend. In Newcastle a friend was cutting me a slice of bread with a blunt knife. She said – 'Time you got this shairpened . . . I could ride bare-arse to London on this gully.' She was parted from her husband and commented – 'Aa wadn't hev another man if his arse wes decked wi' di'monds.'

Seventeen miles north of the city is a place called Ashington. It stands on the edge of the Tyneside industrial conurbation, just short of the lovely sweeps and strands of the Northumberland coast. ('a lad like you shouldn't be livin' down in London,' a Newcastle taxi-man and council-lor once told me. 'It's grand living here in the north-east concubation.') With a population of 25,000, Ashington has been called the biggest village in the country. It is known for the number and lavishness of its working men's clubs. There a ragamuffin crowd of men race the family whippets of a Sunday morning on a playing field. And it turns out great footballers. My friend Cissie Charlton (last night's hostess at Coverdale) taught her small boys Bob and Jackie to play football in her Ashington back street – along with their cousin Jackie Milburn – while father Robert nursed his pigeons up at the allotment. ('Sell me pigeons, Jack? Aa'd rether get rid o' wor [our] Ciss than sell me pigeons.') The reason for Ashington's existence is the pit. The streets and colliery rows are straight and drab. It is not a pretty place.

But in Ashington there is a thriving group of pitmen artists. And in

Ashington there lives a quiet man called Fred Reed who speaks and writes the old Northumbrian with gentle power . . . 'Aw lass! Yo're keel and shy as owt could be . . . Are ye affeared? Luv, rest yorsel' in me . . .' He can be just as moving when he writes about a teenage vandal, an unemployed school-leaver or the industrial junk on the beach near his home. But you have to *hear* the half-tones, the rumbling gutturals, the hesitating rhythms that inhabit every line, to catch the beauty of the language.

> 'Ee! But it's all se grand!
> But Aa'm dazzled wi' the mysteries o' livin', –
> As if Aa wuz standin' in a lane,
> Eftor rain,
> Blinkin' up at the sun.
> And then wi' ye Aa run,
> And laugh, and run agyen,
> The thowtful pethside daisies streamin' by,
> The weshin' air, the lairksong through the sky.
> And then Aa catch ye, and Aa understand.'*

A pitman's voice! There is a pause after 'lairksong through the sky'. The Northumbrian 'r' in the word 'understand', and the final falling syllable, have a value that cannot be explained to users of the mere Queen's English. It is verbal music.

3

Anyway, there I was still at Scotch Corner with my reflections and my way still to choose. I'll tell you what – if ever I embark upon another English journey and come northbound to Scotch Corner I will veer east to Teesside. Lower Teesside, that is, which, since Leicestershire's *Anschluss* of little Rutland, is England's smallest county, Cleveland. I will conscientiously traverse the banks of the river, which hereabouts is black and poisonous. I will explore – as diligently as any Livingstone – the forests of retorts and catalytic crackers and towers and tanks and flues that lie between Middlesbrough and Hartlepool. I will tell of the predicament of Teesside – 'Europe's most dynamic industrial centre' and Gladstone's 'Infant Hercules' – whose chemicals are unwanted by the world in times of slump and whose industrialists, in times of boom, invest in more

* 'Reverence' from *The Sense On't* by Fred Reed published locally by Northern House, Newcastle upon Tyne.

complicated plant that needs fewer workers. Then I will try to understand why half a million people are more fiercely proud of their ugly patch of England than Cotswold men, Devonians or any other Englishmen.

But now rain splashed the Scotch Corner Hotel forecourt and I took the motorway that sweeps past handsome Durham City, the pitman's capital. As dusk fell I came down through Gateshead to the steep-sided Tyne and saw Newcastle piled up on the northern bank. A hundred office windows lit, Norman castle keep, the fantastic Gothic crown of St Nicholas's Cathedral, all silhouetted on a smoky sky . . . the interlacing girders of the Tyne Bridge forming a familiar portal into the heart of the truculent, masculine, awkward, Geordie town.

I cannot know how this dramatic entrance affects strangers. When I write about Newcastle I am writing with affection about home with all its faults. When I peer over the cast-iron parapets past regiments of elaborate chimneys and rococo dormer windows into the deep-cut Victorian streets I stir memories within me beyond my own lifespan. Here began Newcastle. All Saints – an exquisite oval church whose elaborate baroque spire springs from the quayside – is empty now. The wharves are deserted unless a NATO squadron or a Continental fishing fleet is driven upstream for shelter. But here the first true Geordies – and not so long ago – lived head-by-toe and toe-by-head in the steep, crowded staircase streets called chares until Dobson the architect and Grainger the entrepreneur built their wide, handsome, well-planned nineteenth-century city centre on the plateau up above. There the young farmyard genius Thomas Bewick learned his art with home-made engraving tools and bits of steel and blocks of wood, saying – 'I would rather live in poverty and insecurity in Newcastle' than in London 'covered with all the porrige of outside show.' There among the coal smoke worked his masters and eventual partners the Beilbys whose enamelled and engraved glass survives in the collections of the rich. As Georgian England became Victorian, here worked the Stephensons, father and son, transforming England and the world with their railways and their bridges. Here strove Armstrong with his hydraulics and his great rifled guns, Swan with his electric incandescent lamps (at the same time as the American Edison – hence, I presume, Ediswan), Parsons with his steam turbine, among the keelmen, coal trimmers and teemers, makers of besom brooms, shipwrights and songwrights and sellers of yellow clay like Tyneside's comic heroine Cushie Butterfield.

She's a big lass an' a bonnie lass an' she likes hor beer,
An' they caal hor Cushie Butterfield an Aa wish she was heor . . .

I know of no other streets so haunted by the Victorians and their children. The ill-paid shipping-clerks, incompetent ships' cooks and hard-up skippers have paid their last tick at the Crown Pasada with its hand-pumps and coffered ceiling, but I know where I could still buy a first mate's uniform straight from the shop window beneath the railway viaduct. The Customs House is still down there. And among the empty alleyways the Trinity House captains still sit in eighteenth-century splendour with fat Rubens cherubs cavorting round their heads on the Carolingian plaster, with their logs and old accounts and menus of seafaring dinners long digested.

One hundred and ten dinners	£57	15s	0d
Five dozen champagne	4	10s	0d
Two dozen claret	1	16s	0d
88 bottles of port	4	8s	0d
Dessert	6	6s	0d
Fifty teas and coffees	3	15s	0d
Punch	1	10s	0d
Whisky		10s	6d
Ice		15s	0d
Cigars	1	5s	0d
Singers	3	0s	0d
Hire of chaises	2	8s	0d
Waiters	2	15s	0d
	£90	13s	6d

'Sailormen 'ave their faults,' said the nightwatchman, 'I'm not denying of it. But being close with money is a fault as can seldom be brought ag'in 'em. I saved two golden sovereigns once, owing to a 'ole in my pocket. Before I got another ship I slept two nights on a doorstep, and I found them in the lining o' my coat when I was two thousand miles from the nearest pub.'

Ah, yes! The nightwatchman I can just remember. And Ginger Dick from Sunderland, and Sam Small and Peter Russett and all the other ghosts immortalised by W. W. Jacobs. For did I not, as a boy of twenty-one, sit below decks in the tug paddle-steamer *Stag* with the one-legged skipper Ernie Baister, and Dozzler Moon and the other lads just down the coast while the lamp swung from the deck above and we drank red wine and ate crabs fresh boiled in the galley bucket?

Home it is. Too intimate, too warm, too full of ifs and buts for such a book and such a chapter. So the motorway took me on past the new egg-box office blocks, across Newcastle and eight miles on into North-umberland, the queen of counties.

I had missed the flowering of the rowan blossom in my little garden, but I saw the pyramid of berries before the winged raiders descended for their scarlet feast.

4

The place in which I live is still called a village. There are still sharpening marks on the Norman door of the parish church where archers honed their arrows at Sunday morning practice. We still sit round the great, stone, Tudor fireplace in the barrel-vaulted bar of the Blackbird Inn where the Newcastle garrison once caught up with the Scotchies and made them sign a treaty which of course they did not keep. The Wednes-day Club meets there on Mondays, Tuesdays, Thursdays, Fridays and even Wednesdays – led by a Canadian ex-Wing Commander – to mourn the passing of the Empire. But the villagers have long been outnumbered by the executives of a great suburb and Ponteland is now a dormitory of Newcastle. The jet engines at the airport down the road out-din the village clock. Worse still, it has become part of the huge artificial borough of Morpeth, sired by the new bureaucracy, whose far-flung villages have little sympathy with each other's problems. So parish issues are settled by foreigners on the advice of some town-bred clerk or a solemn creature called a Chief Executive. Now the inhabitants who care are concerned about the preservation of their Green Belt and when I got back there was an election so I joined in. There is nothing like delivering leaflets early in the morning for studying the English in all their glorious confusion, council house gardens bursting with late summer flowers, gates and latches and letter-boxes, dogs fierce, dogs friendly, leaflet-eating dogs, how wonderfully undisciplined. Taciturn miners watching the votes counted in the Town Hall at nearby Morpeth. Pretty little clerks clipping the ballot slips in brand new clothes pegs. A peer of the realm bouncing with boyish glee like an ageing Bunter as he sees his votes pile up. I enjoyed it. But one morning I set out again and headed for the Cheviots by way of Alnwick walled and gated against the Scotch, still guarded by stone sentinels and lions on the grandest castle in the frontier county.

You can see the Cheviots from Newcastle's northern suburbs. To the traveller who pauses at the summit of the frontier pass called Carter Bar before descending from a high, treeless England to a low, lush Scotland, they are no more than emerald mounds – conical, remarkably alike, benign and rather pretty. What makes the Cheviots smile is their green disguise. There is little ling or heather. Their bent-grass covering is finer, softer and more even than the vegetation of the Pennines or the Durham moors. Shade and texture reflect and absorb the light and display a changing face of greens and golds.

But all that is a deception. Cheviot flanks are steep, the valleys lonely, known to the golden eagle and the wildcat. From time to time a warplane – a Wellington or Heinkel presumed lost forty years ago – is relinquished by a peat bog and the new archaeologists arrive to take away the pieces. The highest summit – Muckle Cheviot – is 1,730 feet lower than Ben Nevis, but Cheviot names disdain statistics. Black Hag's Rig, Bloody Bush Edge, Windy Gyle, Yearning Law, High Bleakhope . . . Up there the curlew reigns, guarding his domain, signalling intrusion with his melancholy music. There is something immeasurably old and knowing about that lovely cry. It suits the Cheviots.

On the road from Wooler towards Coldstream I left the van. I walked through the golden, scented lace of meadowsweet, followed a drystone wall up the edge of a steep copse, slithered and slipped up silky grass and came to Yeavering Bell, which is a hill that hangs a thousand feet or so above the old tragic road to Flodden Field. Below, Northumbria is a vast stretch of parkland. From the south the Romans came, and to the south they went, leaving in Britain not one Latin verb. But down there their great wall still stands, the greatest mark of their engineering north of the Alps. To the south-east a sea causeway – covered at high tide – runs out to Lindisfarne from which Northumbrian rock Aidan and Cuthbert brought Christianity back to Britain – a Celtic Christianity, wrangling with Rome at Whitby, the beginning of an anti-Continental tradition that served Henry VIII well when he needed it and is echoed to this day in Brussels. North are the blunted tusks of Scotland's Eildon Hills, hiding Edinburgh. And 'Auld Reekie', be it known to every Scot, was once Edwin's Burgh. And Edwin was the first Christian monarch of Northumbria, whose kingdom stretched from Forth to Humber.

South beyond the Tyne the bones of England's first Englishman are scattered. The Venerable Bede – a son of that dark age when Northumbria was one of Europe's few unextinguished beacons – was the first man to see England as a political society and the English as a race.

Northwards came the Normans, laying waste Northumbria but leaving us their monument at Durham to outlast their language and their culture.

East of Bede's shrine – a strange, part-Norman, part-Saracenic annexe of the Cathedral – the ancestors of America's first president lived in Washington Old Hall, now part of Sunderland. The English empire which he helped to shatter was the father of the second. And perhaps that could not have been sustained without the mines of Northumberland and Durham, the fleets of collier brigs, the pitmen, keelmen, steelmen, seamen and engineers of Tyne, Wear and Tees. In the end it was a Northumbrian country gentleman – Sir Edward Grey, the Foreign Secretary, a strange and devious man – who led Bede's England into a Continental quarrel upon Flanders Field, from which she has not yet recovered.

As I turned away from Yeavering Bell I heard the faint blow-lamp roar of a high-flying military patrol – perhaps Englishmen en route for one of those encounters with a Russian 'Bear' or 'Badger' that happen every day over the northern approaches to the island. All round me on the hilltop were the green hummocks, dykes and tracks of a considerable settlement whose inhabitants preceded the English and then vanished.

At the foot of the hill, between the Wooler road and a little stream called Glen, is a small meadow. There at the roadside a curved wall of pink sandstone rubble has been erected. It bears a plaque which reads:

At This Place Was
GEVRIN
Royal Town Of The
Anglo Saxon Kings
Of Northumbria.

Here the missionary Paulinus
in A.D. 627 instructed the
people in Christianity
for thirty-six days.

Here, as Bede told us, stood the palace of King Edwin. And the roots of England?

5

When I resumed my way I saw a road sign. 'Ski-ing is prohibited' it said, and the tarmac shimmered in the heat. Along the road another sign said 'Hold hard hounds – gentlemen please'. The Wat Tyler in me bridled. A little further on another said 'Thank you – forward away!' and I softened at the feudal courtesy. A few miles onward I entered a village with a huge central green and a thatched inn upon the wall of which was the legend – painted in white letters that could be seen from the hilltops miles around – BORDER HOTEL – END OF THE PENNINE WAY. At the other end of the village was a cliff, the abrupt termination of the

Cheviots, and I knew that I had not only wandered into Scotland but had reached Kirk Yetholm, Roxburghshire, and by accident at that.

My miscalculation had not been an uncommon one. The Border does not, as many people think, pass due east to west. It is an irregular frontier that begins far south-west then squirms north-east with many a bend and salient, so that Newcastle in south Northumberland is further north than parts of Scotland. Indeed it is not impossible in these parts to travel north into England and south into Scotland.

I knew about Kirk Yetholm though, and the reason for its vast green. There hundreds of cattle could be grazed overnight in the droving days when huge caravans of living beef were brought from as far away as the Western Isles on their way to English markets. The herds swam rivers and followed drovers' roads – now grass-green and half-forgotten – through a wilderness of hills and were whittled down by rustlers on the way. This traffic, and such villages, were once as vital to the health and wealth of England as the north-east coal trade and the collier ports.

I also knew that Yetholm was once the capital of a tribe of northern gypsies – who believed themselves descended from Egyptians – and was particularly associated with the notorious family Faa which in the eighteenth century bothered the Border from North Sea to Solway. I had read that on the edge of the village there was a small cottage still known as the Gypsy Palace.

In the inn I ordered sandwiches and eavesdropped on a conversation between a Geordie and a Scot wrangling about the merits of their native bagpipes. The Scot said his national pipes made a fine, stirring sound on the hillside . . . 'at a distance' . . . 'but between four walls . . . man, they were a terrible thing'. I knew about the pipes as well. For while the Scotchman's pipes hurl their pibrochs and laments to the wind from a bladder filled by the operator's lungs – with barely time for a sup between blaas – a Northumbrian piper may play a lullaby and sing it all at once. He produces the raw material for his melody from bellows squeezed between arm and ribs. The notes are mellower and more melodious. And although I confess to moments of weakness when the Caledonian pipes stir some primitive current in my part-Scotch blood, I have long been inclined to the more rational sentiment that they are intended as a provocation rather than a means of soothing savage breasts.

The landlord of the Border Inn was a Squadron Leader Townsend, a courteous man with a fine set of Dundreary whiskers, who hearing of my journey introduced me to the customer at my side and said – 'If there was such a thing as a Gypsy King these days, this chap would be wearing a crown.'

The object of this speculation was a sturdy, fair-skinned bricklayer in his sixties wearing a neat, grey suit. His name was Jimmy Blyth. Mr Blyth had received his education in the ways of men with the British Army in India and he spoke quietly about the affinities of the Romany language and the Hindustani he had heard. In a while he talked about his great-grandfather 'King Charles Faa' who, with his consort Queen Esther, was crowned at Yetholm.

'My father,' he said, 'refused the crown and was the first of us to enter a church. He was the beadle for fifty years until he died in the nineteen-forties.'

I asked how much of the Romany tongue he remembered. 'Only a few words now. I once had a big book about it. Had it a long time. Then I was courting a tram conductress in Leith and I lent it to her. We lost touch and I never saw it again.'

I took the road to Carter Bar and thence back into England. I looked at the map and saw such mysterious placenames as Outer Golden Pot, Inner Golden Pot and Gemmals Peth, but at Elsdon (named after a Danish giant called Ella!) I was told they were plumb in the middle of a NATO battle training area and that my inquisitiveness could be settled by a Belgian mortar bomb. However, by way of compensation, I was shown a gallows on a hillside where the body of the last murderer executed publicly in Newcastle had been hung up as a discouragement till the bones fell in the bracken.

A rum lot they were in Elsdon. I was invited to try a stone coffin on for size in the churchyard – and so I did. I was manacled in the handcuffs used to arrest the murderer, Willie Winter. I was told that the skulls of three horses had been found piled pyramidwise in a chamber of the steeple (a pagan dedication?) and that the skeletons of two hundred young and middle-aged men – the skull of each within the thigh-bones of his neigh-bour – had been found packed together during excavation of the church wall. And in the Crown Hotel an ancient man recited me a rhyme which began and ended . . .

> Hae ye ivver been at Elsdon
> The world's unfinished neuk?
> It stands among the hungry hills
> And wears a frozen leuk.
> The Elsdon folk like dying stags
> At ivvery stranger stare.
> And heather broth an' curlew's eggs
> Ye'll get for supper there. . . .

> *Should the Frenchies land in England*
> *Just give them Elsdon fare.*
> *By George! they'll sharply hook it back*
> *And nivvor come nae mair.*

Before nightfall I was in green Tynedale and the sweet but little-known town of Hexham. I would have visited the abbey but the light was failing and all I saw was the statue of some eccentric military man capering on a plinth on the way to the market square. Great clouds had been gathering as I came down from the hills, so although I was close to home again, I camped in a field near the river, meaning to get on with my journey with more despatch.

18

*With brush and dustpan in the clouds of Cumbria I anoint
the silent pilgrims of the Pennine Way, and learn how the
town band marched bootless into the highest market-place
in England.*

1

SWEET HEXHAM stood time-washed in the broad valley. And loiter-
ing in the market-place beneath the Shambles – Abbey at one end,
Moot Hall at the other – I could have been in Rutland's soft southern-
ness, for Hexham gives no hint of the harsh land that lies just beyond
ears-reach of her bells. A few hundred yards along the road, towards the
confluence of the North Tyne and the South, a signpost pointed into a
narrow gap between high garden walls and a screen of trees. 'Alston' it
said, and if I had not known the country, I would easily have missed it
and thus motored on through Haltwhistle and Blenkinsopp to the pink
city of Carlisle. The lane, for it is little more, ascended through a
tree-sheltered suburb of comfortable stone houses, then all at once broke
out on to the moors. It was like surfacing from a deep dream of summer

afternoon and awakening to February. This was Hexhamshire according to the map. And Hexhamshire, unlike Hexham town, is raw.

As I drove along a high, level stretch map-marked as Yellow Rig, I could observe the difference between the two lands from which the Tyne draws life. To right and north the bright undulations of Northumberland across the valley swept far away to the blue Cheviot domes, woods and folds half-hiding half a hundred miles in a multitude of greens – North Tyne country. On my left the south terrain looked dark and featureless and flat, its colours between sombre purple and the dunnest brown, a black and heathery place without a tree.

The road itself veered southwards, and as I travelled on towards the Pennine heart a chimney stack out on the moor – the ruins of a lead mine long abandoned – enhanced the melancholy of the scene. I looked into an empty valley that led into another empty valley, and over a low ridge was yet another, with only half-starved grasses in the bottom beside a trickle of a beck. Yet there are men – and usually they *are* men – who love such country with an emotion almost Slav. They hear a lament in the wind that stirs the surface of the heather. For them the keening of a distant ewe is music, and the rags of tattered cloud that fly across the moor, the sharp, steely showers that come and go in seconds, comfort some obscure region of the soul.

But a mile or so along the road the miniature continent of England played one of those tricks – now you see it: now you don't – that delight the traveller. The road sloped downwards – just a bit at first – a few trees, rowan, hawthorn, ash, and all at once I was on the rim of an emerald valley. I changed down to second, worked hard at the wheel to take hairpin bends, and dropped swiftly through tall, overhanging woods. A hard left turn. A bridge that crossed the brown river Allan, and I was in a small, half-secret land of farms and neat stone cottages, of level meadows, groves and parkland. It was a wooded parkland of that soft sweetness that is found only in the North where streams are fleet, the air is pure and there is no thundering trunk road for miles around. There was a church there with a tall, clean spire, and a smell of woodsmoke. The place was Whitfield.

A curve, another climb, more windbent trees, then wilderness again on either side of the unfenced tarmac ribbon that leads from Tyneside towards the Cumbrian mountains. But first there was Alston.

2

I was sweeping the main stairway of Alston Youth Hostel next morning with a handbrush. It was one of those open stairways and the muck that missed my dustpan fell towards the floor beneath, first on to a damp pile of rucksacks then on to the head of a fellow hosteller who was cleaning out the hallway. He took a couple of paces to the rear and looked up at me with a mournful kind of patience, not even a reproach, an acceptance of whatever life chose to throw at him. After all, he had trudged down from the hills the night before with water running from his hair and down his neck. He had dubbined his boots and dried his trousers in a drying room, and now in a few minutes he'd trudge off into the drizzle again on the next stage of the Pennine Way, and he would probably fetch up that night, unless pneumonia claimed him, at a hostel on the Roman Wall called Once Brewed.

They were an odd lot those hostellers, mostly students by the look of them, and of a ruminative, melancholy kind. Unreddened by wind, apparently unbrownable by sun, they were given to an awkward, self-conscious use of language . . . 'The weather is looking more *human* today . . .' Ron is being the good *Samaritan* . . . he's carrying the sandwiches . . .' They could have been a brood of student curates.

But how did I come to be cleaning a staircase in Alston? Well, it had been almost dark when I reached the town. It was a bit late to look for somewhere to set up camp and I was wondering whether to push on over the last Pennine height and make for the Lancashire plain – for it was raining cats and dogs – when I spotted the familiar triangle sign of the YHA. I had not visited an English youth hostel since one night in 1942 when a friend and I had alone occupied the hostel wing of a near-deserted mansion and had given ourselves such a spooky scare that we took the next bus home, preferring air raids and reconstituted egg to strange noises and empty stomachs.

Tonight, I thought, I'd try again. Perhaps there would be jolly sing-songs with robust young people, an accordion maybe and stories of adventure in high places. I was encouraged by the memory of a night in Lapland when the wine flowed free and half the youth of Europe seemed to be there in the Arctic spring. Somehow or other we all had the gift of tongues and we sang each other's songs as if we'd known them all our lives. Well, it wasn't like that in 1942. Or in Alston either.

To begin with there was a paragraph in the rule book which forbade the use of alcohol on the premises – superfluous precaution, so I thought, for this particular selection of the youth of England looked like teetotallers to a man and woman, and probably vegetarian as well. One of them did speak to me, though. The rain was drumming on the roof and hitting the windows like shovelfuls of gravel. I was cleaning my teeth and I suppose I let the tap run on between rinses. There was this young chap with acne standing at the next basin stealing anxious glances at me. At last he steeled himself to speak, and leaning over, said in a half whisper: 'Excuse me . . . er . . . Nothing personal . . . But . . . er . . . there is a national water shortage, you know.' At this point my natural faith in the future of our country began to falter and my hopes of observing the young of England in lusty relaxation dwindled. They didn't even say much to one another. There wasn't a whistle or a hum between them. So, looking for escape, I remembered that I had half promised a charming assistant headmistress, of whom I'd made some earlier acquaintance, that I would attend a lecture on the archaeology of northern watermills which was to be held in the Primary School under the auspices of the Alston Moor Historical Society. It wasn't really how I'd meant to spend the evening. If I had arrived in November I could have heard a talk on 'The Roman Army as a Career', or in February I could have heard Mrs Bone of Clarghyll Hall speak on 'Witchcraft', which sounded somewhat jollier, but . . .

Considering the population of the parish (1,909), the remarkable weather, and the waywardness of the topography in all three dimensions (blinded by rain, I almost plunged over an unbalustraded terrace, and arrived very late and wet) the event was well attended. A large number of people were seated in a modern hall and the lecturer was a pink-faced young schoolteacher nudging forty. He had size ten shoes and a life mission not only to discover and chart every watermill in Cumbria and neighbouring counties (rather a tall order) but also to record the name of every miller and the yearly grind of every mill. I gather it is not an overcrowded field of study.

Nor is that all. He was apparently impeded in this useful task by an admirable scrupulosity about the law of trespass. He seemed to want formal permission to enter every field and cross every heath, and his energy in obtaining sanction – an area of his work which he explained in detail – can only be described as a revelation. I've never had much trouble crossing a field myself, and have never in my life written an application to do so. If I want to traverse a meadow I just line myself up with a gate or tree on the other side and, barring bulls or crops, start off without confiding my intention to a single soul. I confess it has never occurred to me do otherwise. But that night in Alston I realised I had been leading a life of licence.

However, providence had compensated the watermill seeker, and done so in the matter of his feet. Size ten shoes, he informed us, are exactly one foot long, and thus it was possible for him to heel and toe his way round Cumbria, arriving by footfall at the precise dimensions of the many defunct watermills and kilns which he had recorded in the four learned books with which his name had been associated. I could not help reflecting, as the gale swept across Fiends Fell and beat upon the slates of Alston, what a tragedy it would have been if his interest had been philately or moth collecting. What a waste of feet! And how many size tens there must be in England, I ruminated, idly cocked up on fenders, or uselessly resting on the footrails of all the saloon bars between Land's End and Berwick.

The talk was ended, and coffee was about to be served by the ladies, but there is a limit beyond which hospitality should not be imposed upon. I proceeded to the Blue Bell, and after that got thoroughly soaked as I ran the remaining 150 yards to the hostel.

The dormitory to which I had been assigned was in complete darkness and all the other inmates were in deep and sinless sleep. It was with great difficulty that I shed my clinging clothes, climbed into my top bunk, found the entrance to my sleeping bag and wriggled in with wet feet, without awakening a single curate. And there I lay shivering at half-past ten in the evening, afraid to move in case the bed creaked, missing the privacy of my cosy vehicle, deprived of the hot whisky with which I pamper myself nightly, and recalling one more fascinating fact I'd learned at the monthly meeting of Alston Moor Historical Society – that bracken was once used for making soap. I feel I shall carry that piece of information to my grave.

3

I watched them drift away next morning, singly and in pairs, draped in their nylon shrouds. They didn't sing. They didn't smile. They hardly spoke. They all departed at the same slow plod with their backs piled high and their necks stretched forward, like a migration of huge tortoises. The last man had disappeared before I realised something rather strange. They had all gone in the same direction – north, towards the Roman Wall and Scotland. No one, it seemed was travelling south towards the Peaks. I couldn't account for this strange unanimity, so I asked the assistant warden, an eighteen-year-old from Hartlepool and a keen hosteller himself, to explain. He was very patient with me.

'They'll be going north by Wainwright,' he said.

'Ah, I see. Wainwright,' I nodded wisely.

'Yes. You see, you go north by Wainwright and you come south by Stephenson.'

'Of course. How stupid of me. I should have realised.'

'But most people have Wainwright this year because Stephenson is in short supply.'

So ended my second stay in an English Youth Hostel, and I was leaving more puzzled about the ways of men and women – and certainly about Messrs Stephenson and Wainwright – than when I had arrived. I felt disorientated. That is a state of affairs, however, for which there is, in this blessed land, a well-known cure. It was Jock Bisset the landlord of the Blue Bell who set my feet on *terra firma*, so to speak. He explained that Wainwright and Stephenson were the authors of two guidebooks to the Pennine Walk. To travellers along the roof-ridge of England they were Old and New Testament. It happened that each of them tackled the journey from the opposite end.

'Do you mean to tell me,' I said, my confidence returning, 'that these young fellows are obliged to travel in one direction only . . . just because a book is in short supply. I mean, can't they just . . .'

Jock seemed to anticipate my question. 'Well, it *is* rather difficult to follow,' he said, reaching beneath the counter and fetching out a quaintly printed little cream-coloured booklet whose pages were covered with sketch maps.

'Oh come . . .'

'As a matter of fact,' he continued, 'it is the only book I know this side of China that you have to read backwards. You start at the end and work your way through to the front. Here, look it explains it all in the introduction.'

'I'll take your word for it,' I said, turning my attention to the less sophisticated matter of a plate of Birdseye fish fingers.

4

The belief – particularly widespread in North America – that the English are half strangled by conformity is amusing but untrue and I often wonder how it got about. If there is conformity in England it comes in forty-six million varieties. Each suburban garden, every church and chapel, village, town and tavern protests against the misconception. A traveller who wishes to see conformity should go to Ireland. He should breakfast in Scotland. Or if he has a real appetite for boredom, let him journey up to Sweden! England is the land of Difference and always has been. It is strange that Englishmen themselves don't realise it.

At least half the population of Beckenham (Kent) or Surbiton (Surrey) have no real idea of what life is like in Holloway or Penge, though all four are within Greater London and a bus ride from each other. It would be as fruitless to ask them for an essay on the daily round of Nizhni-Novgorod as to demand an impression of life in a grey stone English town in the northern Pennines where streets have no nameplates and houses no numbers, where a stroll up town requires the same amount of energy as a climb halfway up Box Hill on a bracing day, where there are no supermarkets and the drapery store is heated by a cast-iron stove in the middle of the floor, where pub talk is about real things like sheep or the sighting of red deer, and where you may have to walk outside and climb steps up the front wall to go to bed.

And if you were to tell these good people that there are men and women who actually choose to live in such places, that they abandon semis in convenient suburbs for houses there, and having got the mortgages heave great lungfuls of moist Pennine air and believe they have arrived in the nearest earthly place to Paradise, they wouldn't believe you. I, on the other hand, can barely understand how anyone would willingly live in Beckenham, and most of the population of Alston would share my puzzlement.

If all English towns are different, Alston is more different than them all. Its very appearance confounds likelihood. It snakes up an internal spur of the Pennines, surrounded by even higher hills, when by all the rules of nature it should go slithering down into the peat-brown Tyne. So far is it from garrisons (Carlisle 29 miles, Barnard Castle 32, Newcastle 50), it should have been razed by Scotch marauders centuries ago. But its apparently haphazard construction – all twists and narrow, dog-leg alleyways leading to courts and yards of potted geraniums and front doors built at the back – was actually devised to split up and entrap raiding parties so they could be skewered in small parcels.

The highest market square in England – which is the hub of Alston – is triangular, not square. It also tilts. The corner nearest Barnard Castle is up in the air. The corner nearest to Carlisle is down in the air. Pavements list in different directions to all else. One wonders whether each market stall was built with legs of four different lengths and if potatoes and bolts of cloth set off on their own to deliver themselves from door to door.

The Market Cross (ten stone pillars and a pyramidal roof which, of course, are not situated in the middle of the square) was presented by Sir William Stevenson Kt, who left town in 1764 to become Lord Mayor of London. It was built on a patch belonging to Greenwich – yes, Greenwich – Royal Hospital for Seamen.[*] Until recently all vicars of Alston were retired naval officers, though the present incumbent is a member of Equity and a conjurer.

Places all over England boast about underground passages. No self-

---

[*] Alston was ceded to Greenwich after James Radcliff, Earl of Derwentwater, lost life and lands for leading the English Jacobites of the 1715 Rebellion.

respecting village is without its story of a tunnel from church to monastery or nunnery to inn, and all swear they know someone who knew someone else who saw it before it was blocked by the authorities who don't appreciate a good secret passage when they see one. It's a kind of national obsession – as if once upon a time we all emerged from holes like Hobbits. Nevertheless some of these tales must be true, and Alston beats them all. The deserted hills that almost surround the town rise to nearly 3,000 feet and are the birthplace, within a few miles heathery walk of one another, of the Tees, the Wear and the south branch of the Tyne. Those hills are as riddled with tunnels as a chunk of gruyère. Romans, Germans, Hungarians, Poles, Cornishmen and English have mined them for the last two thousand years for silver, lead, iron, zinc, copper and a whole glittering rainbow of rarer ores, an astonishing collection of which may be seen in the British Museum. Great works of subterranean engineering have been wrought, abandoned, then forgotten beneath the mountainsides. In the first part of the last century Alston Moor was one of the richest mining areas in Britain. Fortunes were made, the population burgeoned. Unlike the coalfields round the lower reaches of Tyne, Wear and Tees where the pits were owned by more ruthless profit-seekers, the mine owners of Alston were Quakers and reformers. They provided welfare centres, medication, schools, churches, decent housing, disablement funds and sick pay before such services were considered a state business or anybody else's. Outside Alston they built Nenthead, a model village with one of the first public libraries in the country. There it stands today at about 1,500 feet with hens clucking in the streets and just a sort of fountain commemorating the departed company.

It is underneath the Nent Valley, however, emerging on the furthest side of Alston, that the finest bit of tunnelling runs. This is an underground *waterway*. It was one of the engineering wonders of the eighteenth century, four and a half miles long and made to bring boatloads of ore down from the mines. Its proper name is Smeaton's Level.* But after the mineral ran out the young people of the town put on their party frocks and blue serge suits, rowed up to a cavern in the mountain, held picnics and dances there, and called it Fanny's Dancing Loft.

I have seen the old exit but the passage is not navigable now. The great days of mining are long past and the population shrunk. Only a few part-time troglodytes know their way through the interior of the fells. I was told there are just a couple of privately owned drift mines employing a

---

* John Smeaton (1742–92) was an innovating engineer from Leeds who became famous by constructing Eddystone Lighthouse and for his work on steam engines, waterwheels and windmills, and his clarification of the laws of mechanics.

few men to win coal for local fires. When I ventured up a track to a farmhouse and asked if I could go down their pit I got a polite refusal.

5

Alston is not just a pretty face, a curiosity to be discovered with delight by the more wayward tourists. There are, for example, two foundries there. They are tucked away. But while you are poking among the humpy little back streets or sunning yourself on a seat near the Market Cross, there is an unceasing bustle and clanking somewhere behind the old archery ground. One of the companies specialises in cast-steel gears, and the other employs a sophisticated process to turn out – among other products – precision-cast golf club heads for some of the greatest players in the world.

And Alston has a long memory. People still talk with respect of 'Mister Macadam' (of tarmacadam fame, 1757–1836) who altered town life dramatically by building the road over Hartside Height towards Lancashire and the Lakes – what they call 'the West Country'. More recently they fought like billy-o to keep the little railway that connected them with Tyneside and the outside world and, for a time, kept even Dr Beeching at arm's length.

I was looking at a large picture on a shop wall – a 'blown-up' photograph of Alstonians in the Market Square dressed in their billycocks and bonnets on the occasion of Victoria's Jubilee in 1897. In front of the town band stood a little long-haired girl in wide sun-bonnet and lacey frock, a lead-miner's daughter called Annie White and ten years old that day.

Now Annie Bramwell (née White) happened to be an old friend of mine, and although she now lived in a pensioners' home and could no longer treat me to tea in her own bright room above the Butts, I went to see her. *Annie on the subject of the Alston lead miners*:

On Monday mornings the men took a week's supply of food on their backs in what they called their wallets. You know what a pillowcase is like – well, the wallet was like a long pillowcase made of callicker and they hooked it over the shoulder and walked five miles to Nenthead along of my father's day . . . They were off to the mine till Friday. They slept in the workshops. Some of them took a joint of meat and ate it till it was finished then lived off rye bread and fried bacon. There'd be a lot of bacon in those days. Everybody kept a pig. It was a great day the pig-killing day in the back yard . . . My father had ten brothers and every one would carry a wallet. All the lads when they left school went onto the washing floors at the mines – washed the lead ore and got the

179

fluorspar out of it. I had a drawer at home with I don't know how many minerals in it, and my father gave lectures on minerals . . . Everybody had a little coffee book when they bought their groceries. The grocer put it all down in the book and waited a month for his money. You were paid by the month then and if you ended up in debt you had to be what you call careful – eh! No bacon and eggs for breakfast then. Everybody got porridge . . . Towards the end of the year they sometimes got a month's lendy money. And when they reckoned up (at the *yearly* pay day) they got a bonus and there was free fights that day and the men got drunk. I've heard my father say that his eldest brother Fenwick was never content unless he had three fights that day. Fenwick put a hole in his manners and he had to flee the district. A woman had a child to him and he went to Penrith and never came back again . . .

I went to see Robin Walton, son of an Alston vicar, former haulage contractor and the best talker in town. Robin's storytelling is an artless art, unimpeded by the disciplines of journalism or broadcasting. A Walton story has many by-ways and may indeed turn into two or three stories for the price of one. *Robin Walton on the subject of the town band:*

> Less than a hundred years ago there were ten thousand people in this valley, and there was a brass band in those days. We still have the instruments. Last time I saw them they were on top of a cabinet in the Town Hall, and those were the instruments used on the particular occasion I'm going to tell you about when the Alston Band went over to Penrith to a festival of bands . . . Well now . . . anything that meant going over the fell tops was like a voyage to America, an adventure.

(Here, in Walton fashion, Robin digressed with a story about two of his relatives who vanished for ever in a snowstorm. And another about an old Nenthead woman who was persuaded to take a horse-drawn church outing across Hartside to Melmerby . . . 'From the moment she left Alston she was in a land of wonder . . . And when she reached the top – Lake District, Westmorland and Galloway Hills in the distance – she looked around. "By Gocks!' . . . she said . . . "By Gocks! . . . Whee [who] would have thowt the waarld was sic a big plyece!"')

> Now it was the same road the band was coming home along . . . *victorious!* . . . from the festival of music, every other house a roadhouse from Langwathby onwards, and they'd had a right skinful by the time they staggered out of the last pub at the far end of Shawhouse Flats in the early hours of the morning . . . Anyhow, I think it was between the Black House and the War Memorial, just coming in to Alston, when somebody who was more or less to their senses, shouted . . . 'Whey! . . . Had on lads!' and everybody was trying to get wocken up and sorted out.

'Get the instruments out!' somebody bellowed.

'What fower?'

'Well ah'll tell tha what. *We won*! An' we'll let the buggers know we won when we get h'yem.'

'What . . . you mean we're ganna start and play . . . *now*?'

'Aye.'

Well they staggered off the gig in a disreputable heap and they were all blowing all sorts of noises till they got the instruments warmed up because everybody was about blue with cold, and they'd just started off again – the gig following behind – when somebody yelled at them to stop again. And there at the Brewery Bridge they all had a tremendous huddle . . . a good discussion, and at the end of the discussion they made various adjustments to their dress and the parade started off again. They tramped away along the Town Foot here, and up to the Town Square where the Boer War regimental parades were held, and the old drums were thump . . . thump . . . thump . . . and they were playing like merry hell. They'd won all right. They were really going at it . . . thawed out . . . thoroughly enjoying it . . . pumping away . . . so of course lights were coming on all over town. People were getting into their overcoats and clogs and gumboots and coming out. There was an awful lot of people standing round and the band stopped for a pause, you see, and somebody that was all eyes and aware of the situation tapped Johnnie Sutherland on the shoulder. He was playing the bugle. This fellow, he says –

'Why . . . what's thou standin' in thee stockin' feet for?' because he'd noticed they all had their boots tied round their necks, you see.

Johnnie says 'Whey . . .', he says, 'like, we thowt . . . tha knows . . . being out that late at neet we thowt we shouldn't mek over much noise . . . an' us tramping in here with hobnail byits this time o' the morning.'

And that is what they'd stopped in a huddle for up by the bridge . . . to tak their byits off.

19

*How the traveller fell among potters in Penrith, trippers at
Kirkstone and campanologists in Kendal and was finally
honoured for his shoes in a pub he can't remember.*

1

ROBIN and I sat long. It would be a pleasure to recount how the
Walton lasses did the lancers in their farm boots at Garrigill, and
why the byre boy went courting with a paraffin lamp, but space is my
master. And as for the tale about the conductor who travelled from Carts
Bog to Whitfield Co-op on the roof of his own bus one wild Christmas
Eve – well, that's one for Alston nights when the pubs are full, the snow
lies deep on Willyshaw Rig and Hexham and Penrith might as well be ten
thousand miles away.

I had to move on. I did not relish another night among the curates. So
I took Mister Macadam's road up Hartside as darkness seeped along the
valley from Shield Water beck. It was about the hour when the hills close
in, watching the intruder with an old intelligence – pagan, impartial,

slightly sardonic. Some people are intimidated by this *presence*. They leave as soon as possible and make for the plains or sea. Others do not sense it. But I think the Romans did. I believe it was to this *genius loci* or guardian spirit that Roman army officers built altars here and there, like the one Gaius Cornelius Peregrinus, officer commanding the 1st Cohort of Spaniards, erected at Maryport in Cumberland just across the plain.

At the summit I pulled off the road on to a flat piece of land where the Helmwind Café used to stand when I was a youth. This is where the Pennines stop. Having rumpled up gradually from the east they reach this line over which they plunge abruptly, and although I knew the scene that lay before me, the night was black as coal and I could just see a few pricks of light down in the Eden Vale.

The Helm Wind – now that is a frightener, I am told. It happens when a cold north-easterly bounces across the Pennines at the weary end of winter and primroses are shining down by the Eden banks. It arrives at this western edge and slams down towards the valley and instead of simply hedge-hopping on towards the Irish Sea, it rises like a colossal wave. The air does a backward somersault, screaming, roaring, tearing at dikes and farmsteads, and people in the plain can tell the Helm Wind is at work by the long, low cylinder of cloud that hangs over the brow of the mountain like a bonnet on the fells.

There was no wind tonight though, and I settled myself with my habitual hot toddy. Here was a fine bedroom and I enjoyed it for a while before deep sleep, awakening next morning inside a cloud. As I prepared food I twiddled with the radio and into my white, confined world came those first five slow and infinitely sad notes of Vaughan Williams's Fantasia on the theme by the Elizabethan Thomas Tallis. The mist dissolved. In came that enchanted little melody played by a viola all alone, then by a violin of elfin lightness, and there beneath me stretching far away was the panorama that has astounded the old woman of Nenthead. By Gocks, what a view for breakfast! And what an overture!

In the distance stood the hills of Galloway – the Merrick Range – where Robert Bruce took sanctuary from the English, where Buchan sent Richard Hannay adventuring and which, as a boy in Scotland, I learned of as 'the Fingers of the Awful Hand'.

To a southerner the names of what, alas, is now called Cumbria may have a northern ring – Keswick and Cockermouth, Scafell and Helvellyn, Buttermere and Patterdale – but they are English just the same. There is, however, an uncompromising, un-English literalness about the nomenclature of the granite walls, secret lochs and quaking bogs of Galloway which is apparent even when the words are from the Norse and Gaelic. *Wolf's Slock. Mullwarcher. Lump of the Eglin. The Cauldron of the*

Dungeon. Clatteringshaws. Loch Nieldricken. The Murder Hole . . . Here is no blending of the vowels in the English fashion, no vanished consonants. They are as hard as hammers. We look across the Solway at the alien peaks and realise that we share the island with another people. Their closeness generates an awareness of our Englishness, and that is rare for Englishmen.

Nearer stood up the big, blue shattered dome of the Lake District mountains just thirty miles away. And almost immediately below lay the broad and lovely Vale of Eden, its river dawdling north towards the Solway. It is so aptly named with its tangle of green lanes and small red-sandstone villages, its woods, meadows, parks and old stone towns like Kirkby Stephen and Appleby (place of the apple tree). If a man from Appleby were to be asked in Baghdad or Seattle where he hailed from he would be justified in saying that he came from Eden and that Eden was in England.

Looking down into that small, green land it was galling to remember that other Englishmen would like to spoil it or cancel its identity. Some years ago a coven of businessmen brewed up a scheme to build a leisure centre on the slopes. Actually, they called it a 'leisure and amenity complex'. They would! There was to be a casino, a disco and a marina among other things, to attract the prosperous, urban, rootless of the north. I'm told local government planners and officials were enthusiastic. But the farmers weren't. It is said that they prepared for sabotage – the real rough stuff. Before it got to that, though, the plan was dropped.

The worst indignity, however, was the one they shared with Rutland, Huntingdonshire and half a dozen other ancient counties. The chaps at Whitehall bundled up Westmorland, Cumberland and a hunk of Lancashire forty miles away across England's highest mountains, for no reason that anyone can now defend. They called it Cumbria. After a bit of a dustup, Appleby – population 2,020, the dearest little county town in England, 800 years old and with its own assizes too – was permitted to call itself 'Appleby-in-Westmorland' with no Westmorland to be in. 'Retain your Loyalty – Preserve your Rights' says the motto outside the Norman Castle. Against a brigade of ambitious bureaucrats and politicians with a theory in their heads? Some hope!

Well, it was no good standing before that masterpiece of land and sky with my blood at boiling point. Down the Hartside face I sailed in the autumn sunshine, brakes, clutch and gears doing overtime. It was now past noon. The tawny Pennine flanks caught the southern sun and, looking backwards from the valley, I saw Cross Fell (2,893 feet), ribbed and coloured like a lion. Someone told me that it was so named because St Patrick – a Briton, not an Irishman, by the way – had erected a great crucifix up there and driven all the demons from Fiends Fell: and furthermore that fifty brass bands humped their instruments to the summit in 1832 to celebrate the Great Reform Bill.

Gamblesby and Melmerby were at bright perfection with squadrons of farmyard geese out on patrol up and down the roadway. And ah, the greens – the humpy, hillocky, hoppity greens! It was like the illustrations of an old children's story book depicting an ideal world safe for geese and men.

I came eventually to Penrith (population 11,300) which I had always thought of as a bed-and-breakfast halt five miles from Lakeland. It solicits passing tourists with a hatful of historic novelties – 'the Giant's Thumb' (a tall stone in the churchyard), 'the Giant's Grave' (possibly a communal burial place), 'the Plague Stone' (a squared boulder hollowed like a dish for disinfecting coin), the stump of an old fortress, and a guidebook which speaks of a charming 'blend of old and new'.

One may feel affection for such tarradiddle but in fact Penrith is a not particularly handsome red-sandstone town on the A6, which road was – until the construction of the M6 – the main west-side route between Scotland and the South. It is 280 miles from London and 10 miles north of Shap, and Shap Fell is to winter drivers what the Goodwins are to mariners. Penrith is also the terminus of the A686 from Tyneside which had just tumbled me from the Pennines. The border is less than an hour's drive away – between Carlisle and Gretna – and to the west, roads that begin at Penrith seek out the entrances to Lakeland. All that makes it not only a decent, hard-working, shrewd-trading market town with sound, un-tarted Georgian and Victorian shops – the sort of place where hill farmers and the working gentry go to buy their britches – but standing at the meeting place of several distinct regions it is a storm-port for long-distance travellers, a frontier town.

Frontier people are hard-headed. They do not embrace you at first sight. They are wary. And as Penrith is also an important post on the uncharted network of the 'travelling people' it is a horse-trading town. A smart turnout with two high-steppers in the shafts attracts no more attention in the market-place than the passing of a pretty girl. And just north of town there is a large camp where the 'travellers' (gypsies, tinklers, diddicoys – they are called 'potters' here) park their caravans. The Grey Bull is their 'local' and it was in the backyard of this inn that this particular travelling man set up headquarters for a few days.

Coming upon the Grey Bull was good luck. As a pub it looked nothing special but its patrons were of a special grain. And so was Alex McIntosh the landlord, former professional footballer and a quiet man with a quiet sense of humour who appointed himself my guide, guardian and interpreter. Conversations that would have sounded strange in Newcastle or Carlisle – let alone Staines or Slough – batted no eyelids among the potters in the Bull. They are most often about long-distance lorry-driving, horse-trading, stupendous sprees, or fabled deals concluded in 'ponies', 'monkeys' and 'grands'.

> 'I took a truck down to Penzance last week, and I couldn't believe the colour of the sea. It was *blue*! As blue as that puckit [bucket] . . .'

> 'One Sunday morning a brand-new Rolls was delivered at his caravan . . . gold plated headlight rims. He's only twenty-three, the lad, and all he sells is hosepipes . . .

> 'Immaculate, he is . . . wears a white suit sometimes . . . went to Gretna with these two locals on the dole. Got £650 for the deal . . .

The potters had a special kind of generosity – masculine, yet almost childlike in its sheer, undemanding, bloody sweetness that you meet more often among northerners (especially Geordies) and Americans than among the southern English. A man in the Grey Bull, noticing me fumbling for the last scraps in my tobacco pouch, slipped out and returned with two ounces of the best, sliding it along the counter to me without a word.

If I had not met Alex McIntosh I don't suppose I would have lingered in Penrith and the Eden Valley. In which case I would not have met Geordie Bowman, scrap and carpet dealer, non-smoker, non-drinker, carriage-and-four racer, said to be on warm terms with the Duke of Edinburgh. Nor would I have gone to see 'Shocker' Bowman (no relation), or met Warren Bruce (whose father used to run the Manchester Ship Canal) or 'Black Tom' Jackson, Andy Barnes, Colin Prince, Bobby Lee, Frank, Wally, Harry or Billy Morrison – which would have been a pity. For they – and not the Giant's Thumb – are the essence of Penrith. The Eden Valley is unique. Even the shepherds, solid men and far from other-worldly, count their sheep in some enchanted language. 'Yan, tyan, tethera . . .' they say, instead of one, two, three.*

I stayed three days and camped behind the Bull. As I left the front bar on the final morning I heard one of the potters say – 'He came in like a gentleman . . . and he's going out like a gentleman . . . so good luck to him.'

---

* Yan, tyan, tethera, methera, pimp, sethera, lethera, hevera, davera, dick (10) – yan-a-dick, tyan-a-dick, teth-a-dick, meth-a-dick, bumfit (15) – yan-a-bumfit, tyan-a-bumfit etc. Pronunciation varies from valley to valley. I was told that some North American Indians use a similar counting system, presumably introduced by early settlers.

I was not completely sure what he meant. It sounded more like a remark from a character in a Jeffrey Farnol novel than words spoken in the 1970s. But that's Penrith.

2

Someone in the Grey Bull had said – 'Penrith is not a kick in the arse from the Lake District.' Geographically he was correct but Penrith feels like a town on a plain at the foot of the Pennines and there is no sense of proximity at all to the great geological upheaval down the road.

You set off in a south-westerly direction along the B5320 which ducks under the Glasgow–London railway line then runs alongside the little river Eamont in fairly gentle country. Then, when you have driven about five miles – bam! – there she is. You are standing by a little pier at the bottom end of Ullswater. The long, fjord-like lake winds away in front of you until it disappears round the prominence of Kailpot Crag. On the north shore to your right – where the A592 skirts the water on its way to Patterdale and the mountains' heart – there are headlong woods and denes. And on the south side the steeps come down like thunder, ledge over ledge, crag over treeless crag, plunging into dark water that looks bottomless. The colours of the world have changed – from Eden's light-hearted civvy greens to the lowering hues and bracken-red flashes of the Black Watch and Rifle Brigade. The land from which you have just emerged was shaped, coloured and laid out by man. Here the old earth dominates. Out beyond there are grim screes and striding edges like gigantic saws, valleys riven by fire and ice, and lonely tarns. England, though marvellously varied is by-and-large such a mild-tempered land, its scenery so obviously the work of husbandmen and builders that we do not go about questioning geology. But here one is bound to ask why Nature took to foreign ways and made this knot of violence, so alien that we have no decent name for it. 'The Lake District' – that is a name that could have been thought up in a council planning office, and 'Lakeland' was surely invented for the travel poster.

We are told in books full of forgetables like 'Ordovician', 'Permian', and 'Miocene' that 500 million years ago the land slept under mud beneath a shallow sea. Then it was buried below two miles of volcanic ash and lava. Then it was buckled into mountains by some subterranean cataclysm. Then sea again – warm and full of coral. Then marsh, a place of giant ferns. More mountains which were worn down to arid desert. And then the last great shudder of the earth that raised a dome, the eroded crest of which is now called Scafell. Ice, frost and water did the

187

rest, tearing and splitting, glaciers gouging out the U-shaped valleys, new lakes radiating from the decaying crown-like fissures in an upturned bowl struck from above. The place is still haunted by the awesome drama. But the story was not over yet. Enter Man, a mere five thousand years ago.

Inquisitive, inventive Man made short work of the forests that then clothed the mountains for 2,000 feet. Charcoal-burners, bobbin-makers, ship-builders, house-constructors, stole the woodland. And on the heights Man's sheep would not let a seedling grow. The hills were shaven of the wildwoods. And now the levels of the lakes are governed by the thirsts of factories many miles away. And armies fill the valleys in their cars and coaches. And the slopes of Windermere echo with the snarl of speedboats.

It was late afternoon when I arrived. Rain mist spilled from precipices like cataracts in slow motion. The grass was soaked. Trees at Ullswater's edge were a lacy froth of reds and browns. The hardiest of remaining visitors were buying rainproof nylon trousers in blues and scarlets in the shop at Pooley Bridge. Pale clerks and teachertypes encased their un-accustomed legs in knickerbockers, put deerstalkers on their heads and walked about wet lanes swinging knobbly sticks, as if they had been countrymen for years.

I chose the wilder, steeper, south side of the lake where the roads peter out in sharp defiles. I drank cheerfully in the Sun at Pooley Bridge and felt my way homewards through hedge and over dike in the sweet-smelling autumn darkness. Along by a spinney that ran with a little sandy shore there was a field in which for years had rested, propped up on the grass, one of those steam pleasure craft that used to ply the seven miles between Pooley Bridge and Patterdale when hats were broad and full of flowers, awnings fluttered and brass shone bright on blazer buttons and deck fittings. I think her boilers had blown up. She had been called the *Lady of the Lake.* Close by I'd made my camp.

There were lights on the further shore, and there was a soft wind in the trees which brought more rain. The big drops spattered on the old hull and deck. Occasionally I wakened to the sound of wavelets lapping on the beach.

3

The coaches from Huddersfield and Manchester skip along the sunlit edge of Ullswater, passing from alpine meadow to green woodshade.

* Since my visit the vessel has been salvaged, refitted, and now carries passengers again.

After Patterdale they begin to climb. Grey drystone walls divide the lower slopes into treeless, cropless fields then soar off into the wilderness and one wonders what sort of men accomplished such gigantic labour and for what earthly reason. Khyber-like slopes close in on either side. Scars lean as if to topple down and block the road. The engines slave. Mist weeps down from screes and drips from dykes. It gathers in great, wet, writhing waves and slowly tumbles, ledge by ledge, till it meets the floor and spreads along the roadside, fingering the windows of the little inn. The trippers step down – Raven Edge above on one side, Raven Crag on the other. They pull at the collars of thin anoraks. They bring out woollen cardigans. They look round and upward at the heights and scurry across the gleaming tarmac to the lights of the low stone building and order hot pies and pasties as if it were November. It is always November here. At least I've never seen it otherwise.

I am standing at the little bar of the Kirkstone Pass Inn built in 1810 by the Troutbeck vicar as a shelter for wayfarers. It is 1,480 feet above Blackpool Beach or Whitley Bay or Scarborough. 'And a bit higher if you go up to the loo,' says the barman. The ceiling is low and the main joist is supported by a tree trunk which still has its rough bark. It is warm. You can smell the pies. A Broadwood upright stands against the pillar – about 1905 to judge by carving. The wireless is tuned to Radio 3. 'A little bit of Handel,' sayd the barman, a young Irishman called Trevor, harried by orders from a new coachload. He has a beard and wears a denim smock.

'What's the National Front?' asks a big, red-faced man who claims he used to be a councillor. 'Fascists!' he replies to himself. 'And fascists are national socialists. This government is national socialist.' He has a November drip on the end of his large nose which he buries in his pint and wanders away sadly.

'P-a-a-a-int ur T-a-a-a-rtan Bittur,' says a long-faced, slow-talking Lancastrian, peering for pennies in a little leather purse. 'No-o-o-o. Ah've changed me ma-a-a-aind. Ah'll 'ave an Exp-oo-oo-rt.'

'When people start talking about coloureds and Indians,' says Trevor, 'I say I'm thankful for them. They kicked us off the bottom of the ladder – us Irish. We're up a rung or two. Everybody's got their prejudices though. There's not many coloureds up here. Nor many Irish either. So it's off-comers they don't like in these parts. The new people who come in and buy cottages.'

The red-faced man comes back. He tells me, for no apparent reason, 'It was a great place for highwaymen up here . . . just look at the prison records in Carlisle,' then wanders off again.

'S'mow gripefroo,' demands a cockney. Trevor pours him another grapefruit, and continues – 'Yes, it's a good place to watch people,

English people. July, August . . . ask anyone round here. That's the time when you get everything nicked. Anything that's portable. It's a national pastime – nicking glasses and ashtrays.'

'Half a lager with a straw,' demands an old lady about five feet tall.

'Straw with a lager? You get drunk quicker that way, love, I'm telling you, you get drunk quicker.'

'You leave that to me!' she snaps, and tappety-tappets away.

Trevor grins affectionately. 'Later in the year,' he resumes, 'we get the brass-and-bullshit brigade. They tend to be southern. There must be something in the air down there that breeds them. More bullshit than brain!'

The old woman's place is taken by a man in a bright orange singlet with blue piping round the armholes and a big showy watchstrap. He keeps his arms tightly folded to show off his biceps but he is thin, his skin corpse-white. He sounds Bradford. 'Shandeh!' he demands.

'Thee 'alf, please!' (Yorks. again).

'Gohnee ginj woin? . . . Glass ginj woin!' (Girl from Brum).

Trevor, surprisingly, knows where the ginger wine is.

'Wite a minit, Doris.' (Cockney).

'Royat!' replies her girl friend.

'When I came back from the war I was a bit of a hero,' says the man with the nose-drip, appearing at my side again.

'Why?'

'Because I was recognised as a Field Marshal in the Indian Army.'

'What were you in the British Army then?'

'A private soldier . . . Well, you see, I was in hospital when the Japs broke through. I took about twelve million chaps out through Siam.'

'Twelve *million?*'

'Twelve million! . . . And they discharged me as a private soldier. That was in Mountbatten's army . . .'

He puts his glass down. 'I'm *walking*,' he says. 'I'm not with the bus. I'm walking and studying the system.' He makes for the door unsteadily, bounces each shoulder of the lintels, steadies, then disappears into the November gloom.

It is three o'clock when I get down to Windermere. The sun is shining.

4

When I was young the Lake District was where school teachers went *hiking*. Well, not only school teachers but all the nice posh people of their kind in tweed sports jackets from the industrial north-east who pressed flowers, chipped stones with little hammers and liked Wordsworth. I liked *them*. Perhaps I even envied them a little, though their damned agreeability got up my nose. They all agreed on everything – from the temperature of a cup of tea to the view from Helvellyn. There was not a rebel among them – someone who, just for the hell of it, would challenge their earnest views on pacifism, Franco, cake doileys, cub mistresses, or whatever else they talked about on the healthy tramps. And as for their Wordsworth – 'Daffodils' was quite the soppiest poem I'd had drummed into me outside Sunday School. 'Jocund company', indeed!

Now, alas, they are but a few bands of ageing stragglers, the courteous and perhaps sadder little parties who say 'Good morning – lovely morning!' on the less frequented by-roads. They have been swamped by the democracy they dreamed about. And the new people, the inheritors, who come in their coaches and Cortinas – do they actually see the Lake District through their steamy windows? A jolly time they're having on the move and in a crowd, and there's not much wrong with that. But they might as well be somewhere else. They are like a great tidal wave that sweeps across Cumbria in the spring, retreating in the autumn, leaving behind their cash and empty beer cans.

I turned back at Windermere. I never did get on with the Lake District – still less teashop towns. The whole place denies me that intimate relationship with men past and present that other parts of England so freely offer. Old money was once made here – from minerals, from timber and from wool – but it was hustled off by absentee capitalists, leaving little mark behind. Where are the wool churches, the great houses, the handsome little manors? Where are the marks of toil? Here I yearn for a colliery headstock, an abandoned tin-mine engine house, a great woollen mill. There are only those endless drystone walls climbing up the steep hill faces, dividing one wilderness from another, so remote from our way of equating work with cost that they could have been built by alien creatures.

So early one morning I drove over Shap to Kendal, taking the M6 until the turn-off at Junction 37. Rain had begun at Penrith and it was the real stuff – a blinder. That was a pity because the M6 is my favourite motorway and the Cumbrian section is spectacular when visible. It sails through limestone country with an arrogance that infects the driver. Purring along between the mountains one can forgive the motoring age for many of its sins.

It was the A6 that lowered me into Kendal. The change of altitude made no difference to the rain. Water hammered the slates of the dark old town. It made oceans and archipelagos in the cobbled weaving yards that run off the grey main streets. It swept along Stricklandgate in translucent curtains slapping the faces of cheerful shoppers, trickling down necks and into carrier bags, sluicing eighteenth-century shop windows, enfeebling their electric lights and making distorted spectres of the twentieth-century goods within. At the foot of Stramongate, by courtesy of the river Kent, it came charging down from the distant, treeless wastes of Bleathwaite and Gavel Crags and, seeming to take leave of all sobriety on encountering its first town, hurled itself at piers and arches as if it would hurry the old bridge to some watery carnival ten miles away in Morecambe Bay.

There are guidebooks that put Kendal in the Lake District and people who think of it as another Penrith. Nonsense! The eight miles that separate it from Windermere – and the twenty-seven from Penrith – might as well be eight hundred. The Lake mountains generate rain, Penrith endures it, Kendal celebrates it.

Here – and all at once – is a warmth and animation that was nourished for six hundred years by the water-driven wool trade. Here is confidence, a town that knows itself, what it has done, what it still can do. Its motto is *Pannus mihi panis* – wool is my bread. To which could well have been added 'stockings are my butter' for as late as 1801, 2,400 pairs of knitted stockings passed through Kendal market every week.

Here is a town (present population 22,000) which, after Bradford filched its first livelihood and the British Army donned short socks, turned its industrious hands to making shoes (now its biggest industry), to dry-salting and insurance, to grinding snuff by water power, to making pipe tobacco ('only the finest dark leaf'), to building organs and tuning pianos and to manufacturing tweeds, rugs, blankets, carpets, rope, beer, water-turbines and half a dozen other products that minister to the comfort and sanity of the human race. There is also a confection known as Kendal Mintcake ('double-wrapped for freshness') which, though not to my own taste, is so fixed in the affections of climbers and explorers (it is said to sustain without creating thirst) that it has been consumed in such unlikely places as Everest (c/o Hunt) and the Antarctic (c/o Shackleton).

Kendal also produced Catherine Parr, the blue-stocking who buried three husbands the last of whom was Henry VIII. Its inhabitants have included Ephraim Chambers the great encyclopaedist; John Dalton, described in *Chamber's Encyclopaedia* as 'the greatest chemist that any country has produced'; Sir Arthur Eddington who contributed to Einstein's Theory of Relativity; and two men[*] whose names few remember but who probably did more for England's fortune by inventing machines

[*] William Pennington and Dover Bayliff.

for wool-carding (thus ousting teasels) than their better-known contemporary George Romney, portrait painter, about whom Chamber's says 'in 1798 he returned to Kendal where he became insane and died'.

The miracle is not only that so small, remote, landlocked and often-drenched a town has produced such multifarious activity (even its music festivals and art collection are renowned) but that it has done so with such grace. Its mountain limestone streets are handsome without too much refinement, its buildings pleasing without pomposity, its manufactories – but for an ill-sited gasworks and an insurance building – all congenial. After the brooding beauties of the Lakes and the austere northern fells it was like arriving in a small bustling capital.

I sloshed round the dripping streets and running lanes of Kendal with good cheer. There are, of course, no longer fifty inns – long-distance packhorse customers having vanished with the wool trade. But I warmed myself in the Fleece (1654), admired the Angel with its roof-top pigeon-cote (the better to provide pidgeon pie for hungry merchants), the Queens, the Globe, the Woolpack and the Victorian-classical Kendal, and finally I ate an excellent lasagne for second breakfast in a fragrant little restaurant called Franco's. After which I paddled against the stream up Sepulchre Lane where I could look across the glistening roofs and observe the unusual structure of the town – a spine from which long, narrow yards, former workshops of numerous small industries, branch off at right-angles.

The yards *are* Kendal. They and the rain and the river are my picture of the place. But my memory of that particular day engages two other senses – hearing and smell. Wherever I walked – even by the bawling Kent down along Goose Holme where they used to hang the wool out to dry on *tenterhooks* – I was surrounded by the sound of bells. The clamour came across the rooftops and round every corner of each alleyway. Sometimes it arrived in a crash of notes, as if some gigantic pile of platters had been tumbled in the sky, and at other times it was that heavenly cascade of slightly imperfect timing that in England has been brought closer to an art than in any other country.* I suppose my perambulation took several hours. The concert never stopped. It was not Sunday. Or any other

---

* Before 1600 bells were hung on a simple spindle but around the turn of the century each was mounted with a large wooden wheel round the rim of which the bell-rope hung. This device – peculiar to England – permitted greater control and facilitated the innovation of 'change ringing' in which the order of ringing may be altered. John Camp, in *The Countryman*, Autumn 1980, writes that it is possible to ring six bells in 720 ways before having to repeat a sequence. 'With eight bells the maximum permutations are 40,320 and with ten or twelve the possible changes run into millions.' The changes possible on seven bells – 5,040 – is called a full peal and takes over three hours to ring.

holiday that I could think of. What was the celebration?

As for the smell . . . Many travellers have remarked that countries, cities, even some towns and villages, have a distinctive odour. I had been in Kendal several hours before I realised that the damp streets were haunted by a certain fragrance that vanished almost as soon as it became perceptible, returning only once more to elude identification. It was pleasant – neither cosmetic nor comestible. Not cigarettes. Not incense. What was it?

Pursued by bells and smells I found myself in Kendal's covered market. I have mentioned more than once my contention that the worth and texture of a place may be measured by its bookshops, as a person may be assessed by his bookshelves. Kendal had an interesting little bookshop down by the river but I dripped rain on the pages so I left. I can now assert that a town that can support a decent cheese shop is also a town to be reckoned with. A cheeseless town may be dismissed with publess, churchless and bookless towns. Kendal covered market was warm and cheerful though steamy with wet raincoats. And beyond the banks of asters and chrysanthemums, and stalls brilliant with fat peppers, red and green, tomatoes, cabbages and oranges, and tables laden with such delicacies as marrow-and-ginger jam (26p), home-made marmalade (25p) and home-made pickled onions, there were two separate pavilions that simply creaked and reeked with cheeses. Outside Paxton & Whitfield's, that Aladdin's cave in Jermyn Street, London, I had never seen such a magnificent collection. In delight I walked from one stall to another and back again. There were grand, old familiar cheeses big as millstones and there were exotic strangers marbled green or brown like Victorian washstands. There was Double Gloucester and Baby Wensleydale, and red Cheshire the size of a foundation stone, something hand-labelled 'Gorgon Zola', and Derby and Mycella and Camembert and Petit Gruyère and Havarti and Reblochon and Jarlsberg and Almond-and-Walnut Cream Cheese, Red Windsor, Cotswold, something from Cumberland laced with rum and butter, heart-shaped Neufchatel, soft, undulating Brie and goaty St Benoit – and the sound of distant bells and that mysterious fragrance – and, ah, the Blue Stilton! 'Do you want to try some . . . goo on!' said a cheery acolyte called Peter Gott extending towards me a broad-bladed knife on which sat a succulent green fragment containing walnut. Who bought all this god-like food, I wondered, looking round. 'Can I 'ave some strong Lancashire?' said a small old lady with a plastic carrier bag from Benidorm. 'By all means, love.'

I bought Cheddar for the van and went out into the rain again with the taste of Stilton in my teeth. I strolled down Stricklandgate to where the road leaves town for the high moors, for Kirkby Lonsdale, Giggleswick and Leeds. And there in the damp and misty air I found my wool church standing back in pride with great double aisles and a square tower embedded in the western end and the ten bells of Kendal going hell for leather and half the campanologists of the northern counties queuing for a turn and the other half calling in at a small pub called the Ring O' Bells on account, said a man called Dick, of one of our ringers has just died. What a way to go to heaven! And what a church – Early English to Victorian, 103 feet wide, 140 feet long, 32 nave pillars holding up the near-perfect rectangle where someone counted a congregation of 1,260 in the year 1831.

In the Ring O' Bells Dick sat drinking below one of those framed cartoons with which the nineteenth-century brewers fought the teetotal industry:

> *Temperance Gentleman* – 'Tom Timkins, if you continue like this there is only weeping and gnashing of teeth in store for you.'
> *The Incorrigible* – 'Ain't (hic) gor a tooth (hic) in me 'ead.'
> *T.G.* – 'My friend – teeth will be provided.'

The room was small. The fire glowed darkly. Rain bleared the windows and every time the door opened a gust of bells came in. The subject was Kendal.

' "The Old Grey Town", that's what Lord Haw-Haw used to call it during the war . . . "We will bomb the Old Grey Town" he used to say. But did they? Did they buggery! The buggers couldn't see it. It was always covered with cloud and fog.'

5

I cannot recall in which neighbouring village it was that I ran the Kendal scent to earth. The night was black and I wearing my new walking brogues. I remember that.

If the weather had been drier and it had not been the weekend I would have spent a day or two more in Kendal. I had asked why such a small inland town had three separate tobacco and snuff companies, an activity more suited to one of the old slave-trading ports like Liverpool and Bristol. I was told that when the wool trade failed the town still had commercial connections with North America and the West Indies to which it had exported cloth. It was before the railway boom. There was spare capital about. So Kendal imported baccy from its former customers and used its water power to turn the wheels and grind the snuff – as it still does. I would like to have watched that process. Snuff-taking has been an intermittent vice of mine and I like old machinery but, of course, the factories were closed. So I set out with my windscreen wipers working hard but no idea where to stay that night and no inclination to squelch round fields and farmyards looking for a berth.

At a crossroads I called in at a recently refurbished Georgian pub, but it was full of young-farmer sort of chaps with their little butterflies in best party frocks drinking Babycham. I didn't think they would have much sympathy for a bedraggled itinerant looking for a kipping place so I drank half a pint of gaseous keg and moved on. A mile or so further my lights picked out a notice board and for the first time since Dover I entered a camping site, paid my few bob to the surprised owner, bounced down a slope and slotted my car between a couple of deserted caravans. I cooked a snack and tried to settle down with a book and a Scotch but the van trembled in the squalls, the rain dinned on the roof and even the dear old BBC offered me bleak comfort. Sad stuff about our economic peril and news of worse to come. The ship of state was foundering. England was waterlogged. There was nothing around me but the sound of flooding scuppers. I needed company. So I put on my rainproof cap, took my torch and set out into the night, which was like walking face-first into a sheet of saturated bombazine.

I was blinded by the storm and could only tell I was climbing up a hill by the effort it demanded. But at last I arrived in a village on a ridge. There was a lighted pub. I could hear the murmur of many voices. Saturday night! I pushed in and it was jammed with men and women sitting at tables along corridor-like rooms. Someone edged up to make a seat for me and asked about the weather as if they didn't know – and they hailed each other and they hailed the barman – and I could smell the strange fragrance of the Kendal streets – and someone asked me if I'd mind taking one of my shoes off – and it was passed around and talked about and nodded over – and passed back – and asked for once again to show to Bill or Joe who'd just come in. Here was no sinking ship!

All through the scorching summer I had walked in fields barefoot or worn some old sandals till they fell apart. The change of terrain and season, climbing dykes and scrambling through wet bracken, had practically dismembered my neglected walking shoes. And so in Penrith I had re-equipped myself with as fine a pair of barges as I had ever owned, with handsome scrollwork on the bows, lined with soft leather and tight as a man-o'-war. They were built by Trickers, a noble name in footwear. And while I had grown unconscious of them on my feet, this was one of the few pubs in England where they would be spotted. Many of the patrons worked at the K-shoe factory in Kendal. Their conversations were as laced with talk of lasts and leather as my Lancashire parents talked of weft and warp and shuttles.

Having been thus honoured for my shoes I got talking with my neighbours about Kendal. When I reached for my pipe someone threw before me on to the table a dark cylindrical object a little thinner than a chipolata and I was invited to help myself. The truth is that I did not quite know *how* to help myself, so I was then instructed in the art of slicing, rubbing and packing Kendal dark brown twist. I did not make much of a hand at it. But I had located and identified the fragrance of the Old Grey Town.

20

In search of a lost childhood in the city of a hundred thousand spindles, the wayfarer finds a mosque.

1

ANOTHER DAYBREAK. The distant barking of a dog across a valley sprinkled with wan lights. Blurred rows of houses down below. Abandoned cotton mills. Small engineering works and tradesmen's yards clanking and bumping into wakefulness. The worn-out moorland rising up beyond, not yet quite emerged from night, and presently the forlorn summons of a factory hooter. The air not cold, not dry, not warm – a tepid palpability of unseen droplets.

Somewhere the day before I had crossed the border out of what had been Westmorland, travelling aimlessly in gloom. Once, high up, I blundered into Yorkshire and turned about. There was some greasy shepherds pie in a dingy pub. Mist. And then in early darkness, down a

198

steep unmetalled lane, I had come to a caravan site perched on a hillside above a small, anonymous, decaying town.

Now in the grey morning light I looked round at the little suburb of aluminium boxes and brightly curtained windows. Neat pathways in immaculate repair led among ornamental bushes from plot to plot. Each non-mobile vehicle had its square of short-cropped lawn, its bed of late autumn flowers, its bright enamelled door – each caravan a small gesture of fleeting permanence, cherished, tended, determinedly respectable, aligned so that its big picture window framed an oblong of exhausted countryside. A kettle sighed gently through its whistle on a Calor stove. Feet bumped on chipboard floors through thin nylon carpet. A figure in a quilted nylon dressing gown jerked aside nylon curtains on nylon runners.

Why? Why had they come up here with their life savings, their pension money and their perennials, only a few hundred feet above their hard-won yesterdays? Why not Devon, the Peaks or even Blackpool?

Well, I was born in Lancashire. At 21 Hollin Street, Blackburn, to be exact. Father, mother, aunts had all worked in the mills. My paternal, ancestors, like so many others, must have abandoned their cottage looms and tramped down moorland paths in peasant clogs to seek survival in the great new textile factories, thus altering the history of the world. And when I was born Blackburn was still queen of the weaving trade though already past her best. Fifty years before there had been 100,000 spindles in the town, one for every man, woman and child. But in 1927 mills were closing, looms rusting, and it was said that former cotton magnates were picking fag-ends from the gutters. The population was declining too – a condition my birth did nothing to relieve as my parents emigrated to Wearside, finding idle shipyards, half-time pits.

There were family visits in the thirties. Aunts and uncles came and clucked at my north-east pronunciation, asking me to repeat words and phrases as if my father had acquired some strange ingenious toy on his foreign travels. And I secretly imitated the Lancashire burr that sounds so gormless* on the stage ('Sam – pick up thy muskit!') or indeed anywhere away from the hills and mills where it seems natural and right.

I marked how Lancashire women bared their teeth and stretched their lips in speech as if chewing every vowel, determined to get full value from each word. It was just the women, the men being poker-paced and slow in conversation like Lancashire comedians. Years later I heard it was a

* Gormless (or gaumless) – a beautifully expressive word heard mostly in Lancashire, meaning roughly 'daft' or 'foolish' and based on the lost word 'gaum' meaning 'understanding'.

habit developed in the weaving sheds where the noise of machinery was so deafening that unconscious lip-reading was practised. Young girls who have never been inside a cotton mill do it to this day.

Another mystery of speech was the apparent inability of both sexes to differentiate between the 't' sound and the 'k' before the letter 'l'. No – that is too simple. They differentiated all right, but got it the wrong way about with a consistency that drove me to exasperation.

'Say kettle,' I would order my young cousins.

'Keckle,' they would reply.

'Say pickle.' 'Pittle.' Even their elders talked about a jar of 'pittles'.

'Say freckle.' 'Frettle.'

As I grew to boyhood I was still haunted by cotton-Lancashire, drawn back there by its melancholy, inexplicably attracted, like the retired caravanners who remained anchored to their past.

I remember long school holidays in Blackburn when, like the descendants of the cotton slaves in *Roots*, I heard family legends. And sometimes left to my own devices, I went mooning along eighteenth-century canal banks trying to imagine the Augustan days filled with bales and barges. I liked the great ship-like mills with their rows upon mounting rows of windows, devouring aunts for eight hours of every day. And always between the dark, brown chimney stacks there were glimpses of the moors – the moors from which the millworkers had emerged long since but which they never could forget. Courting, walking with their families at Easter and midsummer, even preaching and hymn-singing, they would go back to the moors – from the Whilpshire tram stop to Whalley and up Pendle Hill. The moors were their blessing.

How different these kin were to my volatile Tyne-and-Wear-siders who seemed to have expunged all rural memory and become a town-thinking proletariat. And how different their reaction to misfortune. Priestley, a seasoned observer in the 1930s when he made his 'English Journey', was surely comparing Lancashire with the north-east when he remarked: 'these Lancashire towns . . . have not the derelict look . . . the streets are not filled with men dismally loafing . . . You do not see abandoned shops down every street.'

In adversity the Geordies blamed 'them-down-there'. They resented the South and scorned the middle classes for insensitivity. They believed they had been badly used, that England owed them recompense and must be made to see it. Their anger – long simmering in the pits, fuelled by the arrogance of coal-owners and brought to flashpoint by firedamp – produced a fighting comradeship that still survives.

Priestley was right. The atmosphere of cotton-Lancashire was as different as its history. There was as much poverty and desperation here, but it was borne with a fatalistic patience, as if it had happened many times before and was well-understood.

'Aa'm a four-loom weaver – as many one knows . . .' runs the cotton song like a Celtic lament, wanting the gaiety, the spite and humour of the north-east industrial folksong.

> 'Aa've nowt t'eat and a've wore out me clothes . . .
> We lived upon nettles whilst nettles were good,
> An' Waterloo porridge was best o' wus food . . .
> An' a feel in me heart that a'll soon clem to death.' [Clem – starve]

Nettles. Here was the song of a dispossessed countryman – whenever it was written – the words of a family man with pride in appearance.

> 'Our Marg'ret declurs, if her'd clothes to put on,
> Her'd go up to London to see the Great Man . . .'

But Marg'ret was in rhetoric. She, and her mother and grandmother, had seen it all before. In fact she would not go to London. She would stay at home and scrape-and-scheme and make-and-mend, and perhaps survive with the thin-lipped determination that was written on the faces of all my aunts.

The north-east mines had long been in the hands of a few notorious families like the Lambtons and Vane-Tempests. At one time dozens of Sunderland carpenters had built collier-brigs in their own backyards – nine months' credit for the timber – but since the early nineteenth century shipbuilding had been the property of a few big firms. There was distance between employer and employed.

Lancashire women who had been neighbours in the roller-coaster streets for years might cling to their respectability by addressing one another by their marriage names – 'Goodmornin' Missis Rimmin'ton . . . Goodmornin' Missis Entwisle' – very proper like. But weavers and their bosses came from the same stock and in the mill were on first-name terms. Many of the cotton-masters had started in the sheds themselves and might easily end up back at the looms. 'Clogs to clogs in three genera-tions', people said in pubs and chapels without rancour. By thrift or luck or marriage, and then some fluctuation in the world's economy, it might have been their story too. When t'bosses failed, so did t'mills, so did wages. Oh yes, it was understood all right.

The Geordie was – and is – a swashbuckler, a spender when in funds, a born employee. In Lancashire when the mills were built and villages like Manchester, Blackburn, Burnley and Accrington exploded, the men, women and half-children who filled the sheds – or many of them – had been self-employed. Which is to say that every farm and smallholding had a hand-loom shop where the whole family toiled, weaving pieces for local merchants who provided the material. Those who won a reputation for fine work quickly done, who were perhaps more thrifty or better managers than others, such could put away a bit of brass. A man with sovereigns in his pocket was a 'long Oliver'. Long Olivers could get bank loans, buy looms at £5 apiece and start a mill.

What these men and women, spinners and weavers and savers and new-born bosses did – albeit unconsciously – was to buttress an Empire, clothe the Orient and enrich the island. In the 1830s half the exports of the greatest trading nation the world had known was Lancashire cotton. In 1910 – long before synthetic fibres were in general use – 70 per cent of the world's exported cotton goods came from Lancashire. Every Indian man and boy wore a dhoti which was woven west of the Pennines, and Blackburn was the greatest weaving centre of the world – just as Sunderland claimed to be the greatest shipbuilding town. Her finest fabrics were sported in the fashionable salons of Europe. And those innocents, those weavers, spinners, dyers, bleachers and mechanics invested more than sweat. Kay, inventor of the flying shuttle, Hargreaves of the spinning jenny, Arkwright of the spinning frame, and Crompton who made no profit from his mechanical mule, all lived and tinkered within a few square miles. So did John Osbaldeston who invented a vital component of the power loom and died in the workhouse. And many of the mills that profited from such devices were financed – at least in part – by the savings of the workers. At one time Oldham was known as a town of working-class shareholders.

But for all their thrift and ingenuity the Lancastrians of the cotton towns were dreamers and idealists. The aggressive socialism which the Geordies had thrust upon them was a bread-and-butter thing. ('There is a happy land, far, far away . . . where we'll get bread-and-jam five times a day . . .' we sang cheerfully on school bus trips.) Lancastrians dreamt of a new Jerusalem.

Whether their vision sprang from Nonconformity and was encouraged by promises of universal respectability in the life hereafter, or whether it had deeper roots, I do not know. At any rate it took many forms – from conventional Methodism, through political radicalism to a kind of idealistic atheism. My grandfather, Ambrose Entwisle, tinsmith, drinker and leg-fancier, though surrounded by a Bible-reading family of weavers, was a member of the socialist Clarion Club and had atheistic inclinations. Entrepreneurs like the local banker Roger Cunliffe founded missions and academies. Chartism, parliamentary and financial reform, universal suffrage, abolition of the Corn Laws – Lancashire, and the Lancashire working man, were in the van of every progressive movement of the nineteenth century with a banner that was at least sprinkled with the Blood of the Lamb. Free Trade, the cause that Lancashire and its radical newspapers campaigned for with a religious zeal, was an expensive investment for a society with a world monopoly of cotton manufacture.

What a society! And how ephemeral it all looks now. Those kin of mine were, after all, more vulnerable than most. Their spectacular successes were pregnant with the seeds of tragedy. When industrial England suffered – as in the great depressions that followed the Napoleonic Wars and preceded World War II – Tyneside and cotton-Lancashire were hurt most because of their dependence on a few activities. But Lancashire had special troubles. Down came the price of silver and India could no longer pay for cloth. Result: idle mills. During the American Civil War, Lancashire was cut off from the plantations and her raw material. Result: the Cotton Famine. Yet she still backed the Yankees and anti-slavery. Lancashire began to build and export cotton looms, and in her colleges she taught oriental students how to manage them. Result: during the 1950s while the rest of England prospered, 1,140 mills closed down. Between 1912 and 1964, 667 million looms stopped for ever. And by that latter year, after other European countries had closed their frontiers to foreign cloth, Britain was importing, from India, Pakistan and Hong Kong, almost as much cotton cloth as she had sold to India alone in the 1930s.

There is no doubt, though, that whatever paradise on earth or in heaven the spinner and weaver still pinned his faith on, there would be soap and donkey-stone* for all. That was the most visible difference between my Wearsiders and the cotton people – an obsession with domestic order, fanatic cleanliness that many prized even above godliness. This, and a thrift that approached the miserly, were respectability's defence against spiritual decay. Without them – lacking the cheerful truculence of Geordies – the society of the textile valleys might have disintegrated.

Of course there was squalor in Manchester – the perhaps inevitable consequence of a city grown too large. Orwell reported slums in Wigan† – but that was a town of coal as well as cotton. Doubtless there were some

---

* Donkey-stone – a kind of soluble brick rubbed on with water as soldiers smarten their belts and gaiters with blanco, also widely used in the West Riding even by Asiatic immigrants. Called 'donkey-stone' in Lancashire because it was once sold by a packman with a donkey.
† The Road to Wigan Pier (1937).

mucky folks in Blackburn but I saw no slums there – nothing like the reeking tenements of Sunderland, some of which survived the 1950s.

The streets of Lancashire that I remember were parades of gleaming window sills and doorsteps pummelled with weekly applications of donkey-stone. Unlike Mr Priestley I did not – do not – find such townscape ugly. There was a touching beauty about the long rows of two-storey cots laced in a compact urban web – the rhythm of purple rooflines weaving down the sides of the dark bowl that was Blackburn – a bravado in the clusters of mill chimneys at the bottom, each stack an ingenious variation of the bricklayer's art.

I used to set out on my boyhood explorations after breakfast when the trams had started down at 't'Boolyvard' outside the soot-black railway station. Blunt-nosed barges would be gliding on the green canal, moss flourishing between the backlane sets, a few ragmen already keening.

It was then I used to hear the buckets, grey iron pails galvanised with zinc, handles rattling. There was the slosh of water hurled across the rust-brown pavements, the swish of stiff yardbrooms – ten or twenty thousand housewives 'dooin' thur fronts', scrubbing the very streets outside their homes, swilling down the sides of the bowl of Blackburn, the morning ritual.

'Goodmornin' Missis Rimmin'ton . . . Goodmornin' Missis Smith . . . Goodmornin' . . .'

2

The right approach to Blackburn is across the moors touching the old shire of sheep and hursts that was woollen country before it took in Irish flax then US cotton. So when I'd taken breakfast and paid for my night's berth I took the high road.

As I approached a sprawling suburb I stopped to ask three girls if I was still on course. Two stood back a pace, grinning from their pert industrial faces. Their spokesman, a pretty lass, answered boldly in the dialect that still has traces of the Celt, the Angle and the Norseman immigrant. Her face, though, was from far away – like as not Kwangtung – and her eyes were almond-shaped.

The road slid down between houses of brick and rough, rain-darkened stone and from either side ran once-familiar streets. I parked in one of them and made my way on foot. About me were all the roof-shapes, ventilators, warehouse entrances that had first enchanted me as a boy of nine or ten. I recognised small details instantly and knew that here I had formed tastes and attitudes that still existed. But I could no longer make an intimate connection. The boy and I were strangers. Too much had happened in between.

I looked for Bicknell Street where I had spent one August with an unmarried aunt who stuffed me with Rowntree's chocolate and plied me with cinema money she could ill afford. But something quite remarkable had taken place. The woman on a doorstep looking right and left had not the pinched face of a millgirl-housewife, a dedicated pavement scrubber. She was more self-contained, more placid. Her cheeks and jaw-line were less angular. She was taller and had a darker skin. The solemn little girls who graced the streets were not the skinny imps – the Lizzies and Mary-Ellens – I had known. The small shopping streets were animated now, crowded, more colourful and prosperous than I recalled. Where there had been black woollen shawls there were saris. There were exotic names above store windows and different, spicier smells came from the doorways.

As in a dream, my quest became compulsive. I *had* to find the place. I saw two Englishwomen chatting on a corner. 'Which way for Bicknell Street?' They looked at one another and before they gathered wit to answer a tall young man addressed me. 'Excuse me,' he said. His speech was faintly Lancashire, his manner courteous. He looked like a technical college student. 'Excuse me – did you say you wanted Bicknell Street? I am walking that way. Would you care to come along?' As he strode on he said, 'I know Bicknell Street quite well. I'm just going there for a bit pray.'

Bicknell Street was as steep as I remembered. It climbed to a brow beyond which, out of sight, the residences of clerks and middle-class insurance men, then the mill bosses, were said to be. The chapel a few doors up from where my aunt had lived, and into which my guide now disappeared with a grave goodbye, had been turned into a mosque.

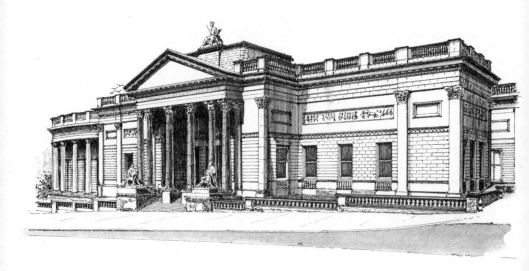

21

Concerning Big Dutchy, old Parchment Face, Ernie Woo, Cockwood Charlie, Frankie Dinn, Billy the Con, and a huge supporting cast in the land of the Mersey Funnel.

1

THE NEXT STAGE of my journey – to Liverpool where I had been told I could camp in a suburban sportsfield – was only forty miles. But beneath the superficial order of motorway and suburb the old chaos bubbles, always ready to erupt. For me at any rate.

You see, I dropped this hitchhiker at an M6 service area called Charnock Richard where I met a large RAC patrolman who was delighted I could tell from his accent that he hailed from Amsterdam. He furnished me with a route to my destination – it happened to be near his home, he said – and suggested that while I was in the district I should call in at the pub where he took his evening glass of Fockink. 'Just ask for Big Dutchy,' he advised. 'That will find me.'

Well, I must have missed a major turning in the sprawl of Merseyside, for within an hour I was fairly lost and had to stop at the Walton Lane 'Bridewell' – which is Liverpudlian for 'nick' – for fresh directions. However, having settled in at last beside a football pitch, I took an evening stroll to get my bearings among the suburban hollyhocks and roses, and seeing a neat, modern public house, I entered and asked for Dutchy. The effect was remarkable.

The barman stared at me, a half-filled glass in his arrested hand. All conversation ceased. After an uncomfortable silence he said –

'Never 'eard of 'im!'

'Big fellow,' I explained. 'Drinks schnapps or something. Dutch accent.'

'I tell you I don't know 'im,' he replied aggressively. The drinkers scowled. I could see beyond the barman into another, bigger room.

'All right,' I said. 'I'll see if he's in there.' He wasn't.

I suppose I should have left then, but intrigued by the hostility I had somehow caused, I returned to finish off my half and made my next mistake. Among the customers I thought I recognised a travel-agency man with whom I had once spent a boozy evening in a Spanish port. He left before I could enquire but I approached his companion, a tough-looking, stocky man with a face like crumpled parchment.

'Excuse me. Do you mind if I ask – Was your mate a courier?'

'A *courier*? Waja mean a *courier*?'

'A travel courier . . . working for a travel firm,' I said.

'Why?'

'Well I think I might have met him somewhere before.'

'No. He never was a courier. Hasn't got the brains. But I'll tell you what *you* are. You're a *busy*!'

That was when the penny dropped. *Busy* – policeman. *Courier* – a carrier of contraband or stolen goods. Even my mention of a travel firm could have seemed deliberately ambiguous. And whoever their Dutchy was, he was not my friendly Amsterdammer.

'A *busy*,' I said. 'Look at me. Did you ever see a scuffer my size?'

'Makes no difference,' he replied. 'They got 'em all sizes nowadays.'

The other drinkers glowered. Clearly they shared my adversary's low opinion of my character. I took time finishing my drink while I considered my predicament, eventually returning to the lounge where I hoped to meet Big Dutchy and clear my name. Within two minutes old Parchment Face had joined me. In the mirrors I could see that one of his companions had placed himself in a chair immediately behind. A third lurked nearby.

'What'll you have?' I asked Parchment Face.

'I buy me own drinks,' he said.

But in ten minutes more we were buying one another beers, we had exchanged names and he was telling me about his grown sons, his police record, and how he would like to do one more 'big job' but he had a bad back.

'Don't be daft, Arthur,' I said.

'Waja mean *daft*? I bet you wouldn't turn your nose up at ten or fifteen grand. An' I got a family. Grown-up sons and daughters. Eight.'

'Eight into fifteen's not much,' I replied.

'Ah . . . you shouldn't have asked for the Dutchman,' said Arthur, shaking his head sadly. 'You shouldn't a done it . . . You caused a lotter stir in there asking for the Dutchman. An' your eyes all over the place, sussing like a rozzer. You're lucky you got away with it, honest. You got to understand us you know. You gotter have a bit of understanding.'

'I'm trying hard.'

'If you'd walked out when I came in 'ere, I just had to give the nod. You'd a got *done*. We got our code a loyalty you know.'

'Of course, Arthur,' I said. 'Thank you.'

I never did see Big Dutchy again. So – decent man – he never knew the sequel of our meeting at Charnock Richard. He was probably on late patrol that evening. Or I was in the wrong pub more likely. Anyway, you don't go to Liverpool for a quiet life.

2

Near midnight in the kitchen loft of the New Shanghai. Ernie Woo, boss, Liverpudlian man of affairs, dispenses sweet-and-sour and whisky at a long bench table to a few chosen friends. Beneath us, on the floor below, black, brown, and white kids – orphans of an expired empire – gyrate in a blue haze to the fanfareless music of the nineteen-seventies. The noise spills out across the surrounding wasteland, lapping at the doorsteps of the tenement cliffs. Little Jimmy Yue, cook and world-observer, pours out more Scotch and forecasts World War III . . .

Mid-evening in a pub where Sam Weller might have felt at home. A big, fair-haired man has been regarding me suspiciously. He looks as though he has just been delivered from the cleaners. Knife-edge pants. Crisp blue shirt. Hands like bunches of bananas. Obviously a docker. He leans across the cast-iron table. 'I'm going to wait one minute,' he says. 'Just one minute . . . then I'll ask you a question . . .'

My companions are three ladies, ample in years and outline, perhaps dockers' wives or daughters, probably virtuous but indomitably flirta-tious. It seems to me that Liverpool women only stop flirting when the undertaker calls. The minute passes. The big, fair-haired man leans over and shouts above the noise.

'Are you a prowletariat-h?' he says, with that light half-lisp that Liverpudlians use for final t's.

'Depends what you mean.'

'Are you a prowletariat-h?' this time with more menace.

It is not the sort of question England teaches you to deal with. But this is Liverpool, not England.

'If you mean, do I work for my living . . .'

'I'm *asking* you – are you a prowletariat-h? . . . If I thought you were going to make one farthing out of *my* people . . . *my* kind of people . . .'

But by closing time it's all Christian names, friendly negotiations having taken place in an atmosphere of mutual understanding, it having been agreed that the Czechoslovakian *solution* was probably a mistake and that the Hungarian *adjustment* maybe was an error. Bearhugs and handshakes. And when will you be back?

'He was round the other night but I'll never have the bastard back,' says the girl behind the bar I can't remember in the club I can't recall. 'One more for the road, Sergeant?' asks the young policeman in plain clothes, fresh as tomorrow morning. 'Thanks, no ice,' says Sergeant Leahey.

Outside, a little whirlwind of brown leaves blown in from the suburbs plays tiggy down the pavement. A dawn chorus of house sparrows outsings the rumbling city for a moment. On a corner in a churchyard a metal Jesus sits like a lanceless Don Quixote astride a metal ass surveying the intersection.

Are you a proletariat-h?

3

In the year that I was born H. V. Morton went to Liverpool. He wrote that a gale from America was delivering itself into the Mersey. He described the largest tobacco warehouse in the world, mentioned the Cotton Exchange and with a touch of imperial pride wrote of the Great Dock Road . . . 'the sound of hooves . . . of iron-bound wheels . . . It is more than a road. It is a barometer of commerce. When the Great Dock Road rumbles, bumps, jingles, gees and whoas from early morning until late at night [a Liverpudlian] knows that men all over England are buying and selling, that ships are loading and unloading, that cities . . . and towns far beyond . . . are thriving and content.' But in the end he said: 'I fled as a man occasionally flies from affection. The city was too full of things worth writing about.'

Six years later – in 1933 – J. B. Priestley took his social conscience and his pen to Liverpool. He called it 'the heart of darkness'. The traffic was thinner in the Great Dock Road, the Cotton Exchange was on short commons and Morton's gale from America had turned very bleak indeed. He put up at the Adelphi and wrote affectingly about the coloured children who had enhanced the grey streets for decades and still do. 'Looking at them, you do not think of the riff-raff of the stokeholds and the slatterns of the slums who served as their parents: they seemed like the charming exotic fruit of some profound anthropological experiment.' He groused about the trams – 'mournful beasts' – and all but recommended the deportation of the Irish – 'What a fine exit of ignorance and dirt, and drunkenness and disease . . .' Back at the Adelphi, which was 'dressed for the evening . . . playing waltzes', he sat disconsolate at dinner. Then, much like Morton, he wrote: 'Miserably I decided that somebody else must give a plain, fair account of this great city. The task, in the time, was beyond me. So I bought myself a good cigar.'

I understand the problem. Even today – with the grand old warehouses of the Victoria, Alexandra, Albert and Canning docks redundant and replaced by a vast computer-operated container port downstream . . . the Great Dock Road an urban desert and its elevated railway, loved by generations, gone . . . with half the city centre disembowelled in the name of some planner's dream that never happened, and its inhabitants dispersed to vast estates – Liverpool defies the 'plain, fair' account. It is big. It is formless. It hums and simmers like a great engine. Its energy spurts out through a hundred valves and vents. Fringe theatre and the oldest rep in England. A huge scripture mural spread on an old gable end with house-painter's brushes, and the biggest collection of fine art outside London. A cacophony of pop clubs and the Royal Philharmonic. Tree-shaded inner suburbs full of mansions, and mile upon mile of seedy terraced streets. Irishmen, Caribbeans and Chinese. Irishmen, Indians and Hungarians. Irishmen, Lithuanians and Scotchmen. Mosques, temples, tabernacles. Shrines, churches, mission halls and brothels. Lob scouse, chip butty, tripe, steak-and-kidney, sharks fin, bisque, caviare-and-bliny. And the densest child population in Europe – cocky, abrasive, urban-wise.

When I first drove in from the eastern suburbs I passed the former residences of the 'Onedins' and the 'Frazers', homes of the shipowning and trading families, elegant and terraced. Then I saw the dusty, broken fanlights, the boarded windows, the graceful, unswept front-door steps. On patches of tired grass Victorian worthies posed on plinths in petrified frock coats, still waiting for the Progress they believed in. I thought, 'Ah yes . . . Liverpool is like Dublin . . . splendid squalor.' And suddenly near the Pier Head – which is not a pierhead, just a stretch of quay for Mersey ferries – I was in Manhattan, in the urban canyons, a kick in the backside from the Bowery. A few blocks further and I was on the

Kowloon waterfront. Cardiff, London, Manchester, arranged themselves in façades and then disappeared. Liverpool was like all of them and none of them. It would not be contained in one description.

As Europeans we expect our towns and cities to have developed gradually from one point – ford, bridge, crossroads, market, church or castle – a point from which we can subconsciously check our place in geography and time. Church, chapel, police station, school . . . shop, bank and railway yard . . . park, cinema and recreation ground . . . architecture changing ring by suburban ring . . . the vocabulary of lamp-post, fire hydrant and chimney pot, the grammar of the streets. But Liverpool seems to ignore such convention. There is no clear starting point. The Pier Head – when you find it – is no hub. The surrounding streets are deep, narrow and commercial, the Mersey three-quarters of a mile wide. Upon a building with no architectural merit except bulk roost the two Liver Birds, tethered with steel guys to hold them in a gale, a landmark only to those who arrive by water. And celebrating what? Life Insurance! I dare say there are Liverpudlians who have seen the Pier Head more on television than in actuality.

There are two cathedrals but even these fail to orientate the stranger. Both were built in the last hundred years and the flow of streets does not draw you to them as in other cities. The Anglican cathedral, though vast and Gothic – twice the size of St Paul's of Ludgate Hill and the second biggest church on earth – disregards the old alignment of pre-Reformation churches. It runs north and south instead of west to east. The Catholic one* is even less traditional, being circular and nicknamed the Mersey Funnel because of its likeness to an inverted cone. It stands gleaming white, surrounded by thirteen apse-like chapels and supported by sixteen props upon a podium which is itself the crypt of a pre-war essay in cathedral building that ran out of peace. A fine and exciting building. But you have to look for it. Or map read. Or take a taxi.

For three days I sought Liverpool in the labyrinth of Victorian streets full of offices and banks with bronze doors like forbidden temples, looking for the pattern that I knew – that I could feel – existed, but ill at ease because like H. V. Morton and J. B. Priestley I was unable to define it. One morning, with the sun slanting through engraved windows, I believed I had come close to the heart of Liverpool in the Vines, which must be the finest copper-countered, mahogany and rosewooded, bevel-glassed and chandeliered gin palace in the country. But by that night I had raised a glass to an MP and a detective in the Nook (where that landlady of landladies Eileen Fitzgerald once ruled Chinatown in her big,

* The Metropolitan Church of Christ the King.

picture hat) and I had to think again, cut loose, just let the city rip and see what happened.

4

'There was this bobby. A hard man. But a good bobby. A character. Birtles. Oh, I could tell a lot of stories about Birtles! He lived in a terraced house and whenever he was on nights – sleeping through the day – the rag and bone man came round. Barrow . . . balloons . . . rags . . . a colourful scene. This feller used to blow his bugle and wake Birtles up and Birtles had had a lot of this. One day the feller stayed rather too long in the street playing his bugle and Birtles had tried blanket over his head, fingers in his ears, couldn't shut this noise out. So at last he jumped out of bed, pushed up the window and told him to go away. "'Who the hell are you?" says the rag man. "Just go away," says Birtles. "Who the hell are you?" says the rag man again. So Birtles puts his dressing gown on, runs down the stairs in a temper, grabs this feller's trumpit, brings it back into the house, runs it through the mangle, throws the trumpit at him and says – "Now go and blow your bloody bugle!" An' the feller's just standing there looking at this instrument.'

The raconteur is a police officer.

Liverpool!

I call on an old acquaintance, an artist working on a sculpture to honour Dolores Ibarruri – 'La Passionara' – and all the other saints of the Spanish Civil War. I am perplexed because he has offered me a plate of Irish stew and seems to be frying it in a flat pan. He is also offering me his explanation of the demoliton of most of Liverpool's best old buildings. 'It's because they want to eradicate any reminder that Liverpool's prosperity was founded on the slave trade,' he says. For afters he's giving me his reason for the removal of half the population of central Liverpool to the notorious council estates.* 'To disperse them,' he says. 'To prevent the revolution. It was a very revolutionary situation there.' Actually, 310,000 scousers were moved out between 1931 and 1971.

Liverpool!

I am sitting on a table in a basement like an air raid shelter beneath a

* The last major racial violence in Liverpool (before 1981) was in 1918 after a black man was stabbed by a Scandinavian seaman. Blacks retaliated, and a white attack on the black population followed. Liquor stores were looted. Police held 700 blacks in the Ethiopian Hall for their own protection. Similar unrest occurred in Cardiff, Barry, Newport, London and Manchester.

block of council flats. A residents' committee is organising meals and haircuts for pensioners, and camping trips for teenagers, temporary jobs for school-leavers, a youth club, art classes, hospital gifts, funeral wreaths, non-dry anti-burglar paint for downspouts. A tall man called Allan, straight as a ruler, skin like a black-leaded grate, asks me about my caravan. Like many Merseyside Caribbeans he came to England as an engineer on war service. * After demob he bought a van, fitted it with bed and cooker and set out to explore 'the mother country'. Didn't I have trouble at nights with policemen asking me to move on? No? Well that had been *his* problem. He'd been sent on his way several times a night. In the end he sold the van. Now in his seventies, he still hopes that some day he might set off again to discover England. 'Just to stop where the dusk catches you,' he says.

Liverpool!

In a clapped-out Drug Squad car we bump across cobbles in a wilderness of houseless streets. The policeman at the wheel wants to show me how the Corporation had preserved a colony of nineteenth-century streets. Church. Corner shops. Kids playing skippy on the flags. Women gossiping on front door steps. An island community spared from the tower blocks that stand on the horizon beyond the wastes, tombstones of the fifties. Back doors painted fresh, well-kept backyards, tidy dustbins. 'See how it is,' he says, 'how they take pride. Still have their neighbours . . . less crime!' He is a disciple of the American Jane Jacobs who has been telling planners they have been getting it all wrong for fifty years. At last somebody in Liverpool has got the message.

I am with Chief Superintendent Frankie Dinn, boss of 'A' Division, in his glass and concrete office above the rubble and he is explaining the robust relationship between cops and dockers – formal enmity diluted by affection. Stories of the days before patrol cars. 'Did I ever tell you about "Cockwood Charlie"?' he asks, explaining that cockwood is the dockers' word for timber pilfered for domestic fuel, a token of family concern for which dockers' wives are said to have shown their gratitude in bed. 'Cockwood Charlie' was a bobby who dedicated his professional life to apprehending cockwood pilferers. Frankie shows me his picture gallery – demolished bridewells, vanished pubs – and talks affectionately of local toughs – 'buckoes and buckesses' – who called in at the station to have fingers bandaged or to 'borrow' a shilling for the meter. 'It's not the same now,' he says, 'but I still consider every one of my men an unofficial

---

* Because Liverpool's large coloured population has been established so long and with much intermarriage, accurate figures are not available. Liverpool City Council has 99 members. I asked how many were coloured. The woman who answered my telephone call said, 'None. They are all *English.*'

213

community relations officer.' So many Liverpool conversations turn towards a lost, golden past.

I pick up a book[*] by an old sailorman. He writes with artless eloquence about Merseyside at the beginning of the century, his childhood homelessness and hunger.

'It was the great days of Liverpool . . . I'm writing about before the 1914 war . . . the river was crowded – and the streets. Seamen of all nations and much-braided people, many of them from poor countries where kids offered themselves for sale on the streets. Rhuie and me and kids like us did. When I was ten, fourteen, and Rhuie a bit younger . . . a Lascar spoke to me. I wasn't new to anything like that . . .'

Liverpool!

5

That small part of England known on Merseyside as 'L8' and comprising the municipal wards of Princes Park, Granby and the Dingle, tilts gently from a highway called Admiral Street towards the river edge. Not long ago, as the English measure time, it was a place of small villages and mansions, and here the pink-purple panicles of reed-canary grass must have grown waist-high. In mid-April sweet vernal on slender stems perhaps dispensed its fragrance. And there were poppies. And butter-cups. And skylarks. And cuckoos in the spring. And maybe on summer mornings the Mersey glinted blue. It was then perhaps still pleasant to occupy a brand new little house in Tupman, Winkle or Snodgrass Streets with great expectations, the brick still pink, the Queen still young, the flag still high. Or to move in from the country and set up modest home in Micawber Street and wait for something to turn up.

What did turn up was Liverpool. It advanced not at a steady march, annexing the corner of a meadow one decade, sending an advance party of smart stuccoed villas to occupy a paddock in the next, respectfully outflanking this quiet country church or that, which was the English way in more favoured places. It came on like a Tartar horde, a host of men and carts and horses bearing bricks and mortar, destroying what was there before, smothering church and cottage, barn and tavern. Its mercenaries were bewildered country lads from Ireland, Wales and even India. The battle cry was Trade and Progress, and to be just, its chieftains believed – sweet, suffering Jesus! – that God was on their side.

L8 is now a postal district. It covers about two and a quarter square

[*] *Then and Now – the Autobiography of an Early Century Street Arab*, by Andie Clerk.

miles of England and contains about 37,000 people. For most it is a prison from which there is no escape.

The sun was filtering through smoke haze on the first day I walked down into L8 with Harry Holmes, a plain-clothes policeman. There was no canary grass, no sweet vernal. A few colonies of willow herb grew on demolition sites, but there was a 'fragrance' in the air. It came from a steam laundry half a mile away – along Tupman, Winkle, Snodgrass and Micawber, investing the ruins of an abandoned bridewell.

We met a young man – I'll call him Billy – who bore the double brand of an L8 address and a police record. Since his last conviction he had been taught some joinery . . . 'I've learned what chisels to use and what wood is what – not by the colour but the shaping of the grain and all that. I've made sixteen Welsh dressers.'

'What happens when you go for a job then?'

'Well two of us, we go for an interview. First we get a brain test. Like what is the difference between two hundred pounds of steel and two hundred pounds of feathers. We get top marks in these tests then the man says "Where do you live?" I say L8 – and that's it, I've had my chips. When they ask if I've been in trouble I've got to lie. If I admit it they say they'll keep your name on their books, but that's all bull.'

What sort of trouble were you in?

'Fighting. And assaulting homosexuals. I got put away for that. It's hard to tell who's queer and who isn't nowadays you know. But around the park . . . everyone knows that's the hangout for them.'

Billy despises the police. 'I don't know one copper that's straight,' he said. 'There's one feller – he's in the C.I.D. – him that got me put away like. He finds out I'm learning joinery and comes round and asks me to make something. "Do me a favour," I tell him. "Do me a favour!"'

What are you going to do now?

'Well, I've got twelve months trade behind me. I can go independent. I can put little cupboards into houses and that. The tax man isn't going to know about it.'

Harry Holmes and I called at a Catholic boys' school to say goodbye to a retiring head. A class of scholars gathered at a window to boo and catcall because they knew Harry was a copper. He smiled back. Outside there was rubble on the road. The tarmac was bruised by the skids of stolen cars used by L8 youths for impromptu stock-car races. As we crossed wasteland three children ran out of a house to tell PC Holmes that they'd been on a trip to the zoo and to show him new toys. And two teenage girls stopped to talk about their voluntary work for a residents' committee – the Southern Neighbourhood Council – which produces a newspaper called *Southern News*. Harry Holmes returned to Admiral

Street Police Station to finish after-hours paper work before signing off for the day. He went out to arrange fixtures for the local boys' football team he runs, then cycled home across the city.

At the end of my first day in L8 I was tired. I sat in a deserted police canteen with a lukewarm cup of coffee and a few cyclostyled copies of *Southern News*.

Letter – 'I would like to thank the three boys Alan, Tommy and George for the wonderful job of decorating they did to our flat, also the good humour and courtesy they displayed . . .' a pensioner had written.

Announcement – 'Any tenants in our area who have housing repairs not yet done, call in at the Neighbourhood Council Centre, Caryl Gardens, and see Margaret bringing your housing chit and she will try to get the repairs done.'

Complaint – 'Number 8 Yard, Grafton Block. Subsidence suspected. When it rains worms and maggots come out of the ground.'

And there was this report from six schoolgirls:

We took 14 kids (aged 5 to 10) to the park (Princes). It was a bit of a bother getting the kids on the bus. We arrived at the swings and we stayed there about half an hour, then we went to the Roly Poly but it was full of bees and the kids were messing . . . Then we went to the small garden and the kids were up the trees and this woman said she was going to tell the copper so we soon shifted from there . . . We had a bit of bother getting on the bus again. – Tina Rice (15), Pat Adams (14), Margie Segar (14), Sheila Hill (15), Eileen Crosby (12), Ann Segar (13).

6

There is an irregular clearing in the Liverpudlian maze known as the Plateau where eight or nine thoroughfares converge as if by accident. There – detached, superior, massive, monumental – stands St George's Hall, one of the finest neo-Grecian buildings in the world. It was designed for civic concerts and a court of law by a 25-year-old architect, Harvey Lonsdale Elmes, who died in 1847, nine years before his masterpiece was finished. In front of great Corinthian columns a young and handsome Queen Victoria sits side-saddle on a charger, her adoring 'Dizzie' only a hip-hip-hoorah away in pedestrian attendance, and Liverpudlian Mr Gladstone very properly at the tradesmens' side in the garden at the back.

On my last morning in the city – still searching for the key to Liverpool – I walked up the steps of St George's Hall. In the entrance, sitting on a chair, was a police constable with twinkling eyes, a full set of silver whiskers and the biggest, brightest, most elaborate badge I have ever seen in a constabulary helmet.

Although this splendid apparition could not have mistaken me for an important visitor he was out of his seat in a shake, asking if he could help, apologising because the famous Minton floor in the main hall was covered with protective timber (which must have cost more than the original bill from the tiler), and enquiring – with that disarming blend of courtesy and cockiness that you keep encountering in Liverpool – if I would like to see a court case. He clearly wanted me to enjoy and approve of his St George's, and he had reason to be proud. The interior is gorgeous, flabbergasting! Outside, the ranks of columns, the pediments and podium, the arrangement of the masses that make up the whole, speak in the restrained accents of the Greek revival and the monotone of jurisprudence. But inside Justice lets down her chignon, appearing but distant kin of the icy maiden on top of the Old Bailey.

The blood-red columns are polished bright. The ceilings and vaults are adorned with all the colours of a Victorian vanity box. A company of giantesses – *all woman* to the last upturned breast – support a serpentine gallery with gilded rails. Among these sirens Sir Robert Peel, a parcel of superior clerics, and Geordie Stephenson looking quite a Charlie dressed in a Roman toga, stand ill at ease. At the feet of these gods and goddesses I mingled with the other earthlings.

At one side of the great hall small groups of advocates from the adjoining courtrooms, in robes of various remembrances of black and wigs of several reminiscences of white, nodded and pecked and flapped, uttering the clipped jackdaw noises that English lawyers make in recess with no purpose but to impress the common sparrows. Across the floor a flight of foreign tourists chattered round a stall of coloured postcards, looking up about them with bright, interested eyes. What did *they* make of it all – of St George's and the lawyers, the Gothic constable at the door, the Adelphi, and the bar counter of the Vines shaped like the curved stern of some fabulous brass galleon, the whole, big, dark, jumbled swaggering city?

I left, walked round the corner into William Brown Street, still pursuing what by then should have been obvious. William Brown Street slopes gradually down from the Plateau. It is one of the most didactic thoroughfares in England. On one side is the backyard of St George's – St John's Gardens – all dripping trees and solemn statues. Across the road stands a remarkable row of buildings, like textbook illustrations of the classical idea. Walker Gallery (1874) – Raphael, Michelangelo and Liverpool's George Stubbs among the Millais and the Turners. County

Museum – aquarium, vivarium and planetarium. Three large libraries – the Brown, the Hornby and the Picton – one modelled on the Roman Pantheon.

I sat down in a room with a pile of books. I read that the town of Liverpool grew on a peninsula beside a tidal creek and that King John granted the first charter in 1229, that it got a castle in 1235, a mayor in1352, a chapel of ease (of Walton parish) in the thirteenth century and the slave trade in the eighteenth. It all seemed irrelevant. In most other English cities you can learn about the institutions, the street patterns, the urban structure of the past, and look outside and see it seeping through the present. But in the industrial and financial explosion that occured in England in the nineteenth century, sending its shock waves round the world, almost every stick and stone of previous Liverpools was swept away. Men built as they had never built before and anything that got in the way came down. A new kind of man was born – industrial man, traditionless, without ancestral ties, conjuring industrial theory to justify his ruthlessness. Liverpool was the Clapham Junction of his upstart world and only the shape of half a dozen streets survived. The population of Liverpool increased from 82,000 to 700,000 in the century, and still the press came on. Other cities were exploding too. But Margaret Simey, in her study of nineteenth-century Liverpool, * writes that here 'poverty was more desperate, housing more squalid, social distinctions more cruel, the state of public health more shocking'.

In the early forties, an agricultural labourer with a family to rear might receive six shillings (sometimes less) for one week's work. Sugar cost eightpence a pound. Two and a half pounds of bread cost sixpence, the price artificially maintained by the Corn Laws (repealed 1846). In nearby Accrington only 100 of 9,000 inhabitants had jobs. To Liverpool came many of these hungry unemployed for work on the new docks which were importing cotton and exporting a thousand million yards of cloth a year. Jews came from eastern Europe. Chinamen, Lascars, Africans – the detritus of empire. Some prospered. Thousands lived – or died – in filthy cellars. Half the streets had no sanitation. Infant mortality was running at 229 per thousand live births. There was a life expectancy of nineteen years for the survivors. In came the Irish!

There have been many migrations in the history of Europe, but was there ever one like this? During the first half of 1847 alone – it was a potato famine year – 300,000 of the Queen's Irish subjects landed at Pier Head. That is an appalling figure. It is twice the manpower of the present British Army. It consisted not of disciplined divisions with supplies and

* *Charitable Effort in Liverpool in the 19th Century*, by Margaret B. Simey.

equipment but of starving families fleeing for their lives to a country where the common people were themselves in distress, where revolution simmered and can only have been averted by some mysterious ingredient of the English psyche. The population of Liverpool at that time was smaller than the number of the newly disembarked. And as they came ashore Cockerell's palatial Bank of England was going up in Castle Street, his newly-finished London and Globe Insurance building a few blocks away. Old churches were tumbling. The cyclopean granite walls, the towers and gatehouses, of Jesse Hartley's docks were rising along seven miles of Mersey shore. It was the year in which young Elmes died, but his red granite pillars were upending on the Plateau, the bronze doors and statues being wrought, the great organ ordered, the Minton tiles of blue and brown for the vast floor being fired, the pediment sculpture for the south portico of his St George's – Britannia surrounded by Commerce and the Arts – decided on. And regiment after regiment of small houses were marching across the fields towards Granby and the Dingle, towards today's L8. What an arrival! What a natal scene!

Many of the Irish left – for other English cities, for America, the colonies and the public burial grounds. But 80,000 stayed, to intermarry with other immigrants, to multiply, to labour in the docks, to contribute cheek and wit, a derision for authority, a Celtic love of ballad and of music to the Liverpool we know, and to become that special kind of Englishman, the Scouser.

I saw now that my search for a city with pre-nineteenth-century roots had been in vain. For Liverpool – the only Liverpool that now exists – was born of the nineteenth century and remains closer to the nineteenth century than any other English city. Whether this unique proletarian culture will outlast the tower blocks, the vast egg-box estates, the urban motorways and the processing by TV and mass advertising, no one can tell; if it doesn't, England will be the loser.

As I left Liverpool the rank wet grass on empty corner sites was yellowing. The colour of the Anglican cathedral was that of ancient rust and half the colossal tower was hidden in low cloud. The statues behind St George's Hall stared stonily towards the river – invisible in murk – and Queen Victoria's nose was dripping. I had a last drink at the Vines and quietly toasted Ernie Woo and the Adelphi and Arthur and Sgt Leahey and Frankie and Birtles and Allan, the girl in the bar I can't remember and all buckoes and buckesses and of course the prowletariat-h, and I promised myself I would come back.

That morning I had received a letter from Bishopsbourne in Kent. It read:

Remember the rings in the 40-acre field? Well, they were Roman burial rings after all. My rose garden is flourishing at the Village Hall. We had a walk and lunch at Charles Fagg's farm on Saturday. There's still the harvest supper. Love Peggy.

22

*How I was shanghaied by a memory, bewitched by magic
stone, fought the Battle of Ay-gincourt with an Irishman on
Birdlip Hill, and left the Cotswolds as time piled up like
pumpkins . . .*

1

NOW I was on my way from Merseyside to Devon, a big leap I know,
but you can only cram so much into one journey and I was trying to
resist the siren calls on either hand. First I denied myself a trip to
Blackpool, that eighteenth-century watering-place that erupted into a
celebration of all the best, the warmest and most kindly kinds of English
industrial vulgarity. Blackpool's sense of fun is essentially Victorian and
all the better for it. It is unexportable. There is nothing exactly like it in
the world. There was Chester too. That was a temptation. I've never
been there and I would like to have walked round the famous walls and
discovered human substance behind the travel brochure prose.

At Spaghetti Junction where M6 becomes M5 in an already dilapidated mess of elevated motorways I ignored all the arrows inviting me to Birmingham. Among big English cities 'Brum' is the least attractive. Interested as I am by the varieties of English speech, the idea of being surrounded by a million people whining that particular tune was enough to set my teeth on edge. Besides, 'Brum' is where pedestrians have been driven into passages underground like Wellsian Morlocks and so deserves a passing insult.

I would like to have turned left for Arnold Bennett country – or to have gone to Lichfield with its three clean, handsome spires and the ghost of Dr Johnson – or turned right for the wooded heaths of Cannock, still haunted by Plantagenet kings on horseback. Swynnerton, Tutbury, Uttoxeter and Stone, Shugborough and Abbots Bromley, I hope I may know them all some other day. Shrewsbury in timber-and-plaster country, Vale of Evesham full of fruit – I let them all go by over one shoulder or another. And as for Stratford, I had no appetite for that perversion of a literary shrine.

It was when it got to early evening and I was thinking of turning off to find a camping place that I saw the sign to Stroud and weakened. I remembered that not far away there was a village in a Cotswold valley with the unprepossessing name of Slad where once I had spent some hours with one of the most enchanting men that I had ever met. It had been the spring of 1962. There were crocuses in his little garden and his wife cooked on a cast-iron range. He was a bit bewildered that a book he'd written had sold a quarter of a million copies. I was younger, and perhaps it was the combination of his modesty and my – well, not awe, but something like it – that inhibited the beginning of a friendship and I saw him no more except on television. But the memory was good.

So, with only half a mind to intrude on him after all those years, I left the motorway, drove through Stroud, and having taken a wrong turning found myself motoring up hills behind the town trying to identify a romantic-looking tower that appeared intermittently above the trees. It turned out to be part of an eighteenth-century folly called Rodborough Fort, and was conveniently near a congenial camping site. I raised and fixed my roof in a hilltop meadow and by nightfall was in bed with toddy. Because of the view across the valley I had not curtained off my windscreen and sitting with my bedtime reading I could see the lights of town below. Along the hills about the rivers Frome and Nailsworth were the strung jewels of other villages and farms. I knew that beyond lay the Severn and the Welsh Black Mountains.

What happened next was thunderstorm. First a few flickers of yellow light ran along the hilltops like distant gunfire. There was a rumbling. Then a heavy spattering on the roof. And then the deluge. It shook the caravan in every bar and strut. There was a time during the wild tearing when I feared for my covering and thought of getting out to batten down and spend the duration in the driving seat. However, I switched off the lights and with the whisky at my elbow sat up and watched the Olympian drama as lightning in forks and sheets illumined the whole world before me, seeming to extinguish all earthly glims, turning the hills into a great amphitheatre bathed in an underwater light.

I must have dropped off in a lull for when I awoke the light outside was cotton white and there was not a sound. A new day was creeping across England but it was far above the mist that stirred about my hilltop. The Fort was invisible. I decided to move off into the silence with no more than tea inside me. Headlamps on and in bottom gear I inched from the gateway and turned right, avoiding spectral sheep that had strayed on to the unfenced roadway of the open heath. I seemed to be in slow descent, then, noticing a sooty darkness to my left that turned out to be a roadside spinney, I eased in and parked in the sound-muffled world and crackled up some bacon. It was while I was drinking sweet, black coffee sitting on my doorstep that the mist first turned to gossamer and then to liquid gold. Leaves and grasses loomed close at hand hung with gems of fire in greens and reds and blues. Then as the mist burned out I looked down into a little sun-warmed vale and upon soft-gold limestone farmhouse roofs with fields and sloping paddocks of such a spring-time green that the earth seemed to have lost its season. What an opening curtain for the Cotswolds!

At this point I must confess my shameful ignorance. I had passed through the Cotswold hills several times before on journalistic errands, but like many of my trade I often travel blind. I had read some books so knew the characteristics of Cotswold buildings and the showplace villages they compose – steep roofs of stone, tall corniced chimney stacks, gabled dormers facing front, mullioned windows with limestone eyebrows to throw off the rain, models for cosy English Christmas cards. Yet I still thought of Cotswold country as material for novels and detective stories in which ageing colonels retired with their sun-crinkled wives. As for Cirencester – well, I must confess I had imagined some half-industrial town. Of course I knew its name was Roman. But so is Manchester's.

Anyway, I washed my breakfast things and trundled through the lovely morning. Soft crests and ridges combined and then diverged, small valleys running at their feet. By-roads which I took at whim lowered me into steep hamlets made of butter-toffee and by old-fashioned gardens full of all the colours of the sweetshop bottles. There seemed to be no system to their wandering. The humps and hills would not assemble into anything that could be called a range. And yet there was a discipline.

223

Centuries ago, it seemed, barns, houses, farms had reached a satisfying suitability for purpose. Proportion, a nice agreement between the horizontal and the vertical, had been achieved. A style had been set and there had been no need to change it. Some critics have called these buildings 'dull', 'obvious', and even 'smug'. I do not understand their discontent. What could be wrong with achieving near perfection, then sticking to it?

Before the thunderstorm the previous night I had come across these lines in a book I'd brought along. They had been written by a private soldier of the Gloucesters in prison camp in World War I:

> Go up, go up your varying ways of love,
> Take each his darling path wherever lie
> The central fires of secret memory;
> Whether Helvellyn tower the lakes above;
> Or black Plynlimon time and tempest prove;
> I will go climb my little heights to see
> Severn and Malverns, May Hill's tiny grove.
>
> No Everest is here, no peaks of power
> Astonish men. But on the winding ways,
> White in the frost time, blinding in full June blaze,
> Village and quarry, taverns and many a tower
> That saw Armada beacons set alight.

The soldier's name was Ivor Gurney, and he said well.

It was still early morning when I ghosted through a town of empty streets. Down what I took to be a by-way I saw a handsome fifteenth-century church tower and circling to reach it I found myself in a market-place – wide, slightly curving street, broadening at the top. And there beneath the tower was a most sumptuous parish church. The eastern light turned buttress, pinnacle and panel into faded persimmon. I walked into the churchyard and found that the east end had four gables – three chapels and the chancel – and by some alchemy they glowed now with a hint of rose. Three storeys high, the south-porch entrance of the church – richly fretted battlements, built in two tiers with corner pinnacles – was a fifteenth-century fantasy big enough to be a town hall, which is indeed how they used it for a century or two. The whole church – soaring perpendicular nave, fan vaulting in St Catherine's Chapel – boasted the prosperity of the Cotswold wool trade. What a building!

As day began and the doors were unlocked at Zachary-and-Co-Wines-and-Spirits-Established-1760, and the first customers arrived at John-

Barnett-Fish-Game-and-Poultry, I stood under a vast tree and watched the citizens of Cirencester move about their early business as if completely unaware that theirs was an enchanted borough. Beneath two Dutch gables French and Sons began their daily traffic in scarves and stockings, and Ettles and Bumford Ltd announced that they had television sets for rent. I was besotted! Devon could wait. I would explore my new discovery, the Cotswolds, for a day or two.

I walked back into the market-place again and judged that the timbered Fleece Hotel was just the place for me. There was a room available. A previous occupant had scratched the date on my window pane – 7th September 1779. The beams in the front bar were the discarded baulks of an Elizabethan man-o'-war and the barman was a Geordie – name of Dave – whose prestidigitation with tumbler and polishing cloth was a pleasure to behold. By mid-morning market stalls were in full sale, and that night there was music and folk-dancing among the cabbage stalks, and the tower of the parish church had turned to silver.

And that, of course, is the magic of the Cotswolds and what bewitched me on that golden morning – what both countryside and villages are made of – the enchanted stone so sensitive to light, so philanthropic with its colours. Up comes the limestone belt from Portland Bill where it is dense, grey-white and fit enough for banks and municipal pomp. At Ketton and Ancaster it may be tinged with pink or blue – elsewhere buff, brown and silver-grey or full of fossils. Bath stone, the favourite of Nash, is honey-coloured. But here tones alter with the clouds, the season and the time of day, turning small towns and villages into places of perpetual delight.

The Romans must have known about it when they arrived at Cirencester, calling it Corinium. They led three roads here, making it a junction and the second town in Britain. There is an entry in my notebook for the day I found Cirencester.

> SEXTUS VALERIUS GENIALIS
> trooper in the cavalry regiment of
> Thracians . . . aged 40 . . . of 20 years
> service lies buried here. His heir
> had this set up.

I must have taken that down from a memorial stone in Cirencester's Corinium Museum, a splendid place where they have tried to reconstruct the environment of a wealthy Roman-British town of 1,500 years ago.

I also noted a tradition that the British princess Claudia, who lived in Cirencester, married a Roman officer and became mother of that Linus who gets a friendly mention from St Paul in the second Epistle to

Timothy. The family turned Christian and it is said that Linus became the second Bishop of Rome in succession to St Peter.

When I got back to the Fleece rather late that night I was served a memorable meal with the greatest courtesy despite the hour. I have the menu still.

Dinner £3.50. Poached eggs en gelée au Jambon. Sauté of Hare Cacciatora with risotto, stuffed peppers, red jelly, croquettes and cauliflower with sauce . . . then Stilton.

The chef was called Pietro Chirizzi.

'Scratch Gloucestershire and find Rome,' they say.

2

For almost a week I put up at the Fleece at Cirencester and in the end I knew I could never tailor a fair account of the Cotswolds to a chapter, chart all the reeling roads or disentangle all the little rivers. I did find that the source of the Thames was at the foot of an ash tree on the Bath Road just outside the town, but apart from that, geography confounded me. I never set out on a single journey and arrived by a direct route. That was for Romans, or maybe American and German tourists. Perhaps a century or two ago when this was one of the most thickly populated parts of Britain and the common trade was woollen textiles it might have been possible to guarantee delivery of a dray of woollen bolts to Chipping Campden at a given time on a given day, though I don't know how they managed. 'To meander' was my principle and I stuck to it single-mindedly.

I give you my last evening. I had fallen in with a public schoolmaster, a charming man who loved music and fine buildings, who could be moved by a row of chestnut trees and who seemed to me, despite his urbane and slow approach to middle age, to have stepped from some sunny Cotswold corner in the 1930s before Mister Chips was married. He knew every village, could tell you in advance what you would see in every church and knew every brew in every inn, but his ability to move directly from one to another was about as good as mine.

At least we knew we were driving east when we left Cirencester. It was raining lightly. We went by way of Ampney Crucis and Down Ampney where Vaughan Williams was born and which inspired him to write 'Come down O Love divine'. And Ampney St Peter where a Mr Barnard, one of the regulars of the tiny local, was so moved when he heard it might be acquired by a brewery chain that he bought the place and thus reserved a small place in heaven for himself. That was our first stop and it was worth it. The inn sign was a fine red lion with a blue tongue and a fabulous S-shaped tail. The car park held three vehicles ('the larger the car park the poorer the pub,' said my schoolmaster) and the interior was a rare survivor of what village alehouses must have been a hundred years ago and long before. The bar-room was about ten feet by twelve – one pump, one choice of whisky. The bar counter was a converted pew.

Running down the bends through Poulton there were still some elms and the building stone wore a faint pink blush. And then we came to Fairford (population 1,840), an old wool town nine miles from Cirencester on the little river Coln. Mark that population figure. For although Fairford is not one of the pop showplaces it contains some of Europe's most precious jewels. St Mary's is one of the finest wool churches in England – which means the world – and from its eaves a wicked company of gargoyles – lolling tongues, drooling mouths, un-Christian leers – observe the passing show. Then there is the great west window depicting Doomsday in horrific detail. That and twenty-seven small windows make up the finest and biggest store of 15th–16th-century painted glass in Britain.

In the town square Georgian façade conceals Tudor interior, nineteenth century leans against sixteenth. The roofline dips and staggers. One building – an antique shop now – is of three periods in succeeding stages, and three varieties of Cotswold limestone have been used with happy carelessness. The Bull Hotel, sixteenth century, is a noble boozer. The beer is from Arkell's of Swindon.

Such art, such conveniences, such facilities, population 1,840 – Lord, how did it happen!

Leaving our empty pint pots glinting in the firelight of the Bull, the blackbirds and the bells in competition in Fairford churchyard, and a dragon that had been chewing its own backside for four hundred years on the parapet, we motored through Quenington and back through a lovely glade to Coln St Aldwyn in a flat-bottomed valley which I might have proclaimed the most enchanting village of the evening had we not come to Bibury. And William Morris said Bibury village was the most beautiful in England so I suppose that settles it. Chestnut trees, double packbridge, Tudor mansion, limestone roofs that turned pink when the grey light glanced at them. And – oh, yes – the largest trout farm in northern Europe, which reminded me of paddy fields.

Dusk was creeping across the hills when we sailed into Arlington Row. Lights were twinkling in the windows of the Tudor cottages down by the river. It was almost too perfect – indeed too familiar. You may not have been within a hundred miles of Bibury, but it's likely you will have seen Arlington Row in some Hollywood confection. When American film companies want a romantic English background they come down here, scatter straw along the roadway, set up their tripods and clap their clapper boards, Gadzooks!

Back on the drunken road we crossed the Roman Fosse Way making its sober way from Lincoln to Exeter via Leicester, Cirencester and Bath, and here calling itself the A 492. More bends and double and triple bends, then a gradual, five-miles drop towards the river Churn by way of a green cathedral nave with piers of bark and vaults of foliage.

Night and storm hammered down as we emerged on to Ermine Street – the western Ermine Street from Silchester to Caerleon. Right turn and up through straight Roman miles until we reached the Golden Heart at Birdlip. How long, how gradual, is the English gloaming, and how right that at the end of every town or country twilight there should be a pub with lighted windows.

'Ay-gin-core!' bellowed Tom the Irishman, waving his George VI beer mug like a battle standard at the ceiling as we entered.

'Ay-gin-core!' he bawled. 'Oh, dear God! The English were outnumbered five-to-one. The casualties were fan-*tast*-ic! Thousands dead. But only twenty-eight among them English. And God Almighty, the longbow was a Welsh weapon anyway!'

'Made of English yew trees, mark you,' a modest English voice cut in.

'No!' hailed back the Irish man-o'-war, not for a moment taken aback by an inconsequential, contrary gust. 'No! Their arrows came from the Pyrenees damn-and-blast! And do you realise why General de Gaulle kept saying Non-non-non? He could *not* forgive Ay-gin-core. He could *not* forgive the bastards. And that's why he wouldn't let the English into the Common Market. Hah!'

Now it may be supposed – especially by Americans, who take simple view of Anglo-Irish matters – that an Irishman has no place in an English pub or a book on England. Not so. The Irishman and his wife and children and descendants have been part of England for many a year. There is hardly an urban pub without its Irishman standing at the bar, barely a municipal body or legislative assembly without its Callaghans and Healeys, rarely a roll-of-honour on a civic cenotaph without an Irish name. And there can't be many English families without a touch of shamrock in them. Paddy is no foreigner and has an honourable place upon a Cotswold Hill.

Tom Primmer lived in a converted pigsty – a big chap, a farm handyman. He was self-taught in ancient Greek and Latin, an admirer of Herodotus and likely to quote Plato at you in Greek. He also had a thirst for cider brewed in Hereford, which brought him almost every evening across three and half miles of fields to the congenial shelter of the Golden

Heart in all sorts of weather. That night rain smote the windows and swept up the die-straight foreign road along which the Legions used to splash, inking out the night view across the Severn Valley, veiling Gloucester, paying no respect to genteel Cheltenham. Against the back wall of the bar-room, piled in two tiers on trestles, stood as many loaded casks as you've seen in any pub in England. And there was a little engine to hoist them up on trolleys, like the carriages on which they trundled guns aboard Napoleonic battleships. The place was crowded. There was hardly standing room – hardly listening room. So Tom would have had to shout even if he had not been such a big, enthusiastic, square-rigger of a man for whom every statement was a comber to be ascended, breasted, and then sailed down again upon the other side.

When we left he had sailed past Agincourt to Gloucester in a full-rigged four-poster bed.

'I've just made a four-poster . . . Nine-by-nine in solid oak and eight-foot-six-inches high. I put my guts into the making of that bed. Once you've expressed yourself like that you've got soul satisfaction and you're not a bit interested in the dough . . . You can make a hundred pounds a week an' put it into the Prudential but it only lasts a weekend so to speak. But if you can construct just one little joint that somebody can look at and admire – then you can stand back and begin to understand your history . . . how all those people made this country and constructed things like . . . Gloucester Cathedral! Just to touch one of those lads,' he said, 'who were responsible for making Gloucester . . . that would be a privilege. And never mind how much you have in the bank, Joe . . .'

3

Next morning I paused at the signpost that pointed down to Slad. The rain had passed. Small clouds like young unicorns hunted their own shadows across the tawny hillsides. I had not, after all, tried to renew acquaintance with the writer I had met in 1962. Standing there I recalled how I had come upon him then, making enchanted music with violin, guitar and tape-recorder and that sometime in the 1940s – perhaps on an autumn day like this – he had written:

> Such a morning it is when love
> leans through geranium windows
> and calls with a cockerel's tongue . . .

When hedgerows grow venerable,
berries dry black as blood,
and holes suck in their bees . . .

When the partridge draws back his spring
and shoots like a buzzing arrow
over grained and mahogany fields.

Such a day it is when time
piles up the hills like pumpkins,
and the streams run golden . . .

I did not go down. *Cider with Rosie* had now sold more than a million copies, and there had been others. Probably he would not remember me.

I went to Hereford to spend that night on the grounds that a cathedral city that had produced people as different as Nell Gwyn and that old puritan Kingsley Martin, and where cider flowed from the brewer's vat in pipes beneath the roadway like mains water – such a place could not be bad.

High above the lazy Wye outside the city someone had climbed the girders of a railway bridge with a can of paint to write in huge white letters:

Pierre love June
June love Pierre

23

How I emerged from Nomansland in deluge, talked of Bren guns at a hunt ball, and observed how – accompanied perhaps by Julius Caesar – the good people of Torrington burned a giant on a Devon heath.

1

'CHANCE' is the blind conductor of most journeys – the best of them, at any rate – however much we trust in forward planning. A storm. A meal. A touch of indigestion. Almost all that happened to me in north Devon began with a plate of lobster soup followed by chicken-and-mushroom suspended in a thick tinned sauce of vilest yellow.

It had been raining. That is an understatement. A waterfall had pursued me all afternoon and on into the night. Tyres seemed to have lost contact with the road. Monsters with great headlamp eyes appeared and disappeared through banks of spray. The wireless, longwave and medium, was a Bedlam of foreign voices – a whine of outdated dance music from Madrid or Barcelona was threaded with a ghost from Paris ('En Angleterre la livre est malade . . . Les Etats-Unis font face à choix . . .') and then was overwhelmed by a rhythmic wailing from Belgrade. The BBC it seemed, had been swamped by the same deluge that submerged my spirits.

I think the cab of a motor car in driving rain at night, even in so densely populated a land as England, is one of Earth's loneliest places. I was misdirected at an isolated filling station and found myself in a town that seemed to be part-populated by half-drowned WRENS. Was it Bridgwater? I passed through a village called Nomansland near which my electric torch picked out a signpost to Black Dog. I asked for directions at a hamlet called Alswear in a big, stone-flagged and empty bar where a woman sat sewing beside a cavernous fireplace. At last, on what seemed to be a rise, I came to a deserted car park outside a factory. And it was there, as a puny declaration of my faith that somewhere out beyond the blackness there really was a world of restaurants and city streets and warmth, that I reached for the tins and concocted my little dish of dolce vita and poisoned myself.

Well, there is but one cure for indigestion and that is time. That time is better spent in activity than lying in a sleeping bag hearing every thunderclap of the intestines. The rain had stopped abruptly. The wind was spent. And through the windows I looked across a twinkling valley. I decided to stroll out in search of company.

Down the silver lanes of Devon I walked beneath a sky of indigo and a moon like a new-washed pumpkin. There was incense in the air. Could thyme be so late? I walked between high banks with no notion of geography. Only the Plough and Pole Star hinted at direction and I was ensnared by roads that saw no virtue in straight lines.

Eventually I came to a thatched cottage, then another gleaming white, and descending steeply through a scent of woodsmoke I entered a considerable village with a lane or two branching left into a world of glowing windows. Here – Kingscott it was called – I imagined I would find a pub where I could renew contact with my fellow men. But there was not a live thing out of doors and the only sound was the chortling of swollen streams. A large bird stood like a stork on a roof-ridge. I beamed my torch at it for half a minute but it did not move and I concluded that it, too, was ornamental. I found no tavern either, and so, with a feeling of exclusion from the human race, I climbed the hill and took another lane.

A clock chimed in the distance and by quarter-hours the sound beckoned me by woods so still, so saturated by moonlight, that they might have been the work of some fantastical silversmith. I toiled up steep ways where long wavelets swilled across the road from rain-laden hedgebanks. I sat on the parapet of a stone bridge and heard four owls exchanging scandal like tree-borne Frankie Howerds.

At last I came to the village with the chiming clock – St Giles-in-the-Wood. Here was a huge lych-gate, a row of handsome estate houses and a lone cow bellowing across the valley. But again front doors were closed and curtains drawn, and still there was no sign of men.

It was then I heard the rhythmic thudding of a dance band. Following, I found myself in an unpaved square, the church on one side and a large hut – apparently the village hall – across the way. A figure in a long, dark coat told me that this was the night of the annual hunt ball of the Torrington Foot Beagles. And this was the place to which the cottagers of Kingscott and St Giles and the inhabitants of half a dozen other villages had been transported.

Now I have never wanted to go to a hunt ball. I had supposed that such occasions were attended by young men with pink faces, red coats and God-awful accents, by arrogant older men with minor titles, and plain young women like those portraits in society magazines. But this was no such gathering. I peered through the door. There were red faces all right. But they were the weathered cheeks of farm-hands bursting out of stiff brown suits. There were young women too, and though clearly of the country they were quite unlike the insipid portraits of those country notables. There were greetings and handshakes, but they were between Jims and Margarets, Pats and Johnnies who jostled and gyrated beneath green paper streamers slung across bare rafters. There were dresses that had never been within a hundred miles of Bond Street, from which emerged soft arms fattened on the crumbling pastries of west-country kitchens. And what was most remarkable to me was that the scene could have been lifted straight from the thirties or the forties. It was a NAAFI dance in Essex . . . a County Durham social . . . any one of a dozen hops that took place in my north-country youth.

'Bless 'em all . . . bless 'em all . . . the long and the short and the tall,' played Mr Perkins. 'Bless all the corporals and double-yew-O-ones . . .'

'Ten years too late,' the man said.

I asked for his name. He was called Michael Blaskievicz. Ah well, if anyone had a right to an opinion about Devon it's a Pole, I thought, remembering the youngsters from Warsaw and Gdinya who were over Exeter in night fighters that May when the Luftwaffe was ordered to wipe it off the map. You meet them all over now, these Poles who learned their drill on Blackpool Promenade. They are as much a part of England, and English history, as the Bren gun from Czechoslovakia about which Michael Blaskievicz talked with affection as only one man can talk to another about a piece of machinery that was once part of both their lives.

It must have been one o'clock or half-past when the landlord of the Admiral Vernon, Torrington – a black-bearded ex-Navy man who looked like Laughton's Henry VIII – called 'time!' and the Foot Beagles and their friends distributed themselves along the lanes and among the cottages.

As I walked up the hillside to my caravan the day's events began to seem unreal. Bless 'em all, indeed!

I needed no toddy that night.

2

The wing-beat of low-flying wildfowl woke me to my first Devon day-break. That, and spears of early sun stabbing between the curtains, and a sharp, insistent message from my stomach that smoky bacon and brown bread were urgently required below. I put on the kettle, trimmed the bacon, and when I jumped out on to the tarmac I saw that Devon had arranged a splendid opening scene for me.

There was a touch of frost. Morning frost and the smell of bacon make optimistic harmony. The car park which last evening in the deluge had seemed like a precarious ledge had now become a gallery. Below me was a relief map of my blundering between barn and hamlet, hedge and dyke. The square tower of St Giles was hidden, but I heard the clock strike seven. Down there was the stone hut in whose doorway I had taken refuge from a passing car on the narrow way to Kingscott. And I could see the rise upon which I had paused at a signpost to decide which invitation I should accept – Roborough, Kingscott, Torrington, Weare Giffard. The valley which had seemed so steep was a mere ruckle in the bed of a wide vale through which flowed the river Torridge. And twenty miles away, across a quilt of hills and woods, lay the long, blue barrier of Dartmoor – about whose quaking bogs I'd heard and read so much.

I chose to walk the four miles to Great Torrington. It stood among the gentle northern hills of the country on a small green cushion of its own – a heap of grey-blue roofs, pleasant but quite ordinary from my high road. I entered between rows of unremarkable stone houses and past an artificial insemination centre ('Visitors interested in cattle breeding and allied modern procedures . . . would be welcome after proper application to the appropriate officer', said the guidebook.) Two filling stations guarded the main crossroads. (Why have planning authorites allowed the oil companies to become the ill-mannered louts of the environment?) There was a small market square carelessly left about between shops and offices, distinguished only by a small town hall portico (classical, 1861) and by a drinking-fountain-clock-tower (St Pancras Station Gothic) which had lost a skirmish with a passing lorry. There was, however, an inviting passageway which led into a charming little shopping lane (the old Pannier Market) and thence on to the town's main car park.

Now there are many towns and cities with dramatic views and I am not suggesting that people will ever flock from the four corners of the earth to stand on Torrington car park. But when you go to Edinburgh, Bath, Paris or Manhattan you know what to expect. Here there is no warning. Population three and a half thousand, architecture unremarkable – it lulls you with its ordinariness and it is probably by chance – the need to park your car while you shop or buy a meal – that you step over the edge and discover that the town is perched on a considerable cliff, and that from this backyard, even in November, you can look down into a lovelier, greener valley than any other English town possesses within a few hundred yards of its town hall. It is an astonishment! And once you have stood on the edge of Torrington car park you cannot think of the place as you did before. The unspectacular streets have become the muted backdrop to an extraordinary piece of geological theatre. The scale of the approach through the little market streets is part of the enchantment.

When I got there the day was new. Long shadows of tree and hedge down in the valley were still printed on the turf. The pattern of fields was emerald green and earthy pink. Wisps of early morning mist survived. And the river Torridge swung into view from between bright red woods and passed silver-blue below. A helicopter inspecting power cables chuntered along the valley and I looked down through the Perspex bubble into the cockpit.

The physical character of a place is often reflected in the temper of its people and I did not have to look far in Torrington for a mirror of topography – sudden Celtic drama in a placid Saxon milieu. As I sought lunch I overheard two men talking on Well Street corner. One, a thick-set, good-natured fellow, asked a lanky man in a hat with a woollen pom-pom to direct him to the church. Actually, St Michael and All Angels was not two hundred yards away but the reply he got was so churlish and confusing that I was tempted to volunteer the simple information. And I might have done so had not the enquirer betrayed the fact that he knew the way quite well and that his question was just a pretext for a quarrel. The voices mounted. Violence seemed close. But after a last exchange of insults the contestants parted. I proceeded to the Admiral Vernon where I was served with a steaming plate of faggots and told that the street scene I had witnessed was no more than a customary charade performed between some Torringtonians for their own amusement and the possible bewilderment of passing strangers. The man with the pom-pom was one 'Lardo' Alexander, shoe-shop owner, builder, artist and the creator of the large picture painted on the wall behind us. It was a spirited evocation of the battle in which Vice-Admiral Vernon captured the town of Portobello on the isthmus of Panama in 1759.

My informant was none other than my Henry VIII of the previous evening. He greeted me like an old friend and furnished me with the supplementary intelligence that it was not the Vice-Admiral's victories but his trousers that were famous wherever in the world mainbraces were still spliced. Vernon wore nether garments made of a coarse taffeta-like fabric called grogram which earned him the disrespectful soubriquet 'Old Grog'. And it was he who first ordered the naval rum ration to be diluted with three parts of water (Port Royal, Jamaica, 1740) since when sailors have referred to rum as 'grog'. Which, of course, has nothing at all to do with Torrington.

The lunch-time company expanded. More faggots were served. The landlord got out his treasure-trove of Spanish pieces recovered from a galleon. Torringtonian tales grew thick, and even taller. But one which I was able to check later in the public library told how Torrington exploded into history in 1645 when two hundred cavaliers were imprisoned in the church too close to a powder magazine. No one knows why for sure – or at least nobody would ever tell – but all at once the place blew up, distributing king's men and bits of medieval architecture all over town. Now if that was the biggest firework display that Torrington ever saw, it was certainly not the biggest bonfire, as I would soon discover.

3

I am still wondering what really happened at Torrington the night before I left. I saw a town parade, there was torchlight and music, I watched a firework display and I met a few men in a muddy field singing a sentimental song. But there were times when I felt I was witnessing something other and far older than a celebration of the events of 'gunpowder and plot' that took place in the vaults of Westminster 370 years before.

Why do we do this all over England once a year? The old quarrel means little to us now. And nobody mentioned Mr Fawkes of York that night. It wasn't even the fifth of November – that had come and gone. What is the attraction of pyres and effigies? And why, in this Devon town, was there a special *otherness* in the occasion?

I felt it from the moment the door of the Black Horse clicked behind me and my eyes adjusted to the shadows of the small town square. It was populated by dolls.

I call them dolls. They were, I suppose, guys – Guy Fawkeses. But they wore such a grotesque motley of frocks and coats and pullovers, and hats and beards and moustaches, that no subject of King James I would have recognised them as contemporaries. They were carried high, in no apparent rank or order, and they leaned this way and that, gazing stiffly round and catching the light from the Town Hall portico. They were a gathering, a congregation, with an odd family resemblance to one another. It was as though *they* were the citizens, and we the spectators were incidental.

Someone began to ignite torches. There was a tarry smell, a drift of smoke, a few ragged notes from the band getting into spit around the corner. Then the dolls began to muster in the roadway, swaying slowly side to side, haughty faces flickering in the eddies of orange flame. I took a short cut round the church to miss the crowds and met them all moving towards me up a bent and narrow street. In most processions there is some military order. Or if it is a religious celebration there is the discipline of church music, the slow gait of clergy. There was none of that in this ragged little host. Torrington Silver Band was playing some martial air I do suppose, but no one had told them that caps should be worn straight and heels lifted high. And as for the rest – the torchbearers and followers – there was no pretence of keeping in line or matching step as they skipped and shuffled up the deep channel of the street in the dance of torchlight that glanced off the walls, fired window glass and made unlikely shadows on the stone façades. Thus surely passed the Athenian artisans on their way to meet in Palace Wood 'a mile without the Towne, by Moon-light' when Theseus and Oberon and Puck were abroad that other magic eve.

The piece of land where we eventually assembled – five or six thousand of us – was an extension of the plateau upon which Torrington was built, a headland jutting out into the dark. There was the sour smell of bruised grass and earth. We ate pasties and drank ale and cider bought from tented stalls. There was another audience out there on the hills that stood round three sides of us – sitting in motor cars, standing at dykes, farm gates, barn doors, waiting for the sacrifice, a galaxy of parking lights and twinkling electric torches.

Ahead was a roped area and in the middle, sitting on the biggest bonfire I had ever seen, was the patriarch of all the dolls. He was 85 feet tall – three times the height of a suburban house. The sword at his waist was eight feet long and at the end of one outstretched arm he held a flickering lantern. He wore a great belt with a square buckle, and a round, shallow, buckled hat. His face was framed by yellow ringlets and a rough, corn-coloured beard.

Beyond the ropes, in the arena, I joined a small group of humans. One was the mayor. It was the first sharp night of winter. Our breath steamed and we began to stamp the ground and slap our sides. We chatted inconsequentially about carnivals and fêtes and the mayor told me about

237

his family and how proud he was of Torrington. The throng swelled behind us. But even when the first fireworks went up and sky-blossoms of red, green and blue burst above the Common, and the crowd-sigh of *Ah-h-h-h* ascended, even then the great contemplative figure astride the pyre dominated all.

A small man-shape ran forward with a torch as puny as a match. He touched the kindling and sent rivulets of fire running beneath the giant's feet and there was such a stillness you could hear the first dry staves begin to crackle. I looked about me. There were no smiles. All stood there as if struck by an enormous guilt.

It was a savage spectacle. First the legs took light. Billows of black smoke rose in the red light and grew crimson as if they might explode. The heat scorched the front ranks of the watchers and people shaded their eyes. I looked at the mayor. He seemed as awestruck as I felt myself. Now something blew up inside the fire mountain and sent red streamers writhing skywards. As the effigy burned, the head tilted downwards and slightly to one side. And now the whole body was enveloped in a pall of black smoke. For twenty minutes the great face hung disembodied in the sky above the road to Bideford. Then thin white jets of smoke began to issue from the nostrils like the breath of a terrible anger. 'Look, look!' cried the crowd. And that was all. The beard caught fire and the show was over.

I was told afterwards that this finale, the suspended head and the smoking nostrils, was quite unplanned. If the creators of the great Torrington guy had tried for such an effect, they said, it would probably never have happened. But if a stranger on the Bideford road had passed by that night between the hours of nine and ten and seen that apparition in the sky he might well have thought his Devon trip had coincided with the end of the world. And he would certainly have had some difficulty staying out of the ditch.

It was a rather solemn crowd, I thought, that walked back across the Common. I would have set off back to town myself if I had not heard the singing. The heath was almost empty. The sound came from a tent-like stall, the voices male, the song lachrymose.

> *In an old Australian cottage,*
> *With ivy round the door,*
> *A girl received a letter*
> *From her boy shot in the war . . .*

As I passed, a lanky man in denims, gumboots and a woollen hat thrust a cardboard cup half full of undiluted whisky into my hand.

Why should I wee-ee-p
Why should I cry?
My love's aslee-ee-p
So far away.
He played his paa-aa-rt
On that August day,
And left my hea-aa-rt
At Sulva Bay.

I joined the party and saw that the lanky man was he who had dominated
the mock argument in Well Street about the best way to the church –
builder, jack-of-all-trades 'Lardo' Alexander. He and his dishevelled
group had been the high priests of the evening's saturnalia. They called
themselves the Cavaliers. Some were businessmen. There was a plumber, a carpenter, a garage-owner. One dark-haired youth said he was
descended from shipwrecked survivors of the Armada.

They had planned this Devon night for months and there had been
others. There was the night they burned the *Scharnhorst* before an invited
party of German survivors while ships fired from the surrounding hills and
mock aircraft screamed down on cables. And there was the time they
sailed down the Torridge in a galley, fought the Saxons of Appledore,
then bore King Hubba their Viking leader along country tracks to be
burned in a great funeral ship upon the Common.

. . . there's one thing more I ask of yew.
I ask for nothing more.
Jes bring me back the girl I love,
The girl that I adore-ore-ore.
And to those that will not merry-merry be,
They'll never share our joy-oys.
Sing, sing, the boys in blew,
Are bound for vic-tor-ee . . .

they chorused as the whisky warmed them. By now they were singing to
an empty heath in Devon, England.

I had that evening been thinking of a certain passage I had read quite
recently, and when I got home I looked it up.

Some tribes have colossal images made of wickerwork, the limbs of which
they fill with living men. They are then set on fire, and the victims burnt to

death. They think the gods prefer the execution of men taken in the act of brigandage or guilty of some offence; but when they run short of criminals, they do not hesitate to make up with innocent men.

The author was Julius Caesar. He was telling of his campaigns among the British.

24

In the little white town by the Torridge I meet the Wizard of the South, examine the case of the scrumpy-mazed butcher and contemplate the Tale of the Curried Cat as told by Cap'n Cox (ably assisted by the man from Fowey).

1

A WHOLE OCEAN has flowed through the twenty-four arches of Bideford Bridge since I first fell in love with the fair Ayacanora and along with ten thousand other classroom seadogs, weighed anchor and set sail with Amyas Leigh, Will Cary, John Oxenham and Salvation Yeo of Clovelly – 'a tall man and black' who 'sweareth awfully in his speech, the Lord forgive him'.

He has a lot to answer for, that prejudiced old Christian-Socialist Parson Kingsley. He is charged with taking his romantic Victorian morality, lock, stock and Bible-thumping barrel, stuffing it into the poops and berth-decks of Elizabethan men-o'-war, and unleashing it upon the Caribbean to frighten the whiskers off all the black-hearted papists of Spain. Worse still, he is accused of haunting the imaginations of generations of Englishmen with tales of glory – which is surely as grievous a felony as kissing girls. I wonder how many young sailormen went to Jutland and the Falklands, or even chased the *Graf Spee* and the

Scharnhorst, with some scrap of *Westward Ho!* in the ditty boxes of their minds.

For shame!

In the first paragraph of *Westward Ho!* Kingsley describes Bideford thus:

> The little white town [sloping] upwards from its broad river . . . and many arched old bridge . . . The hills close in, cushioned with deep oak woods . . . till they sink into the wide expanse of hazy flats, wide salt marshes and rolling sandhills where Torridge joins her sister Taw . . . Pleasantly [it] stands there beneath its soft Italian sky, and pleasantly it has stood there now for perhaps eight hundred years . . .

Well, sure enough – pleasantly and white it stands there yet. The bridge too. I glimpsed that first as I coasted down the winding road from Torrington through red oak woods on a bright November morning. I took a bend a mile back from the town and there it rode – 677 feet long across the river with arches of oddly differing widths because of the varying lengths of the old timbers. A few curves later I slipped into the town itself, standing back, eyes-front upon the river, with little ships along the waterfront which is part tree-lined boulevard and part wharf.

And there stood Charles Kingsley, the old villain, on his plinth at the end of Bideford Quay, looking as though ship's biscuit would not melt in his mouth.

How peaceful it all looked! How could this sleepy place of 1,200 gentle English souls have ever been spoken of with awe in the far-off Caribbean? And those polished local faces carved on the church screen three centuries ago – like the faces in the bar of the Royal Mail today – how could they have been known and feared in Eldorado? It is all very well to have a fanciful tale or two to tell the tourists in the summertime, after which you can count your profits and go respectably to church on Sunday, but . . .

But . . . hold on! The first person I noticed after my arrival in the town was wearing a white top hat – a dirty white top hat that had seen much cockier days. It graced a youngish, lanky man who brushed past me in the market hall just up the hill. And I found myself recalling how, when John Oxenham first appears on Bideford Quay in *Westward Ho!*, he wears crimson velvet 'a little the worse for wear' and a whole Quetzal bird upon his head – a not dissimilar circumstance.

The first man I actually spoke to was a waiter who tipped me off that the police had hired a quayside flat from which they could covertly observe a moored vessel suspected of running contraband (for all he knew I was a smuggler myself) and then told me with even more delight of such goings-on in the borough and neighbourhood of Bideford that sexual good taste forbids me to repeat them.

The second man I spoke to was a Persian magician.

I had been walking with some difficulty down the steep High Street when I noticed a large sign running the length of a Georgian housefront. 'The Supreme Magic Company Ltd' it declared, and I could not resist knocking at the door. I was let in – reluctantly, I thought – by a young woman who asked me many questions about my business then left me standing in the hall between two piles of brown paper parcels addressed to Istanbul and Havana. Having apparently completed my security check she admitted me to an office inhabited by a number of busy typists and a small dog in a tiny kennel, over all of whom presided a plump gentleman called Mr Edwin Hooper.

You may not have heard of Edwin Hooper, MIMC (with Gold Star) and MIBM (Order of Merlin), Hon. Vice-President of the Wizards of the South and Member of the Society of American Magicians. Nor had I. I can tell you now, however, that he is well known among all those gentlemen who pull whole Kew Gardens-full of flowers from tiny boxes, saw half-clad women in half, and chop off the limbs of uncomplaining accomplices. People – magicians, that is – come to Mr Hooper for their equipment. And if they can't come, they write. A man in Belgrade, for example, wants to make vampire bats appear. If he knows his onions he will get in touch with Mr Hooper. Someone in Milwaukee wants a vessel that will keep on pouring water after it should, by all the normal physical laws, be empty. Bideford is where he will get it. There are two hundred or so such requests daily.

Mr Hooper was on the telephone. 'A Voice from the Tomb? . . . Yes, of course,' he was saying. 'Death by Thought and – ah! – The Vampire Cometh . . .'

As I waited, a slight, pale man with black hair and dark eyes was admitted. He had a sweet, self-deprecating smile and was so very soft of foot he did not so much enter as *appear*. He tried to explain where he came from and what he wanted, but with small success because he had hardly any English. Some intonation, however, told me he was Persian and as I have a few words of the language, I intervened.

'How are you this morning?' I was able to say, and 'Please sit down', though there was not a free chair in sight. His face lit up and he was off on a stream of ornately polite Persian from which I could only make out his name and the fact that he was a sorcerer from Teheran. Somehow, Supreme Magic managed to take his order, and while I was introducing myself to Mr Hooper who had now put down the telephone, I heard a courteous 'Salaam Aleikum' behind me and turned in time to see the visitor make a small bow and leave as softly as he had arrived.

Mr Hooper was charming. He stood up, shook hands, stuck a dozen nails through his arm, fired a broadside of executive instructions at his staff and offered me a guided tour of 'the biggest magic factory in the world . . . fourteen permanent staff . . . another twenty working from their homes'.

He had, he informed me, been a plumber, but inspired by a performance of 'The Great Levante' one night at Bideford Garden Theatre, he had earned enough in the streets with a Punch and Judy show to start 'Supreme Magic Ltd'.

I cannot say I learned much about the deceptive arts that morning. It was all too confusing. One minute I was in a room like the inner sanctum of an oriental temple – 'on this altar,' explained Mr Hooper, 'you can set fire to a human head' – and the next minute I was in a room crammed to the ceiling with 'disappearing flowers'. 'Watch your step – that's a bed of nails,' said Mr Hooper on the landing.

In the printing and publishing department two magazines – *Magigram* and *Peter Warlock's New Pantagram* – and thousands of books were being despatched to domestic and exotic destinations. The periodicals contained such headings as 'Carlos Corda's Silk Sensation', 'The Ultimate Hand Chopper', 'Two Ideas Using the Brass Nut Release', 'From the Land of Chiana by Arun Bonjerjee of Calcutta', and 'Oh Mummy!'.

A book jacket advertised:

> *Adair's Encyclopedia of Dove Magic.*
> Fifteen thousand volumes already sold.
> VOLUME 4
> The final volume to complete your set.
> The biggest of them all.
> Three Years In The Making.
> Autographed Copy . . . First Edition Only.

I would make a poor industrial spy. As I stepped out again into the steep, white streets the only secret of the prestidigitatious arts I'd positively learned was that all those flowers that appear from the fat lady's bodice and other unlikely places are made from goose down, because it – the goose down – can be compressed into small spaces.

2

It is entirely owing to my appetite for knowledge about human affairs and the machinery of society that I was obliged to spend some time in the back bar of the Royal Mail at Bideford where – a glance at my notes confirms it – the window light struck brown fire into my glass of ale and the best cottage pie for miles around was served by a pretty, brown-haired maid with cheeks like peaches. It was there, for example, that I realised that the chief industry of Bideford, and its twin town of Appledore downstream, is storytelling. It seemed to me that every other man had a yarn to spin, the time to spin it and a thirst to match.

I sat beside a very old man that morning with the gaudiest repertoire of lewd stories I'd ever heard. Victorian tales they were – mostly about coachmen and what they got up to with the lady of the house – harvested in his sunny youth and carted, mildewing, down the years till, ancient friends all gone before him, they were his last companions.

'You ought to go down to the Seagate at Appledore,' said a man called Jimmy Cox. 'Go in the seamen's bar and ask for Wobbles. That's his nickname, see. His real name is Charlie . . .'

And in the Seagate – ''Ave you been to the Royal Mail at Bideford? There's a chap gets in there called Jimmy Cox. He'll tell ee a tale or two.'

Jimmy Cox! *Captain* Jimmy Cox. Five years before the mast. Thirty years a pilot.

Do you remember *Many Cargoes, Night Watches, The Monkey's Paw,* and Ginger Dick of Sutherland, Sam Small and Peter Russett, and that little pub down the Commercial Road where they and all the other ghosts of W. W. Jacobs's world of little coasters met . . . the dirty wharves and the treachery of skippers' daughters? Well, that was Jimmy Cox's world, and Wobbles's world, and here it was again, alive and supping.

'I went to sea a month before the First World War began . . . in sail . . . a schooner,' said Captain Cox. His accent had a ring of Dublin – one of the mysteries of these parts – and labelled him a man from Appledore.

'First month, when me wages is due in Cardiff, the 'ole skipper says "Go and get washed than come down and get yor wages." An' I 'ad a wash an' goes down thinken I was going to pick up a pound.

'He says "Sign 'eor" and 'ee shoves over two 'alf-a-crowns.

'I says "What the hell's this then?"

'"Who brought yew up?" he says.

'"Me mothor and fathor."

'"Well, I'm allowen *they* fifteen shillen a month . . . and five bob for *yew*," he says.

'Five bob! That 'ad to keep me in cigarettes and soap ecksetra. An' I got shipwrecked twice in *her*. Got dismasted in a gale er wind. Washed ashore on the rocks at Anglesey . . .'

Jimmy Cox went deep-sea, but by the late twenties he was married and was back in coasting.

'Then I got a skipper's job. Four-pewn-ten a week, send three pewn 'ome to your wife and find your own food. Cap'n, mate and two engineers would grub together . . . buy the groceries and cook it, and 'ave it out o' one dish like, see.

'I durn't take a bloody pilot. 'Cos if you took a pilot – like into Fowey – anywhere where it wasn't compulsory . . . heh . . . next port you got to there was another cap'n waiting for ee. "I've come to relieve ee," he'd say.'

Sacked?

'Sacked! Yes, oh by Chrise-cor-buggor, yes!'

Now it turned out that Wobbles of Appledore was Jimmy Cox's brother.

'You know there was these two – my brother that went engineer and the Cap'n – they used to trade a lot out of Bridgwater, see. An' every time they go to Bridgwater they'd buy five gallons of scrumpy cidor. They used to pay a shillen a gallon back in they days. Oh, they was fly they two buggors – they was fly they was. Any'ow, from Bridgwater they used to go to Cardiff an' load for Bristol and they'd go ashore there – heh! – an' they knowed a little butcher's shop. He was *mazed* about this scrumpy cidor, the butcher, but he couldn't get it in Bristol, see. So any'ow, what they used to do, they used to fill up a gallon can an' take it up to un.

'"Hullo Cap'n!" he'd say.

'"Here y'are . . . brought you up a gallon o' scrumpy," Cap'n would say to the butcher. An' oh my Chrise he'd smack it up he would. He'd lap it up. He enjoyed et! An' he'd say "How much do I owe you?"

'"Nothen. I jus' want a bit o'meat. Cheap meat."

'"There y'are," says the butcher. "What's in the shop . . . pick what you like. Beef . . . pork . . . or leg o' lamb. Shellen a pewn to yew."

'So th'ole skipper used to go off. He'd 'ave a bloody, big, nice piece o' roasten beef, y'see. Then he'd come back aboard an' he'd say – "Wobbles! . . . All right . . . your turn now." An' Wobbles would fill the can.

'Butcher would say – "Hello Wobbs!"

'"Hullo Butchor. I brought ee up a drop o' cidor."

'"Oh, fine boy . . . fine!" he'd say, and o' course he'd 'ave another two, an' the buggor was drunk then, see.

'"What d'you want?" asks the butcher.

'"Oh . . . 'Ave you a bit o' lamb by any chance? Or 'ave you got a nice little piece o' pork?"

'"Aye . . . Pick what you like . . . *sixpence* a pewn!"

'When he come to wrap it up, the 'ole butchor he'd say . . . "It'd be better for me to close this damn place down and go to sea with you buggors."

'Ah, they used to see 'im off, they did. He was drunk on scrumpy!'

Captain Cox has by now been joined by a mate from Fowey. I go for refills and when I get back and put down the dripping glasses, Jimmy says: 'I'll tell ee one now . . . 'tis trew as I'm sitten 'eor . . .'

'The – Tale – o' – the – Curried – Cat!' says the man from Fowey, as solemnly as a Sunday School superintendent.

Sorry. What was that?

'The Tale o' the Curried Cat,' he repeats. And Captain Cox began again . . .

3

The Cap'n o' this little ole coaster – about two-hundred-an'-fifty ton an' called the *Radstock* – he come down to Bideford an' he wanted an engineer so he asked my brother.

Now he'd never been in an engine room in his bloody life, but he went as Chief Engineer and he *drove* 'er, and 'cause times were a bit quiet he stopped in 'er several months.

Any'ow, one trip they loaded in Cardiff for Bridgwator an' they got outside the bar at low wator, an' they'm going to stop there four hours for the risin' tide for her to go up the river.

Now whilst 'em at anchor, her come into dense fog, an' it lasted three, four days. An' as I told yew on these boats they 'ad to find their own food. An' they only bought twenty-four hours grub usually.

Well, the fourth day come . . . Mornen . . . dense fog all the time . . . they couldn't move. 'Course tedn't like today. They got radar today an' everything, see. Any'ow, fourth day come. There's nothen aboard to eat. Same tea pot . . . they pour a kettle o' boilen wator on the same tea every meal, see. Well this mornen they was all there down the fo'c'sle playen cards. All their tongues was 'angen out . . . *starven!* An' th'ole skippor was walken about on the deck. Now they'd got a black cat aboard there . . . this is trew, innet 'Arry? An this 'ole cat came rubben up against 'is leg.

'Right you buggor,' says 'ee. 'I'll give yew a birthday today.'

He caught the cat. He killed en . . . skinned en . . . an' he put en on, an' he made a stoo. He 'ad a bit o' curry there an' he put that in too. An' when the time come he went down to the fo'c'sle an' he said – 'Come on boys. All 'ave yer dinnor!'

'*What dinner?*' they say.

'*Bloody* big pot o' stoo . . .' which was the cat, mind, but they didn't know it.

They 'ad a feed! An' whilst they's eaten thor dinnor, all smaken their lips, th 'ole skippor he say – 'Now don't throw away they bones, boys. Save they fer the cat. He's got to live jus' like us.'

Well, they put all the bones on a sheet of newspaper after they'd sucked en an' all that, to take them up on deck fer the cat. 'Oh,' says th'ole skippor. 'I'll take them up and give the poor buggor somethen.' An' he took 'em up an' what he do with the lot, he 'eaved et over the side.

'Chrise!' they say, 'Arthur. That was bloody 'andsome. What was that?'

'Nevor mind,' he says.

Any'ow . . . that afternoon the fog cleared up. They got up to Bridgwater all right, went ashore and got grub. At last . . . when they've eaten . . . somebody said: 'Aven't seen anythen of our cat for a bit. What became of he? Yew must 'ave poisoned the buggor with they bones you gave un.'

Arthur said: 'Ee-woan-see-ee-no-more.'

He said what?

EE-woan-see-ee-no-more-ee-say.

I'm sorry, You'll have to translate that. That's Devonshire to me.

You would say it Yew . . . won't . . . see . . . him . . . henny . . . more. An' I say ee-woan-see-ee-no-more-ee-say.

I see.

Then one of 'em said, ' 'Eor Arthur (the crew never called you Cap'n on a coaster) . . . 'eor Arthur. Mek us another feed like you did that day, Arthur. That was 'ansome,' he said. 'What was in it?'

Arthur said: 'Yew 'ad Kitty Curry.'

'Kitty Curry?'

'Cat curry.'

'Cat curry?'

'Ah . . .' he said. 'I killed the bloody cat and put it in that buggor.'

'Trew, in't it, 'Arry?' said Captain Cox.

'Trew,' said the man from Fowey.

25

Lotus-eating among November fuschias the traveller de-
scends into Clovelly, goes kernobbling, is shipwrecked on
Dartmoor and is warned about the inhabitants of the isle of
saints.

1

IT WAS almost mid-November but the fuchsia was still tumbling over
walls into the steep village of Clovelly as it had done when Kingsley
lived there and Dickens walked down to the lilliputian harbour with
Wilkie Collins. Woods of a rustier red plunged over the 400-foot high
edge of Devon into a mill-pond sea. Out in the Bristol Channel, twelve
miles off Hartland Point, the cliff-bound disc of Lundy Island lay like a
big round cheese. Palm trees rustled. The touch of frost I'd felt on bonfire
night in Torrington was just a memory.

By now I had enough material for half a dozen books on England. All I
had to do was to turn the car due south, fire a few words in the direction of
the Fleet at Plymouth, cross the river Tamar into Cornwall (which some
would argue isn't England anyway), perhaps haul King Arthur from the
signal locker of national sentiment as I passed Tintagel way, salute an

Atlantic sunset at Land's End, and this part of the job at any rate – the travelling part – could be finished in a day.

But it was not so easy. Each chance encounter led on to yet another and there was an enchantment in the air that increased the density of time itself. I told myself it was the untimely weather (at least to me, a northerner, it seemed untimely) that threw reality a little out of focus and seduced resolve . . .

I was not finished yet with Bideford but next day I rambled and came first to Appledore – the name itself is an argument for tarrying – and there I visited a shipyard. I used to know a bit about building ships. In my north-east youth the noise and squalor of the yards was part of life. But here were no stocks and slipways or acres of industrial litter. There were lawns and palms and rhododendrons and a big, blue swimming-pool for shipyard workers. Steel plates were stored as neat as books on library shelves and ships were constructed in a row of 'halls' – the 'preparation hall', the 'panel hall', and finally a hall as big as a cathedral which contained a drydock. On one side of this a vessel was being assembled from prefabricated parts placed in position by men in shiny hardhats who operated cranes by remote control with electric handsets. When, on the other side, a new hull was completed, there was no clumsy trip to a marine engineering yard a mile – or even a river – away, attended by manoeuvring tugs. The dock was flooded. The powered vessel, complete to the last coat of paint, sailed out for ocean trials. A new shell was moved across to take its place for fitting out. The dock was pumped dry. And the elements of a third hull, already fashioned in the prefabrication area, began to take ship shape at the vacated quay. The chairman and managing director – the man behind this feat of timing – occupied an office in a small Georgian mansion behind a moat of flower beds. He was a bluff, swashbuckling Geordie called Jim Venus.

Hard by the shipyard a writer worked in his small cottage upon a monograph of Bernard Shaw, advertising his literary products in the front window to passing shipyardmen. Outside in the estuary a family of amphibious tanks wallowed like playful porpoises.

On the sea wall I fell into disagreement with a man who said the combined Taw and Torridge rivers emptied into Barnstaple Bay although the map – with my thumb obscuring the words 'Barnstaple or . . .' – clearly said Bideford Bay. The name is a matter of choice, of course, unless you came from Bideford or Barnstaple in which case you stood up and fought like a man. I plumped for Bideford for the love of argument. My opponent was from Barnstaple and chose to ignore my thumb for the same reason, I suppose.

In a nearby pub the handsome barmaid, discovering I had a caravan, warned me against sudden frosts at this time of year. 'Wrap up well at night,' she said. 'The frost can play hell with your vegetable patch. Many a fine man has seen his prize carrot wither on such nights.'

With that dire warning in my ears I wandered off through Fairy Cross, Woolfardisworthy, Alfardisworthy and Stibb and Shop. Past Hartland Point where the eighteenth-century lighthouse stands at the foot of the great cliffs while high on the headland a great steel gantry, like a metal sculpture of the fifties, dwarfs time, topography and distance – the radar scanners nodding soundlessly.

Bare Hartland almost broke my lotus-eating mood, but driving east I coasted three miles down a road called Hobby Drive among dense, exotic trees. And when, from time to time, there was a clear view of the bay below, the sea looked still as glass. So, by this wayward route, I came upon Clovelly. Or rather I arrived at a large car park and wondered where Clovelly was.

Clovelly is a mystery. For the last thousand years (there is evidence of Norman habitation) it has clung to its Devon cliff face in defiance of both gravity and commonsense. What advantage could there be in stringing a settlement half-way up a cliff when there are so many other places where sheep might safely graze or one's fellowmen be more comfortably fleeced? When a parishioner of Clovelly needs a bag of dolly blue he or she must assault a precipice to reach the general store. If he or she forgets some essential item – such as a postage stamp – it becomes necessary to run all the way back like a mountain goat. Elsewhere men have built settlements in inconvenient places. They have done so for the sake of gold or water, to be safe from their enemies or closer to their God. Clovelly has me beaten. Every Englishman (and woman) should, sometime in his life, go to Clovelly – if only because it is a great deal handier than the Pyramids of Gizeh or any of the other riddles of the world. He should avoid the summer months when it becomes a half-mile cascade of human beings of almost every nation. And ideally he should arrive at about that time of a balmy afternoon when some softening of the light unmeasurable to the eye, a deepening of the colours of the plunging headlands or an infinite-simal darkening of the sea, informs the senses of approaching dusk. So I was fortunate enough to do.

I walked to the car park's seaward side and, hearing voices, looked at the water far below and realised they came from a lifeboat on permanent station outside a tiny harbour, her riding lights already burning. The village lay between – barely disclosed by the surrounding trees, the sounds of its 434 inhabitants inaudible. So it had hung between sea and sky, unknown to the outside world, till 1855 when Charles Kingsley, son of the Clovelly rector, used it as a set for *Westward Ho!* Then came the other writers. Then the artists with their easels, then the pleasure steamers, from Ilfracombe and Weston-super-Mare, the tuppeny photographers, and now the chrome-trimmed super-coaches.

Dickens tried to do Clovelly justice in the opening lines of 'A Message from the Sea' (to be found in the *Christmas Stories*).

> The village was built sheer up the face of a steep and lofty cliff. There was no road . . . not a level yard. From the sea-beach to the top two irregular rows of white houses . . . rose like the sides of a long succession of crooked ladders . . . The old pack saddle, long laid aside in most parts of England, flourished here intact . . . As the beasts of burden ascended laden, or descended light, they got lost at intervals in the floating clouds of village smoke . . . Captain Jorgan struck his leg with his open hand, as some men do when they are pleased – and said – 'A mighty sing'lar and pretty place it is, as ever I saw in all the days of my life!'

S. P. B. Mais, in the 1920s, wrote of 'wandering in the darkness and at dawn up and down the deserted way in order to inhale the amazing atmosphere [of] night-scented stock, the fuchsias, honeysuckle, hydrangeas, japonica and rhododendrons . . .' And Arthur Mee in the 1930s called it 'the place incredible . . . still laughing at the motor car'. Morton went in tourist time and only found it 'quaint'.

I set off down a cobbled path that at first paralleled the sea – the rich leafage of the cliff-face on my right, a wall adrip with flowers and lichen to my left, and entering the village a little further down, found all they had described. Here were all the flowers that had kept faith with the weather. The smell of the sea. The white houses looking as rooted in the rock as if some Herculean mason had carved them out on site.

A boy passed me with a burden on a sledge.

The road twisted right and into a small canyon with a spring gushing from a moss-green wall opposite some troglodyte's front door – then left again to tunnel beneath the very houses and plunged on. At last the causeway widened, becoming more gentle in descent, then swinging subtly left, emerged with a sideways curtsey on the quayside.

Immediately before me was a three-storeyed inn with a row of blind arches along the lowest level. In days of trading yawls and ketches this lower floor must have been a storehouse for village goods supplied by sea. From a nearby house a balcony on sloping props craned out above the tideline. Boats were drawn up on shingle. The main pier of the tiny port was built of pink boulders in three receding tiers. There were tilting bollards, timber buttresses shaped by time and tide, and worn flights of steps from water's edge up to a navigational lightpost on the pierhead with a little cast-iron crow's-nest.

Compact, diminutive, an exquisite fragment caught between cliff and sea, it is tempting to describe Clovelly harbour as a little operatic stage with the climbing village up behind as backdrop. But whatever made the earliest inhabitants fix their dwellings in a fissure on a cliff face, and however it is seen by summer visitors and the West Country Tourist Board, it was not built for entertainment.

There were no other strangers at the inn. A local woman in the bar, mistaking my recorder for a transistor radio, frowned with a disapproval I quite understood.

Someone told me that in 1652 three Turkish ships carried off the inhabitants of Lundy into slavery and that several times Clovelly men had put out to the island to deal with foreign pirates.

Someone else said that Lundy Island had once been an Irish settlement, that a Barnstaple MP with contracts to ship slaves to America had leased Lundy and transported them no further – for which sleight of private enterprise he had been fined £5,000 in the courts of George II – and that one W. H. Heaven had bought the place for £10,000 in 1834, declared it 'free territory' and successfully defied the jurisdiction of the Devon magistrates. Which is why for years Lundy was known locally as 'the Kingdom of Heaven'.

A man in a white sea-jersey told me how HMS *Montagu* – a pre-dreadnought battleship with 12-inch guns – struck Shutter Point and sank one foggy night in 1906. However, all were rescued and the only casualties were the captain and navigation officer who got a wigging.

An old salt called George Lamey, aged eighty-three, who lived in a cosy grotto of a house above the harbour, topped me up with tales of intelligence work among coastal shipping in World War II, of German airmen rescued from the sea, one of whom came back to thank Clovelly, and of hard times when storms closed the harbour for weeks on end and the fishermen of seventy Clovelly boats poached river salmon to feed their families. He had been paid in Woodbines at thirteen when first he went to sea, had served ashore against the Turks at Suvla Bay while in the Royal Navy, and was Clovelly's lifeboat cox for twenty years. 'The lifeboat business runs in our family like wooden legs.'

It was all good, seaside, happy-ending, *Boys' Own Paper* stuff, sanitised by time.

Now the trading ketches are all gone. Half today's inhabitants are newcomers from as far inland as Birmingham. There are just a few fishing boats; the harvest is not herring but a multitude of tourists, and most of the old sailormen are sepia shadows on picture postcards sold to the visitors.

Outside the inn there was now an inshore breeze and the tide was lapping at the harbour steps. A light flickered far out at sea, one short flash for each five seconds of receding time – the Lundy light the *Montagu* had failed to see in 1906.

My footfalls rang and slithered on the cobbles as I climbed. The trees folded over and the village was buried in the dark.

Back at Bideford the Royal Mail was crowded. Captain Cox sat where I'd left him yesterday. Through the din I heard him saying: 'One ole sailen vessel I was in . . . ole skippur used to make me clean 'is shoes. One mornen after breckfuss 'ee say to me "Y'eor boy, clean they! An' put a shine on!" Well, I cleaned 'en, polished 'en, rubbed a nice bit o' cloth over 'en, an' I put a shine on like a cat's arse in the moonlight . . .'

A large man in a red pullover leaned across and told me he had a farm at Holsworthy and that I would be welcome.

2

That was one of the pleasures and the hazards of the whole journey. I would arrive in a town or village I had scarcely heard of and soon there would be a network of acquaintances, an eagerness of informants, and downright generosity of that quiet, undemonstrative kind that is an English speciality. That was fine. The danger was that I would become too involved, too comfortable, and linger on gathering too much moss.

I make no bones about it, that is what occurred in Devon. My journey was drawing to an end. The last opium days of an Indian summer lay over an Arcadian countryside. Cornwall was still ahead but I felt like those sailors who, landing on the breadfruit islands and finding friendly natives, were reluctant to move on.

It is perhaps pertinent to note here how so many people urged me to see their local historian. Parish history seems to have become an obsession of the English lower middle class. But unless I had some special interest to pursue I avoided them for fear of being overwhelmed by detail. I gave a wide berth to town clerks as well, for with some notable exceptions they are a muttonheaded tribe. The local rascal, the intelligent policeman or the energetic farmer took me closer to the essence of a place and were anyway more entertaining.

Which is why next forenoon, accepting the invitation of the man in the red pullover, I made my way to Leworthy Farm, a rambling, white-painted house with a little lake in park-like countryside and with a far view of Dartmoor.

My host, Eric Cornish, was a large man of large humours and large appetites. I could not at first make up my mind whether he was formed on the John Bull model and Tory to the core, or if he was of the Mr Wardle pattern like the liberal-minded yeoman who lavished such hospitality on the Pickwickians at Dingley Dell – both admirable templates – but, I concluded in the end that he was an out-and-out original.

I arrived in time for a traditional Sunday dinner after which family and guests retreated to the front room to recover. All at once the post-prandial calm was shattered. Eric leapt from his armchair, grabbed his double-barrelled shotgun, fired two rounds through the front window, recharged, and then subsided into his seat muttering 'Damn those birds!' It was an unnerving interruption and no sooner were we all resettled when he was back on his feet – bang-bang, click-click and 'Damn those birds!'

Apparently he had stocked the lake with trout at great expense, a benefaction much appreciated by a pair of heron whose ambition seemed to be to polish off the lot before anglers could get them. Eric's pyrotechnics were just a warning, but he might as well have saved himself the price of cartridges for a few minutes after every volley the lovely birds sailed back.

My first evening with Leworthy's host was memorable for pubs and eggs. He took me on a tour of neighbouring villages and in every one a hostelry blazed cheer into the night. It was grand country for connoisseurs of beams, hearths, great oak tables and all the impedimenta that make the English pub so mysteriously more than the sum of its delightful parts. We also enjoyed the hospitality of Leworthy neighbours and it must have been one o'clock when we returned to the farm kitchen, the scrubbed table, the agricultural calendars and the plates warming on the Aga.

'What about a fried-egg sandwich?' asked Eric John-Bull-Wardle Cornish. 'Three eggs or six?'

I am not sure if Eric Cornish was really a Devonian (I think he told me he was from Somerset or Dorset) but the sheer abundance of the man, his appetite and zest for life, stamped Devon for me during those last truant days when I made Leworthy my base. But for him I would not have found myself in a farmers' cooperative depot helping to rig a carnival float. (There seemed to be carnivals everywhere and all held at night – but why in winter? Unless to celebrate the departure of the 'grockles', the Devon name for summer visitors.) Nor would I have encountered, at one such festival, a party of men in crimson britches and wide, feathered hats singing 'Suvla Bay' from pub to pub. They turned out to be my old 'Cavalier' acquaintances from Torrington. 'Where are you drinking Frank . . . come on with us!'

Had I not lingered I would not have learned to play Kernobbling (pronounced Kernobblen'), a pub game in which you guess or calculate the number of coins concealed in the hands of your opponents – which sounds innocent enough for any parson's parlour but not the way it's played around Dartmoor. Losers buy drinks all round. 'Kitty' games in league matches can end in £100 celebrations and disputes have been settled with Kernobbling that might have gone to court.

Nor would I have taken part in an even fiercer game called 'Buzz' in which twenty or more men sat for a whole evening in a hired pub room snapping out numbers like naval gun crews rapping back their orders. I can't remember much about the rules of Buzz and little wonder. An elected chairman was given dictatorial powers to change them all at whim. It was a game of wit, arithmetic and memory in which clearheadedness fought with the contents of a brown, two-gallon jug. I forget how it came to a conclusion except that there was much singing and embracing.

In daylight I explored the labyrinthine lanes that tunnel through the county like wormholes in a piece of timber. They are so deep and their hedgebanks are so high that, traversing them, one is in a half-subterranean world through which opposing armies might pass within a quarter-mile without a sighting. One assumed that roads existed to conduct goods and people from one place to another. If so, where were the starting points and destinations of these wayward trenches? I consulted my old mentor Hoskins. In *English Landscapes** he suggests they began as boundary ditches setting one man's land apart from that of his neighbour and that some were already ancient a thousand years ago. But why in this west country and not elsewhere?

Pondering such pleasant riddles I came on houses made of mud – that is to say 'cob' which is a mixture of clay, chopped straw and bits of slate which can last for centuries. There is an old Devon saying that all cob needs is 'a good hat and a decent pair of shoes' – a watertight roof and good foundations. Cob was tread-mixed by farm animals and men. Each foot-high course was forked on in lumps and allowed to dry before another course was added. Thus it could take a year to raise a storey after which, whiskery with straw-ends, it was shaved before whitewashing. There are clay-built dwellings in other parts of England, but more buildings of unbaked clay survive in Devon than in any other county. And the English countryside offers few more pleasant scenes of habitation than a cob hamlet with its rounded corners and rippling walls, looking as though it had sprouted like a colony of mushrooms.

* Professor Hoskins records that in 1844 a surveyor showed that the hedges of but ten East Devon parishes totalled 1,651 miles – half as long again as the Great Wall of China – and the hedges of one single parish equalled the distance between Land's End and Edinburgh.

I have remarked elsewhere about the subtle yet immense variety of the English landscape and the fact that common institutions have not erased all cultural differences. Nowhere is this more striking than in Devon. How different was this land and people from the moorland and lean faces of Lancashire just 200 miles behind me. The benevolence of the warm Gulf Stream and the presence of two coastlines might be advanced as reasons. But Cornwall has these too and yet it seems to me that Cornishmen warm more slowly to strangers, their humour is rougher, more aggressive. It has been said that Devon is a land of Saxons while Cornwall is all Celt, the implication being that Devonians are of sunnier disposition (which is true) and less imaginative (which is not). My observation is that there is an even greater readiness for fun and games and fantasy east of the Tamar. Perhaps, after all, all Celtishness was not expelled from Devon when the Saxons came . . .

One day I trundled down to Exeter. Of course I was three decades late to see it at its best, for one spring day in 1942 the German radio announced: 'We have chosen as targets the most beautiful places in England. This Exeter was a jewel. We have destroyed it.'

Ernst von Kugel, pilot of a Junkers 88, declared: 'I saw whole streets on fire . . . People were running everywhere . . . We thought of the thousands of men, women and children, the victims of our deadly visit . . . but we thought of our Führer and the word of command he had given – "Revenge!" '

Well, you could see old Exeter afire that night from thirty miles away while the bombers came in low enough to identify nurses' uniforms and machine-gun them for the Führer. But Exeter was not destroyed. As Pevsner has written since: 'The German bombers found it primarily a medieval city. They left it . . . Georgian and early Victorian. . . . the close-knit pattern of medieval streets and alleys, parish churches and houses irretrievably gone.'

Now the town centre on its little rise has been rebuilt in the architectural idiom of our own times – the same old chain-store kit parts you will find from Calais to Cumbernauld – yet with a modesty that is almost charming. Nothing – apart from the unforgivable tower block at the head of the high street – throws its weight about. And it is curious and rather moving to find the little old bits of parish churches that Kugel could not raze among the stores and offices. One of them sits sugar-pink a bit self-consciously in the middle of a shopping centre and you look twice to be sure it is not a clever bit of advertising. Time, I suppose, will mellow the incongruity.

And the cathedral is still there, lying like a great grey creature behind the bustle of new shops. How privileged the citizens of Exeter to walk by the foot of that fantastically carved west front on their way to the bread shop or the office. Or to enjoy at will the longest run of Gothic vaulting in the world. But someone scuppered that. They stuck a great organ half-way down the church and blocked the view. Such insensitivity baffles me. The perpetrators should have their names engraved on a plaque as a warning to all developers – ecclesiastical or not – to mind their bloody manners.

The Guildhall survived the Führer too – the oldest municipal building in the kingdom, already more than four hundred years old when Drake was a little lad. And the Turk's Head, where Dickens, seeing a corpulent youth of torpid mien, begat Mr Wardle's fat boy. But all that is in the guidebooks, along with the amazing Maritime Museum and its remarkable collection of craft – steam, sail and oar – moored alongside the oldest inland waterway in England (1567).

But what is most remarkable about Exeter is that despite its population of 100,000, its bright, contemporary shops, and the broad ring of respectable, if comfortably seedy, Edwardian and Victorian streets, it still feels like a county town where country neighbour might meet country neighbour. Somehow, it retains a connection with the hills and fields and creeks of Devon. The old curves and contours have not been erased, and surviving scraps of the old sailors' town preserve a sense of continuity.

'Next to mine own shippe,' wrote Francis Drake, 'I do most love that old "Shippe" in Exon, a tavern in Fyssh Street as the people call, or, as the clergie have it, St Martin's Lane . . .' Well, I took the alley called St Martin's Lane – round the corner from Mol's Coffee House where the Queen's Admirals met in the Armada Room – and found the three-master painted on the signboard. The first customer I met there gave me a guide to the real-ale pubs of Devon. The names of town and tavern spoke of England in a Devon accent. The Double Locks at Alphington, the Lobster Pot at Hope Cove, the Hungry Fox at Broad Clyst, the King William at Budleigh Salterton, the Old Thatch at Cheriton Bishop, the Nobody Inn at Doddiscombsleigh, the New Inn at Sampford Courtney, the Devonshire Arms at Sticklepath, the New Fountain at Whimple, the Peter Tavy at Peter Tavy, the Sloop, the Royal Oak, the Digger's Rest, the Mare and Foal, the Black Venus, the Royal Marine, the Minerva, the Ferry House, the Archer, the Artillery, the Dartmoor Railway, the Live and Let Live, the Traveller's Rest, the Journey's End . . . thatch and panel, pickled egg and handpump . . . thank you stranger, but, alas, life is far too short.

Instead, I took myself to the White Hart in South Street (which is on the way to those splendid quayside warehouses that pretend to be Onedin's Liverpool in the television series) in the hope of finding my

Professor Hoskins. Someone told me it was his local and though I had never met him I had for so long been nourished by his works on the meaning of the English landscape that I thought it would be pleasant to tell him so. Well, he was out of town but now I owe him another debt for the White Hart turned out to be a jewel. The façade was unpretentious and late Georgian but passing through an arch straight off the pavement I found myself in a little crooked courtyard full of foliage among which stood a half-naked lady on a plinth said to have been left by a customer who could not pay his bill in cash but overpaid in marble. Beyond and on either side rambled the perfect English city pub, a gleaming darkness of comfortable old bars, of pewter jugs, wine rooms, hallways, staircases, stone walls and plaster and it was all pickled in the incense of good cooking served in substantial pots across the counters. The company was native and therefore excellent.

I returned to Holsworthy that night by way of Copplestone and Zeal Monachorum.

3

Up at Leworthy the year was on the change at last. One morning there were frozen puddles in the farmyard. Trees were bare. The hedgerow oak was in his winter dotage, sporting a few rags of red and yellow motley, and the sun was diluted gold as I set off one late afternoon for Fowey by way of Dartmoor. I might have chosen a more direct route had I known that there were demons in the air.

The storm struck soon after darkness. I have experienced typhoon in the South China Sea. And Arctic Snow. I am old enough to recall, and with nostalgia, how we felt our way down Fetter Lane and along the Strand to report blindly on the last great London fogs. But no other territory has so promptly and dramatically confirmed its reputation as Dartmoor did that night. Trees lashed out then hurled their broken limbs into my path so that I had to turn about and seek other ways. The rain was not just rain. It was a seething, hissing, blinding torrent that wiped out the windscreen view and killed the headlamp beam.

I have a good compass in my head, but that soon failed to function. When I reached a crossroads I had to get a torch and climb up banks in saturated trousers to read signposts pointing to places I had never heard of then and have not heard of since. I was completely lost.

At one moorland fork I came suddenly upon a sharp-prowed building like a storm-stranded ship showing a few lights. It turned out to be an inn. I worked my way round the walls feeling for a door. At first none yielded and no one heard my knock. But on my second trip around I managed to push one open and entered a large room where at first I was almost as blinded by the light as I had been by darkness.

There were only two men there, the barman and another. They gawped as if I were an apparition, for who but an idiot ghost would be about on such a night? I asked for a double whisky and directions, explaining I had telephoned ahead to book a berth in a village called Polruan. They had never heard of it, but when I mentioned its proximity to Fowey they gave me what instructions they were able, which ten minutes later proved of little use.

We have all been in storms. But one is affected too by time and place. I knew that beyond the walls of my little cell of steel lay the wastes of Dartmoor, the notorious bogs, the tumuli of long-forgotten people, the tors protruding from the moor like broken ribs. It was a Dickensian tempest, worrying, yes, but oddly comforting as well. I was moving over the great wold like a character in a gripping yarn read beside a well-stacked fire. The fallen trees, the roads that had become watercourses,* the very name of Dartmoor, were like something in a storybook. Even when I descended to the coastal plain – by good luck more than my instinct for direction – and I could see familiar road signs, the sense of unreality persisted.

It was still raining. Plymouth and Devonport were a wet blur of lights over on my left. I joined a queue of cars for petrol. Two vehicles ahead a police car was refuelling and, still uncertain of my way, I got out to ask a woman constable. 'Ah,' she said, 'Polruan – that will be in Cornwall. I'm sorry, I can't help you, but I think it will take at least three hours.' Then, as if musing on the edge of uncharted country – 'They're strange people down in Cornwall.'

Damn it, but Cornwall was only streets away! The Tamar was just along the road, Polruan less than thirty miles. And she a policeman! It was not the first time I'd realised the Tamar ran so deep, and that some Cornishmen think of Cornwall as a separate country† which should be called Kernow. There had been that water bailiff back at St Giles who told me of the missing racing pigeons released in France. Where did I think they got to? Fallen in the water? Nothen of the sort. Landed in Cornwall for a rest they did, poor things. Snaffled by Cornishmen they were!

---

* Annual average rainfall in the Thames estuary is 20 inches. In Exeter it is 31. On parts of Dartmoor it is well over 100.
† Indeed, Cornwall is almost an island. The Tamar runs along all but five miles of the county border.

I paid my emigration fee to cross by the new toll bridge that now accompanies the splendid railway structure built by Isambard Kingdom Brunel in the 1850s and found myself in Saltash – an English enough sounding name that would be dismal even on the lower Tees among the chemical refineries.

It is only when you move down the peninsula with the Anglo-Saxons at your back that you know you've crossed a frontier. In Devon geography may be 'jog-a-free', a gramophone a 'grammer-fone', and furniture 'furny-toor',* but the link with formal English is apparent. And place-names, though more poetical than in most other parts of England, could belong to no other tongue. In Cornwall an unfamiliar poetry besieges you. You are beckoned by old Brythonic syllables to Egloskerry, Treneglos and Tregadillet. There are names like Gwithian, Marazion and Lezant – Rosemullion, Seworgan, Perranzabuloe, Feock, Germoe, and Crawsandra with the accent on the 'ra' which means witch's cross. The words are from a tongue that was old before the English came to England. It sounds different from the Scotch and Irish kinds of Celtic and its relationship with Welsh seems only rhythmic. There are places named for Cornish saints as well – dozens of them. St Erth, St Enodoch, St Ia and St Ewe. St Issey, St Mawgan, St Pirran, St Tudy and St Teath. It is as if, in some misty age, Kernow had been swept by a religious mania which – thank God! – could not have happened to the English. Never can sainthood have been so common. A chap called St Kerri arrived in Cornwall from the sister land of Wales. He had three wives, uncounted concubines, twenty-four sons, twenty-five daughters, and every one of them became a saint, they say.

Beyond Saltash when the rain stopped I was lost in another labyrinth of deep west-country lanes. Pausing to read signposts I could smell the sea, but I was entangled among the dripping trees and banks with new-washed stars above and no way out. At last, though, as I passed a sign pointing to St Veep, the woods released me. I topped a rise, left trees behind and saw a lighthouse flashing far ahead. The sea stirred somewhere down below and all at once I plunged into Polruan and down the steepest high street since I'd left Clovelly. It was narrow too, and when I found my destination, a converted dairy, I had to run down to the little harbour, turn round on the quayside and drive back up again to a car park on a promontory between the top chimneys of the village and a cliff drop into the English Channel.

The air was sweet. Beneath me were the gleaming rooftops. Beyond

* From *The Devonshire Dialect* by Clement Marten, published by Clement Marten Publications, 15 Castle Street in the City of Exeter in the County of Devon England.

and running inland was the Fowey River, * and the lights of Fowey town strung along the other shore sent a glinting, shifting lacework of reflection across the darkling water. I could hear the faint slap and tinkle of swaying mainmast tackle and I thought I could see the rigging of a three-masted schooner down the midstream moorings. I found a steep, deep alleyway to take me through the backyards and the chimney pots and I slept well at the dairy.

* Fowey is pronounced 'Foy'.

26

Recounts how the traveller smells a rat in Troytown, is challenged by a gravedigger called Mister Puck, hears about the socialist republic of Cornwall, and comes at last to journey's end among the eucalyptus trees of St Just in Roseland.

1

I AM GOING to stick my neck out. I am going to say that there is no better place in the whole Duchy* in which to seek out Cornwall than in the port of Fowey and its surrounding creeks and hamlets.

Others, smitten by the full-blown beauty of Polperro, will disagree. They have been enchanted by the tiny harbour at the bottom of the coombe, the old houses and artists' studios propped and piled up around, plants of a Mediterranean luxuriance pouring down the walls and jagged rocks forming a barbaric gateway to the sea. Polperro is indeed spectacular. But hers is the obvious gorgeousness of the professional beauty queen. Even in the winter there is a whiff of greasepaint about Polperro.

---

* Cornwall was the first English dukedom. It was instituted by Edward III in 1337 to support the Black Prince. The monarch's first son has always inherited the Duchy.

Some people find their Cornwall in St Ives, in Falmouth or Penzance, and each has merits. But each – and each in a different way – has had its Cornish elbows blunted by rubbing up against the world. Fowey has somehow resisted such erosion. However well it sits among its woods, looking like an eighteenth-century engraving, it is not a set-piece. It has not become an artists' dormitory, nor has it given in, hat-spade-and-bucket, to the tourists. Perhaps a certain isolation and an entrenched squirearchy have had an influence, providing an unseen barrier behind which a wiry sort of independence and a mischievous awkwardness have been able to survive.

Fowey is almost as far from London as is Newcastle. It is avoided by the 'Cornish Riviera' railway line. It is served by two fairly unimportant roads. One comes from the west against the current of pleasure-seeking traffic and the other is a B-road down from Bodmin. Both end at the river Fowey. From seaward the way into Fowey is but a break in the rampart of cliff and headland that guards the southern coast. Two little forts – an arrow's flight apart – stand at the entrance. Between these they used to raise a chain to dismast intrusive strangers. You do not chance on Fowey, you have to want to go there.

But inside the harbour entrance the estuary broadens, becoming a lagoon-like haven with room enough to hide a fleet. To starboard Polruan village tumbles its old, sunbleached houses down to the water's edge. On the other shore St Fimbarrus' Church rings out the hours and Fowey backs up the hill in broken terraces, as prim as if she'd never heard of piracy or sent a king's emissary back to London with his ears cut off. Upstream, beyond the quays and Customs House, the woods spill down the heights from either side. Past church and manor, by abundant gardens, close to kitchen windows, seamen's taverns, the sitting-rooms of retired Cornish captains and through fleets of fallen, drifting leaves, glide the oceangoing ships. They moor just where the river bends and disappears among the trees, to load great off-white bellyfuls of china clay. There is an old New England air about the place.

Fowey has not been ignored by the writers, though. It is Daphne du Maurier country for a start. As a girl and young woman she lived next door to the Ship Inn at Bodinnick where the woods begin. There she heard the tales of Fowey's private wars with France, the sport with Spain, the carelessness about the laws of contraband and occasional short-sightedness when it came to distinguishing between English ships and those of any other flag if there was a little business to be done with cutlasses and a bit of profit to be made. From her window young Daphne watched the cargo ships sail in – one day a yacht that brought her future husband – and there she wrote *Frenchman's Creek*. Out walking she saw a house called Menabilly beyond the woods behind Fowey town. She dreamt of living there. In time she did and it became 'Rebecca's' Manderley and half the English-reading world recalls the first sentence of that cracking yarn: 'Last night I dreamt I went to Manderley again. . .'

'Q' – Sir Arthur Quiller-Couch, the classics don who compiled the Oxford books of English Prose and Verse – was a mayor and freeman of the town. In his rumbustious novel *The Astonishing History of Troy Town* (1888), which I have never read, 'Troy Town' was Fowey.

> 'O the harbour of Fowey
> Is a beautiful spot,
> And it's there I enjowey
> To sail in a yot . . .'

wrote the illustrious 'Q' for some reason I cannot possibly imagine.

It is also 'the little grey sea town' of *The Wind in the Willows* which I have read a dozen times and will read a dozen times again. Kenneth Grahame wrote it as a bedtime story for his son on visits to his friend 'Q'.

There, said the Sea Rat in a chapter that haunts a million grown-up Englishmen, there . . . 'through dark doorways you look down flights of stone steps, overhung by great pink tufts of valerian and ending in a patch of sparking blue water . . . at its destined hour, the ship of my choice will let go its anchor . . . and then one morning . . . I shall wake to the clink of the capstan and the rattle of the anchor chain. We shall break out the jib and foresail, the white houses on the harbour side will glide slowly past us as she gathers steering way . . . And you, you will come too, young brother; for the days pass and never return, and the South still waits for you . . . I will linger and look back; and at last I will surely see you coming, eager and light-hearted, with all the South in your face!' Well, as we know, Rat packed his satchel and took his stick, but being one of those English, upstream, inland sorts of animal, dreamed first of the great voyage, and then, by stages, dreamed of sheaves and reddening apples, the towering harvest wagons and their straining teams, and stayed at home.

It is not surprising that the town of Fowey inspired these and other storytellers. For not only does it *look* like a sailors' town and a pirate town and a smuggling town and a town where rascality – or what would be counted rascality in Orpington or Slough – was part of the common traffic of the day, but it really *was* such a town, and not so long ago at that.

There is a booklet* on sale at the stationer's behind the quays. No

* *Fowey – A Brief History*, by Kerdroya (I. D. Spreadbury, BA), Jorey & Son, Printers, Fowey.

tourist catchpenny, it is a scholarly little work and it tells the story of the town as plainly as can be. Here and there among its pages there are accounts of loyal deeds and celebrations that would threaten no man with the gallows . . . 47 ships and 770 men sent to the blockade of Calais (1346), 'the greatest contribution in all England', 100 archers shipped to Agincourt (1415), Fowey's part in the rout of the Armada (1588), high jinks at coronations and royal jubilees, D-Day preparations, the purchase of a new town crier's costume (1954). But otherwise it is as brave a catalogue of roguery as would inspire a whole shelf of boys' adventure books.

It tells how the men of Fowey – the Fowey Gallants as they were know far and wide – set out to taunt the Cinque Ports fleet and to flout its royal privileges. It records complaints from France, Germany, Spain and the Low Countries about their spirited behaviour . . . 'these Foye men were grown so rich and formidable by taking . . . prizes, that by force and arms they would enter many ports . . . and carry away all the ships they could conquer . . . and what they could not, they would use means to set on fire . . .'

It recalls that Edward IV ordered the arrest of all masters, mariners and ships of Fowey, Polruan and Bodinnick – and even the victuallers who supplied them – for persistent piracy, to which the Gallants made reply by removing the ears of the Sergeant at Arms who bore the news. When a squadron of Spanish bullion ships sought refuge in the harbour from pursuit by Frenchmen the Gallants obliged by relieving them of their cargo. In 1666 they sheltered the Virginian tobacco fleet of thirty ships from the Netherlands navy, mounting fifty guns against the Dutchmen who retired after a six-day siege.

Smuggling was bread and honey for rich and poor alike. The Mayor of Fowey escaped prosecution in 1824 by emptying his brandy casks at the back door while the Revenue men knocked at the front. Even Coast-guards joined the sport.

However, at about the time of the Reform Bill of 1832 Fowey seemed to change. There had been some questionable manoeuvring by the squire's party during the 1820 elections and Fowey lost its parliamentary seat. The mayoralty-and-corporation – suspected of diverting funds – was dissolved. An official receiver was appointed to administer the town's charities and its inhabitants were placed under the 'protection' of the county magistrates. There was a spectacular haul of contraband by the Revenue cutter *Fox* in 1835. But thenceforward – to judge by the histories and guidebooks – the civic energies of Fowey were devoted to such elevated works as the foundation of hospitals and schools and the opening of golf courses.

I smell a rat. In fact I smell several rats. Though reluctant to abandon the doctrine of the perfectibility of human nature, I feel that histories and guidebooks change their ways more suddenly than men.

I can't recall which charming, beer-drinking Cornish rat it was who directed my attention to the matter of the multiplying cannonballs. Each summer, I was told, skin-divers come to Fowey to explore the waters, and each year there is excitement as they bring ashore large quantities of shot thought to be relics of the Dutch siege and similar amusements. Diver competes with diver for the biggest haul, the veils of history are stirred, and diving being a salty sport, there is much celebration and generosity towards the helpful locals. At season's end when visitors have gone a number of small boats may be seen on some errand in another corner of the port. And next year – lo! – there is another find of cannonballs. Never was there such an arsenal as the bed of Fowey harbour, according to my witness – for whom story-telling proved a thirsty business too.

And as for smuggling – 'well, everyone knows that's all over now', another new companion told me. There was this local man, he said, whose neighbourly visits to the ships moored in the harbour excited the suspicions of the excise men who pounced on him one day as he was about to go ashore. Naturally alarmed at their abrupt appearance, he cleared the gunnels at one leap and struck out for the Albert Quay, the Customs boat in close pursuit. A number of idlers on the quayside cheered at the uneven contest and were quick to lend a hand to their fellow townsman as he reached the wharf with dripping clothes and empty pockets just as the Customs posse arrived. There was an unusual amount of flotsam on the tide that morning – cigarette cartons and the like – but no prosecution.

A strange, reflective lot, those Customs men. I was crossing the harbour with one of them one morning in the cutter when sadly he began to shake his head. 'They can't help it, you know,' he said to the passing water. 'It's bred in them. They have a fly, quiet, cunning nature.'

By that time I had met Mister Puck.

2

The morning following the storm was sparkling. I went out early to seek Sunday papers but everything was locked and there was only one other man about. He was down on the quay outside the Lugger fishing his pram out of the water.

A pram is not a receptacle for infants. That is a perambulator and there can't be much use for those in precipitous Polruan. A pram is a little boat of shallow draught with bows squared off as well as stern. It floats lightly on the water like a coracle. I lent a hand and after we had landed it the man talked about feuds with foreign fishing boats and how to fox the Frenchies over the whereabouts of mackerel. Then all at once he cast me a quick glance, shut up and turned away as if he felt he'd said too much.

I found a path behind a church. It mounted sharply and took me inland, first skirting gardens and boatyard, then wending high above the estuary's eastern shore entered steep woods where the way was slippery with fallen leaves. Breaks in the trees revealed a fine spectacle. Moored in midstream was a small armada – dinghies tugging and dancing at their painters, sports yachts shifting together in the current, and two tops'l schooners that perhaps had taken shelter from the gale. Smoke in pale streamers was whisked from the chimneys of the 'little grey sea town' across the water. Sunlight gilded cornices, flooded quays, flashed the occasional window. And then the Penny Ferry began its daily round between Polruan and Fowey, sputtering across its blue half-mile with standing passengers as easy on the deck as Londoners strap-hanging on the Central Line.

Upstream the Bodinnick car ferry awakened with a diesel Splat! that echoed through the woods and then began its ungainly sidling across the green-brown water of the upper reach. Yachtsmen sculled out to their varnished darlings. Someone was at work with hammer and plank. Reflecting sun and water played on the flanks of big, slumbering, unladen ships from Germany and Greece and there ascended from the empty hulls mysterious bumps and clanks like stabled shires stirring in their sleep. A splendid amphitheatre, a golden opening for a Sunday morning, a little world entire.

But then the path veered from the harbour. It plunged to a winding inlet called Pont Pill,* hidden from Fowey harbour by the trees that clothed its sides and big enough to conceal a brace of galleons. Here was a bridge, an old mill, signs that the place had once been busy and frequented. There was not a soul about. I sat on an abandoned baulk and wondered how I would describe the conundrum of a county that gives itself a foreign name and yet is as inseparable a part of England as Lancashire or Cambridge.

Musing here on the tail end of the whole island I could have composed a soft lament about the slow death of Cornish mining, how Cornishmen invented engines and devised mining methods that have been used wherever men have tunnelled the earth, and how Cornwall missed the profits. The moors and cliffs are studded with ruined winding-engine

---

* Pill is an Old English word for tidal creek, still used in the West Country.

houses as tall and gaunt as pele towers in Northumberland. Arsenic, antimony, bismuth, copper, cobalt, lead, silver, gold, tungsten, pitch-blende – now all dwindled except the china clay shipped out through Fowey, Par and Charlestown. I could have deplored the condition of the fishing industry, then finished with a celebration of the tourist trade, the saviour of the West. But that would not do at all. The decline of mining is an old story better told elsewhere, Grimsby is worse off than Looe and I distrust too hearty a commitment to the tourists. It is no accident that when Devonians call holiday-makers 'grockles' (a little nonsense word for which I can find no etymology) they do so with an indulgent smile. But the Cornish call them 'emmets' and 'emmet' is an old word for 'ant'.

The rasp of a ship's siren rattled round the harbour and came up the Pill in broken echoes. I resumed my trek, emerged with the path on to the heights again, passed a monument to 'Q' that overlooks his town and river, and took the road down past the inn at Bodinnick to catch the ferry outside the old Du Maurier home. I had intended to traverse the crooked streets that cram the Fowey shoreline and take the Penny Ferry back to Polruan, thus completing one of the finest four-mile walks in England. But the pubs were open and stepping into one of them to quench the morning's thirst I came face to face with Mister Puck.

He sat opposite the door, a lanky figure with legs akimbo, a knitted woollen hat stuck on an eagle head. Worn, faded jeans with matching jacket completed his ensemble. He was lean, fit and straight. A Gilbert and Sullivan producer looking for a pirate would have booked him on the spot.

In case I fell in with some inferior brew I enquired about the bitter and cannily bought half a pint.

Mister Puck commented loudly about people 'oo come down 'eor tryen to change the place to their own liken.

We looked one another over.

I stood my ground.

Mister Puck became a little ruder. His audience roared with laughter.

This, I thought, is going to be a stubborn case. And so it proved.

Some people spring from the earth on which they stand, like the weird sisters in *Macbeth*. Such a man was Mister Puck the Polruan gravedigger. No other county, perhaps no other town but Fowey or village but Polruan, could have produced him. He was as native and appropriate as the stone forts at the harbour bar. I learned later that he had borne the name of Puck since schooldays, retained it through a lively manhood, and now sixtyish, a little grizzled and stiffer in the knees, he had no mind to change it for a Jonesian or Smithsonian old age. I never did find out what name his mother gave him at the font or what surname he inherited. He was Mister Puck – or simply Puck – to all.

During the next few days he turned up everywhere. He was aboard the ferry, in the pub or on the street. The more skilfully I parried his cutlass thrusts the more he sharpened to the fray. To him, it seemed, I was the year's last emmet and he was going to let me know it.

The weather changed one morning when I had been buying sausages at Fowey. Squally showers swept the streets. Returning by the Penny Ferry to keep an appointment in the Russell I had a choppy passage, and a ship that had come downstream as serene as a Cunarder checked way between the forts and lunged off with a corkscrew roll into a world of spray and white-capped waves. At the Russell I barely noticed a group sat round a table beside a new-made fire. My companion had not turned up. ''Ad to go to sea this mornen . . . Left a message to say 'ee would be back d'rec'ly.' I knew about that word 'd'rec'ly'. It is the Cornish version of *mañana*. It means nex'-time-we-'appen to meet. I stood up at the bar with a sandwich.

The conversation at my back might have been entitled 'Notable Funerals in Polruan Since 1927'. One tale concerned the obsequies of a well-known writer whose ashes had been scattered on the sea on such a day as this.

Voice 1 – Flag was histe 'alf mast at the Coas'guards an' we set off at ar-past six. No buggor arrived on time an' I thought What's going on . . . ?

Voice 2 (female) – Well, I was in the Seagull 'aving tea. An' there they all were, the family, sitting at the table with the poor soul's ashes in the middle. I felt 'orrible really . . .

Voice 1 – We 'ad to go three miles off, an' t'was rough. Th'ole mother got as sick as hell an' we layed her in the bottom of the boat an' covered 'er with coats . . .

Voice 3 – Mind, the *Boy Bob* could move across the water then – she could so!

Voice 2 – Really 'orrible I felt, drinking my tea there . . .

Voice 1 – 'Alfway across the bay I said to 'er – Where do you want this to go? I said . . . I 'ad to speak p'lite to 'er . . . D'ye want to keep this, I said, for a flower vaise I said, in your bedroom? *Good idea,* she said. So I unscrewed en. It wor the ashes! OO-oo-OO-oo . . . the tears was flowen . . . Well, th'ole lady, she was delighted. She said to 'er daughter-in-law she said – *Now, I think we'll all go to the Riverside and have a good piss-up,* she said. That's the very words she used. Away we goes. Dear old lady – she cuddled my arm. I told 'er – Look Missis, I said, 'fore we go any further I got no money, I told 'er straight . . . *Money's no object,* she said. *Come in, come in . . .*

(*Pause*)

270

Voice 1 – 'Ee 'ad always said to me – When I die, Puck, you can bury me at sea. And so I ded!

Puck!

I turned, resting my tape recorder on the table, and saw that Mister Puck himself was president and chief mourner of the fireside party. A jolly party it was too and prepared at last to tolerate this emmet.

'I reckon the best time, Jimmy, was when we buried th'ole Vicar's 'orse.'

'I was away with the football but my son was there,' said Jimmy.

'Switch that buggor on an' I'll tell you this story,' said Mister Puck, nodding at my machine. Someone fetched the drinks and he began.

'I got a young niece you see, an' I was 'eor in this pub one Good Friday she came knocken on the door and asked the landlord if Uncle Puck was 'eor. "Oh," she said, "come up 'ome Uncle," she said. "The Vicar is standing in the court with 'is missis crying." I thought "What's gone wrong with they pair?" Well . . . I goes up . . . an' poor ole Vicar was cryen . . . an' 'is ole woman was cryen. "Good Morning, sir" I said.

'"Oh, Mister Puck, ahr *horse* is drowned. Can you bury *him*?" 'ee said. The 'orse 'ad fallen in a ditch up in the hills behind the Pont river. The farmer couldn't get there with a tractor.

'"All right Sir," I said. "Can't do nothen today though . . . Good Friday . . . Our Lord was crucified today . . . I'll see to it tomorrow."

'Well, me and my old mate Ivor works out a plan for using blocks and tackle and a telegram pole. We goes up with a harmonium and all in the bloody boat. And fourteen able-bodied men jumps in another boat with whisky, rum and two cases of Bass, an' we holds a proper service. Me brother Arthur acts as vicar an' I'm the gravedigger.

'We get the the tackle round the horse's legs and pulls the buggor out the dike and the others grabs 'old an' puts en down the beach. Then me an' Ivor tows en up to the old cold stores – you know where that is, Jim! – come back and rings Mister Peake at the knacker's yard. I says "I've got a horse down 'eor, Mister Peake. Can you fetch en at seven o'clock in the mornen? Fit for dogs' meat – 'ee's only been drowned." "All right, Puck," 'ee says. "Seven-poun'-ten!"

'Well, we finish off the whisky an' the rum then we ring up Sergeant Hawkins at the police station at Fowey to warn 'im we are coming back to 'ave a drink. All hands was in the boat – organ an' all and it was just a small boat. The quay was packed with visitors and the sergeant and three constables waiting. An' we capsize 'or! Oh, we make a proper show! And we get into Missis Harvey's at the King of Prussia at opening time. Oh my Crise the water was streamen out the lot of us . . .

'Well – the Monday afternoon the Vicar come down . . . wants to

271

know where the 'orse is buried. I said – "I'll tell you what we'll do, Vicar, we'll got out tomorrow evening in your little car, Ivor and I." Of course me an' Ivor 'ad to go out to the hill then and heap up a great pile of earth. No 'orse there, you see. The 'orse was out in the knacker's yard.

'"Oh," 'ee said when we all got there on Tuesday, "Wot a wonderful job you *have* done. Now," 'ee said, "we will go back to the vicarage and *have* a little drop of whisky each!" So 'is missus – she was a dear old lady – she says – "Puck, for the wonderful job you *have* done, the Vicar and I will give you another pound each."

'"Thank you very much madam," I said.'

3

When I left Fowey and Polruan I wandered round the old peninsula of granite never more than twenty miles from sea for the excellent and bracing reason that in Cornwall the sea is never more than twenty miles away. I did not go to Land's End to stand on the tip of England and pronounce a valedictory. I had been there before with a pasty in my hand. I had mingled with the jolly crowds from Belfast, New York and Philadelphia and peered with them at the multi-fingered signpost which points out over the Atlantic at just such places and even gives the mileages. But it was not worth another visit.

I am happy to report, though, that I met more honest rascals like Mister Puck than in any other part of England, considering that the population is less than half a million outside the grockle season. I have not consulted all the figures but I bet there's not a town with more than 20,000 souls, and that is a civilising influence. The Romans had it right. I read somewhere that when a city reached a certain size they stopped. Not just because there should be food and services enough for rich and poor but because they thought that too large a city became a social mess. I have enjoyed the monster cities and go back to them. But only for a time. All the best towns can be traversed with ease in much less than half an hour by the vicar's mother on a bike. That is my private scale. It covers Exeter, dismisses Plymouth but includes every town in Cornwall.

I worry about some Cornish towns, though. I called at St Ives (pop. 9,760), the town that proclaimed Perkin Warbeck king and so revered John Wesley and his Methody that it named one thoroughfare Teetotal Street. It has not improved in spirit since. It is picturesque – which is why it has more artists than anywhere but Hampstead – but it seems to be parting from its roots. Its real Cornish roots, I mean, not the anaemic culture that makes plastic piskies for the tourists.

I went to Penzance, mainland Britain's most western town, and had no worries there. Is it the only place in the kingdom that can grow banana trees out in the open? I dined on quail in a restaurant close to the harbour and hard by a Trinity House yard in which green wreck buoys, dan buoys, can buoys, bell buoys and mooring buoys lay this way and that. And for the first time I remember I watched men hand-working a cast-iron capstan with wooden bars like weighing anchor on a sailing ship. In fact, they were opening the dock gates.

Penzance is not ancient, the Spaniards having burned it down in 1595. But it bustles. As a terminus of the old brass-funnelled GWR line from Paddington, it was to generations of Victorian, Edwardian and even thirties children, the magic capital of Cornwall. Down they came in their straw hats and sailor suits, with cabin trunks and nets and spades and nannies, to renew old summer friendships in the elegance of Chapel Street and Clarence Place and the little squares and terraces round Morrab Gardens. And off they went in gigs and omnibuses to see Mousehole (He-he-he!) and Sennen Cove (Yo-ho-ho!) and the granite ramparts of Land's End (Lawks!), then carried off their golden Cornish-summer memories to Coulsdon, Orpington and Delhi, to Spion Kop and Picardy and Alamein.

But Penzance is not just a holiday town, though the only place in the county with a seaside promenade. It makes shoes. It repairs ships. It imports coal, seaweed, fertilisers, and, most famously, it imports and re-exports flowers and spuds from Scilly as well as selling produce from its own market gardens. In the middle of the tilting market-place – which was built for drays and long-distance coaches and still looks it – stands a fine porticoed town hall and a statue of Sir Humphry Davy with his miners' safety lamp. He lived across the road. It has public gardens of tropical luxuriance, a maritime museum, a museum of nautical art, a geological museum, tennis courts, a helicopter port and bags of Cornish swagger. All this with a population of under 20,000. I have known bigger villages. I love it!

At last I turned back eastward, and so doing called at Falmouth as a million travellers have done before me. Its high main street looks out on what is said to be the third-largest natural harbour in the world – five miles long, two wide, and eighteen fathoms deep. Standing on its small peninsula with Pendennis Castle at the end where the broad sea-tongue of the Carrick Roads and the Penryn and Percuil rivers meet the salt water of the bay, its setting is a fair one. For more than 150 years it flourished as the main packet port of England and a communications post for the British Empire. (The local newspaper is still called the *Falmouth Packet*.) Fast, well-armed, sloops carried mails, bullion, ambassadors and passengers to the Iberian peninsula, the Caribbean and the Americas. It not only meant trade for victuallers, repairers and hoteliers, but it made of Falmouth one of the greatest smuggling ports on earth. It is said that every seagoing man, from cabin boy to captain, was in business for himself. After the Royal Mail steamers took the postal trade to Southampton and London River the railway arrived and Falmouth became a Victorian holiday resort, and a romantic one as well, for until marine radio was universal it was still a famous port of call for signing and discharging crews and picking up instructions. 'Falmouth for Orders' was almost as well-known a term as 'A1 at Lloyds'. The great days are over but you can still stand on your hotel steps, or glance across a shop counter through the window, and see a supertanker against a background of green hills. Now the holiday trade fears the idea of Falmouth's revival as a container port. They should be ignored.

One blue and silver morning I found myself in a white village near St Mawes looking down and away across a prospect of inlets, headlands and distant hills. It was a memorable morning, the air so still that each piston beat of a small fishing boat – no more than a silver splinter in the sunlight – was as clear as a rifle crack as it crawled across a distant bay. Looking westward, one might have been in Scotland's western isles.

Yet how un-Scottish, how far from oatmeal austerity, were the white, well-stuccoed houses standing stoutly on the hillside in a steep labyrinth of lanes. From one nearby house I heard a piano and a half-remembered tune, one of those melodies to which thirties children marched to class from assembly in the hall. Turkish Patrol? I knocked, knowing what would happen. I was invited in. I was given a plate of biscuits, and white coffee in a little cup. There was a picture of HMS *Barham* on the stairhead – fat funnel, sturdy lines, familiar, alas! long gone – and round the front-room piano the Methodist minister and three gentle ladies were at their little, morning glee-club meeting. They sang more songs for me that I had all but forgotten. Ah, Hampstead, Brixton and ah, Chelsea! – there are still dear people abroad in England singing round their Broadwoods. A little later, looking for a Dr Whetter, I was tempted down a side-street by the sound of hymns. It seemed like a well-practised choir, adult and predominantly male. I found the singers were the customers of a sun-filled pub. And then I could have sworn I was in Wales.

I found my Dr Whetter. He was no medico. He was a revolutionary of sorts complete with revolutionary moustache. He was in a farmhouse kitchen where he lived a bachelor existence, married to his dream of a Cornwall free of what he called 'English imperialistic exploitation and oppression'. His walls were hung with posters from South America, the Caribbean, Spain, almost everywhere where people consider themselves downtrodden and sometimes are. There was Comrade Ché. There the raised fists, the banners, handsome toilers in heroic poses, the strong, raw colours.

James Whetter sat in an old armchair about ten feet from a fire whose ashes spilled out on the hearth. There were books beside him on the floor and he did not have to interrupt his reading to fuel the flames. Between chair and fireplace stood a pile of bricks. Across the bricks lay a builders' plank. One end was in the fire, the other at Dr Whetter's expert, nudging foot.

There was a pile of magazines. 'An Baner Kernewek – the Cornish Banner – Voice of the Cornish People', contents announced boldly on each cover. 'Bodmin Rides Again', 'The Curse of Kernow', 'England's First Colony' . . . then on to 'Brittany – An Oppressed Nation', 'Swedish Finland', 'The Russyns of Czechoslovakia', 'Nationalism in Flanders'.

I liked them. I particularly liked a piece entitled 'Cornwall is Nobody's Playground' in which the writer said the Cornish were becoming slaves of the tourist industry whose profits were not spent in a Kernow of fast-fading beauty. There was a fine tirade against bureaucracy. And a cartoon of a Breton greeting a Cornish visitor with 'Bon Jour, me 'andsome!' And there was a report about a Mr Harold Orman of Pensilva appealing against a Caradon Council order to pull his house down. An inspector testified that when he called he found a pony in the front bedroom. Throughout the hearing Mr Orman referred to the building as a stable – for which he had planning permission. When it was pointed out that the doorways were the usual domestic width he said that was the right size for Shetland ponies too. Asked about the elaborate Cornish fireplace in the lounge he said it was ideal for shoeing horses. Challenged about his ornamental garden – fishpond, granite mushrooms, rose arbour – he said he made it attractive for his pony. Told it looked like a modern bungalow he said – 'It is a stable because I have a horse living there.'

Oho, that's my Cornwall!

Dr Whetter was Chairman of the Cornish Nationalist Party. He was something important in Mebyon Kernow (Sons of Cornwall) and Editor of An Baner Kernewek. When he looked into his fire he saw not fading embers but a sunny socialist republic whose sturdy children used the old language in which 'love' was kerenza, 'joy' lowena, amma meant 'to kiss' and a thumb was a 'crack-louse' pronounced crakkya-lewen. * When he

---

* The Cornish language, descended from an ancient British dialect, fell from use in the seventeenth century, lingering only in the far west and the Lizard into the nineteenth. It is closer to Breton than to Welsh, the Bretons being descendants of Cornish settlers. It has been resuscitated and renovated in recent times, and a dictionary appeared in 1934.

looked from his window he saw not only sky and trees, he looked into a golden dawn beneath whose sun lay a federation of six nations – Alba (Scotland), Eire (Ireland), Mannin (Isle of Man), Cymru (Wales), Kernow (Cornwall) and Breizh (Brittany) – 'a model society that would be the envy of the world . . . the Celtic Crescent . . . Six Nations, One Soul!'

He was a kindly man. He saw no violence through that optimistic haze, though he had once written: 'If by some law contrived in Westminster Plymouth City Council acquired one yard across the Tamar, Mebyon Kernow would feel sympathy for the militants who would disrupt and disorganise the administration of the occupied land.'

He would have me know that Kernow was once part of a great Celtic empire that dominated Europe from Eire to Turkey; that the segregation of English immigrants from Cornish natives (apartheid?) would, in his view, be no bad thing; and that it might have been better if the English had been conquered in World War II . . .

Well, we talked for an hour or so, and I enjoyed it, and he enjoyed the provocation. Eventually I asked him how he made a living. Farming, a garage, and he had some rents in the district.

'Ah,' I said. 'You are a kulak.'*

Citizen Whetter liked that. 'A kulak,' he chortled. 'Yes, that's right, a kulak!'

4

H. V. Morton wrote that when he crossed the Tamar he saw a name on a map. It curled itself round his heart so he drove through the darkest tunnel of a lane he had ever seen and, turning a corner, came to St Anthony in Roseland.

'Well,' said the rosy woman at a door where he sought lodging, 'I've nothing for dinner, sir, but eggs and cream.'

Eggs and cream! I first read that as a schoolboy in Sunderland in the 1940s.

He stayed and wrote about pink cottages hung with briar roses, surrounded by great bushes of veronica, and Canterbury bells, and London pride, foxgloves, and palm trees twelve feet high – and of deep, deserted lanes and sudden glimpses of a tiny bay where the sea broke in the dusk.

---

* Kulak – Russian peasant who employed some labour or owned a little land and so was persecuted as an enemy of socialism and the revolution.

Roseland 1926. Morton has been invited home by a farmer to listen to the wireless set. A paraffin lamp illuminates two pictures on the wall – Kitchener in scarlet, Victoria with crown and sceptre.

. . . Ah, here we are! . . . Just listen to that, sir. '*London calling the British Isles!*' . . . Oh . . . we're getting Morse! I reckon the battery's running down . . . Listen! cries the farmer, beating time. The Blue Danube! That's a real good tune that is . . . !

Across the miles of emptiness came the sound of the Savoy. The door opened and a cat walked in. I could hear people in London putting down their liqueur glasses . . . the old man was smoking, the two women were sitting with their hands folded, and outside was the wildness of the night and the rain and sea . . .

As I walked down the little path I turned and saw, framed in the yellow window, the new picture of rural England . . . heads bent over the wireless . . . Queen Victoria and Lord Kitchener watching . . . London coming to them out of space.

Nineteen-twenty-six was the year before I was born. Morton painted that 'new English picture' only ten years before public television.

Next day he went to St Just in Roseland. 'I have blundered into a Garden of Eden . . . The church is grey and small . . . but I would like to know if there is in the whole of England a churchyard more beautiful . . . You stand and look down into a green cup filled with flowers and arched by great trees. Beyond the church . . . trees form a tracery through which you can see . . . the creek . . .'

He met a clergyman training a plant over a wall. 'Which do you prefer – those wine-dark rhododendrons or the pink?'

'Who was St Just, sir?' I asked.
'St Just was – I want you to admire those pansies . . .'
'You were saying that St Just was . . .'
'Ah, yes, forgive me! – oh, the trouble I've had with those japonicas.'
'St Just?'* I murmured hopefully.
'That tall tree over there came from Australia . . . By the way, I have a tropical garden behind the church which you must see . . .'
'You have made this garden?'
'With my own hands I have made it. It took a long time . . .'†

Well, more than half a century had passed since that conversation.

* St Just, or St Jestyn, son of Geraint, one of King Arthur's Knights of the Round Table.
† Quoted from H. V. Morton's *In Search of England.*

This was to be my last day in Cornwall – the last before I turned for home. I had driven up the A39 from Falmouth and taken a bosky east-bound side-road short of Truro. I had passed some splendid gardens at a great house called Trelissick,* then I had come again upon what, to these north-country eyes, is Cornwall's most amazing *coup d'oeil* – big, seagoing ships moored not among wharves and warehouses in the middle of a city, but deep in woodland. The river Fal was wider than the Fowey at Bodinnick. But King Harry's Ferry – another pontoon-like, car-carrying contraption – chuntered me and my Marina-home from one bank of forest to another. I brewed up. I sat with tea on my back doorstep and looked at a map. I was on the edge of Roseland. A good place, I thought, to end my journey. I decided to look up St Anthony.

At last I found it. I had passed the little confluence of loanings several times before but the hamlet had been screened by trees and hedges. I stepped out into a fragrance of byres and unseen sea. It was as he had described it – the few cottages, the palms – and just as at the hour of his arrival, there was not a soul about. Then a head rose from behind a dyke. A hat that might once have been a deerstalker surmounted a nutbrown face that seemed to be astonished at my intrusion from the outside world.

Could it help me? Was I looking for something in particular?

Yes, I said, I was looking for the house where H. V. Morton stayed in 1926.

It did not recall that name but . . . ah, did I mean the writer chap? Yes, he'd stayed in that cottage over there, but there was no one in just now. It was as if Morton's visit had been last weekend. But of course the briars were not blooming. I found the farmhouse too, as confident and prosperous as it must have stood for centuries. I looked in through the window. Queen Victoria had abdicated, Kitchener had been dismissed, and indeed there *was* television.

Now, setting course for St Just in Roseland I saw an old man fairly hurtling up a hill. I stopped to ask him for directions but by the time I got out he had hurried by and I was obliged to run up the bank to catch him. He was lean and fit and had a brimming smile. 'Go down and see the new rector,' he advised. 'He's the happiest man in St Just. Tell him I sent you,' and he named his name.

'Thank you for *your* help,' I said. 'You look a pretty happy man yourself.'

He grinned, delighted at the compliment. 'Well, so I am,' he said. 'But not so happy as I might be. You see I lost my wife just before our golden wedding. I've just been to the grave. I know I shouldn't mention it . . .

---

* The 'tre-' so common in Cornish names means 'homestead' or 'hamlet'.

278

but . . . well . . . sometimes I stand there and say – "I wish I was down there with you, me 'andsome.'" By the time I'd turned he was pounding up the hill again.

The road he'd indicated went up, not down, towards the rectory. It stood in a wooded garden on the rise. Opposite, just over a stone wall, was the churchyard – Morton's cup of green. Beyond lay the creek. I knew Roseland stood in the Gulf Stream's wash but not even Morton could have prepared me – an Englishman standing on his own soil – for such an extravagance. It was like a picture in a boys' adventure book, a South Sea island hideaway.

A churchyard noticeboard gave the rector's name as Peter Durnford, and when I knocked on his substantial door it was answered by a burly, sun-tanned man in a dark-blue seaman's jersey who invited me into an untidy study mountainous with piles of books and papers. I mentioned Morton's visit. Yes – the Durnfords had read the book in Bonn. 'You would like coffee!' he informed me. He hurried to the kitchen, returned with pot, jug and cups on a silver tray, placed them on a foothill of sermon notes where, with slow inevitability, they tipped over. Back to the kitchen – and while he was away I marked a row of hats on a high shelf, among them a dark bowler, a gold-encrusted RN hat as worn by commanders and above, and a topper. Reading from left to right I guessed correctly that Peter Durnford had been a naval officer, that he had retired early and become an embassy chaplain in the West German capital before settling in Roseland.

I told him about the old fellow who had directed me. 'A dear man!' replied the rector. 'I was with him a day or two before his wife died. She was making him a pasty. One end of this pasty was savoury and the other end was sweet with jam. So he had a complete meal. It was the bit in the middle that worried me.'

The Reverend ex-Commander Durnford was full of affection for his parish. He explained that when the villagers referred to the *new* rector they meant *him*. When they mentioned the *last* rector they meant his predecessor. But when they simply said *the* rector they meant Humphrey Davis, maker of the church garden – 'yes, garden: I prefer that word to churchyard because that is what it is' – and the man that Morton met.

'He baptised them all . . . helped in the school . . . taught them chess. The heart of the village was the blacksmith's shop. There was always a fire there. That's where they used to congregate and there they used to sit round the lantern playing . . .' He paused, relishing the picture. 'You take two lumps, I think . . .'

I leaned back in my chair balancing my cup. I was conscious that this was the last hour of my journey and that this would be the last conversation. We were two Englishmen of entirely different backgrounds, playing that comfortable old English game of guessing about class, education, family, native region, noting small mannerisms, speech variations (he was from Hertford), understanding one another perfectly.

We talked about the BBC and tourism and Gilbert Harding, pre-war England and Cornish nationalism. 'It's always been fun having these various cultures. There's always been rivalry in England. It would be a pity to take it too far, though,' he said.

The talk drifted gently back to Roseland. He told me how the Fleet, back from Trafalgar, lay off the shore here with Nelson's embalmed body, and I recalled having read that the nation's hero had been preserved for the voyage in a brandy barrel.

He said Roseland may have been the fabled Isle of Ictis – a centre of the tin trade when Levantine merchants frequented England's southern shores. 'Look at the little rivers. When they are running hard you can see it as an island. This well-sheltered little harbour may have been where they laid up their boats in winter and took aboard provisions. The water here is wholesome, there are lots of springs. Others have said it was a holy place, perhaps with a temple where seafarers would give thanks for safe arrival. That tradition is associated with the legend.'

'Legend – what legend?'

'Well, it is said that St Joseph of Arimathea used to come to these parts. He was a merchant, and the story is that on one of his voyages he brought his nephew, the child Christ, and that while Joseph was dealing in the tin trade further inland Jesus came across and talked to the people here.'

'What a story – and in such a place!'

'No one speaks of it much, but the local people hold it very dear. They don't go bandying it around.'

I strolled out into the warm, moist evening – down among the azalea and rhododendron bushes, beneath the gum trees from Australia. I came to the tiny church, once Celtic, before that, perhaps, a site of pre-Christian worship. Inside it was cool and still. Peter Durnford had told me that up to 70,000 people sign the visitors' book each summer – 'but the church never loses its tranquility'. The light was pale. The stones seemed faintly luminous. Like pebbles at the bottom of a sea-pool.

I walked down a few yards to the little inlet which was almost enclosed by small green hills. There was an arc of sand and the place was fringed with trees. Below the trees were gigantic broadleaved plants of a kind I had not seen before in England, for all I knew the progeny of some Caribbean plantlife whose seeds had been brought by the warm Atlantic current – or something let fall from cargoes long forgotten. It was not hard to imagine a brown-legged lad running across the strand.

I turned away reluctantly. Almost all my departures had been reluctant on this journey. None more so than this.

INDEX